Wolfgang Schivelbusch

The Railway Journey

The Industrialization of Time and Space in the 19th Century

The University of California Press
Berkeley and Los Angeles

University of California Press
Berkeley and Los Angeles, California

© Wolfgang Schivelbusch, 1977, 1986

The German text of this book was published under the title
Geschichte der Eisenbahnreise by Carl Hanser Verlag, Munich, 1977

English translation first published in the United States by Urizen Books, 1979
This new edition published by The University of California Press, 1986

Library of Congress Cataloging-in-Publication Data
Schivelbusch, Wolfgang, 1941–
    The railway journey.
    Translation of: Geschichte der Eisenbahnreise.
    Originally published: New York : Urizen Books,
c1979.
    Bibliography: p.
    Includes index.
    1. Railroads—History—19th century. 2. Railroad
travel—History—19th century. 3. Space and time—
History—19th century.   I. Title.
HE1021.S3413 1986   385'.09'034   86-11226
ISBN 978-0-520-05929-0 (alk. paper)

Printed in the United States of America

13   12

15   14   13   12

The paper used in this publication is both acid-free and totally chlorine-free
(TCF). It meets the minimum requirements of
ANSI/NISO Z39.48-1992 (R 1997) (*Permanence of Paper*). ♾

The Railway Journey

The Industrialization of Time and Space in the 19th Century

Contents

[v]

Contents

Illustrations

Acknowledgments

For their hospitality and assistance I would like to thank the following American libraries: Library of Congress, New York Public Library, New York Historical Society, New York Academy of Medicine, the Boston Athenaeum, the Kress Rare Books Library and, especially, John McLeod of the American Railroads Association Library.

W. S.

For Shirley D. Carse

'I thought of railway travelling.'
— Lewis Carroll

Foreword

Nothing else in the nineteenth century seemed as vivid and dramatic a sign of modernity as the railroad. Scientists and statesmen joined capitalists in promoting the locomotive as the engine of 'progress', a promise of imminent Utopia. By the end of the century their naiveté came home to them, especially in the United States where railroad corporations were seen as the epitome of ruthless, irresponsible business power, a grave threat to order and stability, both economic and political. But in fact from its beginnings the railroad was never free of some note of menace, some undercurrent of fear. The popular images of the 'mechanical horse' manifest fear in the very act of seeming to bury it in a domesticating metaphor: fear of displacement of familiar nature by a fire-snorting machine with its own internal source of power. Once it appeared, the machine seemed unrelenting in its advancing dominion over the landscape — in the way it 'lapped the miles', in Emily Dickinson's words — and in little over a generation it had introduced a new system of behavior: not only of travel and communication but of thought, of feeling, of expectation. Neither the general fear of the mechanical and the specific frights of accident and injury, nor the social fear of boundless economic power entirely effaced the Utopian promise implicit in the establishment of *speed* as a new principle of public life. In fact the populations of the industrial world, including the American Populists who aimed their profound hostility toward corporate capitalism at the railroad, accomodated themselves to the sheer physical fact of travel by rail as a normal fact of existence.

Now, as the railroad recedes in importance as a mode of personal travel and of economic distribution, it reappears as an object of study, of historical contemplation. Scholars have weighed its importance in the making of industrial capitalism, as transportation and as the business of organization. Not only was its economic function of first importance, but that function exerted itself in many indirect ways upon what seemed to be simple personal needs for getting from one place to another. Personal travel by railroad inevitably (if unconsciously) assimilated the personal traveller into a physical system for moving goods. Behind the railroad's 'annihilation of space by time', wrote Karl Marx, lay the generative phenomenon of capital. The 'creation of the physical conditions of exchange' was 'an extraordinary necessity' for capital, which 'by its nature drives beyond every spatial barrier'. Products become commodities only as they enter a market. They must be moved from the factory to the customer. Entering a market requires a movement in space, a 'locational moment'. The industrial system also requires the movement of resources from mine to factory — a movement which is already a transformation of nature. Thus the railroad fulfilled inner necessities of capital, and it is this alone that accounts for its unhindered development in the nineteenth century.

The 'railway journey' which fills nineteenth-century novels as an event of travel and social encounter was at bottom an event of spatial relocation in the service of production. By exposing this hidden nerve within mechanized travel, Wolfgang Schivelbusch has placed the journey by rail in a new and revealing light. It was a decisive mode of initiation of people into their new status within the system of commodity production: their status as object of forces whose points of origin remained out of view. Just as the path of travel was transformed from the road that fits itself to the contours of land to a *rail*road that flattens and subdues land to fit its own needs for regularity, the traveler is made over into a bulk of weight, a 'parcel', as many travelers confessed themselves to feel. Compared to what it replaced, the journey by stage coach, the railway journey produced novel experiences — of self, of fellow-travelers, of landscape (now seen as swiftly-passing panorama), of space and time. Mechanized by seating arrangements and by new perceptual coercions (including new kinds of shock), routinized by schedules, by undeviating pathways, the railroad traveler underwent experiences analogous to military regimentation — not to say to 'nature' transformed into 'commodity'. He was converted from a private individual into one of a mass public — a mere consumer.

This puts too crudely and schematically the form of Schivelbusch's astute analysis. But the brief summary does suggest the special kind of light that flows from his insights. He wishes to recover the subjective experience of the railway journey at the very moment of its newness, its pure particularity: to construct from a magnificent display of documents written and graphic what can be called the industrial *subject*. In this enterprise Schivelbusch writes in the spirit of Siegfried Giedion, Walter Benjamin, Norbert Elias and Dolph Sternberger — cultural historians who look for evidence of new forms of consciousness arising out of encounters with new structures, new things. One feature of modernity as it crystallized in the nineteenth century was a radical foregrounding of machinery and of mechanical apparatus within everyday life. The railroad represented the visible presence of modern technology as such. Within the technology lay also forms of social production and their relations. Thus the physical experience of technology mediated consciousness of the emerging social order; it gave a form to a revolutionary rupture with past forms of experience, of social order, of human relation. The products of the new technology produced, as Marx remarked, their own subject; they produced capacities appropriate to their own use. In their railway journeys nineteenth-century people encountered the new conditions of their lives; they encountered themselves as moderns, as dwellers within new structures of regulation and need.

Schivelbusch has undertaken to reconstruct the immediacy of encounter through an extraordinary richness of detail. The book is rich in proportion to its breadth as well as its intensity of concentration. It brings into focus a single system that underlies a diversity of partial facts: the design of under-carriages and cars, compartments and corridors, platforms and waiting rooms. It explores the nodal points of juncture between railroads and cities and shows the effect of the new mode of travel upon traffic circulation and the segregation of urban spaces. It also discloses hidden connections among journeying by railway, walking on city streets and shopping in department stores. It is not only the changes in physical behavior that concern the author — the new demands upon the nerves, for example — but the cultural perceptions and definitions of such changes. The book is itself a kind of journey, from the railway experience to the larger formations of culture within industrial capitalism. It suggests that we look for evidence of culture at those minute points of contact between new things and old habits, and that we include in our sense of history the power of things themselves to impress and shape and evoke a response within consciousness. There is nothing here of nostalgia for a lost 'romance' of the railroad, but a great deal that compels us to conceive of that romance in

a new way. The book contributes provocatively to a much-needed
critical history of the origins of modern industrial culture.

Alan Trachtenberg
Yale University

[1]
The Mechanization of Motive Power

L'industrie est devenue la vie des peuples.
[Industry has become the life of the nations.]
— Marc Séguin, 1839

In the economic life of the pre-industrial era, wood was the prime material, universally used in construction and as combustible matter. The shipbuilding industry of the European maritime powers, the iron works and the machines built in the manufacturing and early industrial period were all based on the use of wood. Werner Sombart, the economic historian, regarded the exhaustion of this resource (i.e., the deforestation of Western Europe in the eighteenth century) as an essential factor, or perhaps even *the* main incentive for the development of industrial capitalism. In the pre-industrial era, 'wood affected all areas of cultural existence, being the prerequisite for the prosperity of all branches of economic life: so general was its use in the production of material goods that the characteristics of culture before the eighteenth century were decidedly wooden, and thus that culture retained an "organic" quality in its material and sensual aspect'.[1]

Next to wood, water and wind power were the main energy sources of pre-industrial economic life. The Industrial

1. Werner Sombart, *Der Moderne Kapitalismus*, vol. 2, p. 1138 (1st ed., Munich, 1902).

Revolution, generally seen as having begun in the last third of the eighteenth century, was a complex process of denaturalization. The abolition of 'live' workmanship by the division of labor, a process first described by Adam Smith, corresponded in terms of materials and energies to the 'emancipation from the boundaries of nature' (Sombart) which occurs when 'live' natural materials and energies are replaced by mineral or synthetic ones. Thus wood lost its universal function. Iron became the new industrial building material, coal the new combustible.[2] In the steam engine, the prime mover of industry, these two combined to produce energy in theoretically unlimited amounts. The technological development of the steam engine in the eighteenth century exemplified the gradual process of industry's emancipation from nature. The initial economic utilization of steam power occurred in the early part of the century when Newcomen's atmospheric steam engine was deployed in the Newcastle mining region to pump water out of mine shafts. The Newcastle region can be regarded as Europe's first industrial landscape in that coal began to determine the physical aspect of the environment. Thus Daniel Defoe, who had a clear understanding of the economics of his day, traveled through the region and expressed his astonishment at the 'prodigious Heaps, I might say Mountains, of Coals, which are dug up at every Pit, and how many of those Pits there are; we are filled . . . with Wonder to consider where the People should live that can consume them'.[3] The Newcomen engine was a crude contraption, only capable of a back-and-forth motion, consuming incredible amounts of fuel, and comparatively weak in performance. However, as it was used in the coal-producing region, its excessive fuel (i.e., coal) consumption was no problem. As early as 1767, fifty-seven Newcomen engines were working in the area.[4]

The waterwheel remained the main energy source for Eng-

---

2. Lewis Mumford (following the Scottish sociologist Patrick Geddes) has coined the terms 'eotechnology' and 'paleotechnology' to describe this epoch-making change in materials and energy: 'The eotechnic phase is a water-and-wood complex; the paleotechnic phase is a coal-and-iron-complex.' (L. Mumford, *Technics and Civilization*, New York, 1963, p. 11.)

3. Daniel Defoe, *A Tour Thro' the Whole Island of Great Britain* (1st ed., 1724–7; repr. 2 vols., London, 1968), vol. 2, p. 659.

4. Conrad Matschoss, *Geschichte der Dampfmaschine* (Berlin, 1901), p. 55.

land's manufacturing industry in the eighteenth century. Yet, following the evolutionary pattern characteristic of the Industrial Revolution, the water-wheel was to be aided by a curious intermediate adaptation that pointed the way to mechanization: water-powered factories attempted to end their dependence on seasonally variable water levels by installing the Newcomen engine to pump back the used water (i.e., the water that had already passed through the wheel and would have been lost otherwise).[5] This recycling process was a kind of mechanization of the mill race: it regularized the previously natural and erratic stream of water and transformed it into an aqueous driving belt. Thus water-power became a merely incidental element in a uniform and regular mechanized process whose true mover was the steam engine.

That bypass became obsolete with the development of a steam engine capable of rotary motion. Watt's low-pressure engine, perfected in the 1780s was such a technological advance. Thus steam power left its original 'natural' habitat, the coalfields, and became an essential part of the manufacturing industry. Watt's engine used only a fraction of the fuel required by Newcomen's. Its performance was also far better and it produced the rotary motion required by industry. (The immediate incentive for Watt's development of the low-pressure engine was the saturation of the coal mine market with Newcomen pump engines. Its manufacturer, the firm of Watt & Boulton, urged Watt to develop an engine for the new market of the manufacturing industries. The success of this speculation demonstrates that industry had in the meantime indeed developed a need for mechanical power.)[6]

At the turn of the eighteenth and nineteenth centuries, the evolution of the steam engine reached its culmination in Oliver Evans' high-pressure engine. Once again, the improvement was tremendous: the engine's performance was no longer based solely on condensation, but on the immediate effect of steam pressure. This made it possible to further reduce the size of the engines, which had been quite unwieldy, while increasing performance and reducing fuel consumption. On the other hand, it

5. Thomas Ashton, *Iron and Steel in the Industrial Revolution* (1st ed., 1924; repr. ed., Manchester, 1951), pp. 99–100.
6. Matschoss., op. cit., p. 77.

became necessary, in order to meet the requirements of increased temperature and pressure, to improve the quality of machine technology and its materials.

The intensification achieved by the high-pressure engine — maximal work performance with minimal machinery — permitted the *mobile* use of the steam engine, that is, its use as locomotive. This first occurred at the beginning of the nineteenth century in the coalfields around Newcastle, where the Newcomen engine had found its first application a century before. In the wake of the now full-blown Industrial Revolution and its increased demand for coal, the region, already transformed by coal production in Defoe's time, underwent further changes. The land between the mines and the river Tyne became covered by a dense network of railways up to ten miles long — descendants of the rails used in mountain mine shafts since the late Middle Ages. These railways were appendages of the mines and were used only to move coal. The wagons were first pulled by horses, but after the end of the Napoleonic Wars these were progressively replaced by steam-powered locomotives. The changeover to mechanized motive power was possible because in the mining region, fuel (coal) was cheaper than food — which latter had to be shipped from other regions. From 1815 on, coal became cheaper to use than food throughout England and in that year, Parliament, dominated by agricultural interests, passed a Corn Law which, by imposing steep taxes on imported grain, forced grain prices to rise.[7] Obviously, the artificially high level of grain prices helped to replace horsepower by mechanical power in much the same way as the shortage of wood in eighteenth-century Europe had accelerated the development of coal production. Confirmation for this is provided by a contemporary, Thomas Grahame, who, in 1834 when steam locomotion was an accomplished fact, described the

---

7. Concise information on the history of the English Corn Laws can be found in: Eric Hobsbawm, *Industry and Empire: From 1750 to the Present Day*, Pelican Economic History of England, vol. 3 (Harmondsworth/New York, 1968); Asa Briggs, *The Age of Improvement, 1783–1867* (New York, 1959), pp. 202, 312; R. K. Webb, *Modern England* (New York and Toronto, 1970), pp. 153, 185–6. The corn legislation after 1815 can be seen as a temporarily effective skirmish conducted by the land-owning class against the rising industrial bourgeoisie. No later than 1828 the pressure of free-enterprise interests caused the law of 1815 to be modified, and by the mid-1840s it had been abolished entirely, after the industrial bourgeoisie and the working class (i.e., the Chartists) had joined, in 1838, to form the Anti-Corn Law League.

choice the English industrial capitalists had to make: 'The landed capitalists of Britain . . . have by the taxes on corn and provisions more than doubled the price of animal labour, whether of man or horses. To avoid the effects of these taxes the monied capitalists of Britain have been for years devoting their capital to the promotion of those inventions by which taxed animal power may be dispensed with; and their endeavours have been crowned with eminent success'.[8]

From the beginning of the nineteenth century, there were plans to develop the railroads into a general and national mode of transportation. The 1820s saw the origins of a fully-fledged 'railroad movement', whose main promoters were agreed that the railroad, which in the meantime carried not only coal but other goods and passengers, must be powered by steam. The high cost of grain was a recurrent and standard argument. According to Adam Smith, the upkeep of a horse was equal to the feeding of eight laborers. Thus, it was argued, when the one million horses kept for purposes of transportation in England were made redundant by mechanization, they would release additional foodstuffs for eight million laborers.

Thomas Gray, the most important railroad promoter of the time, whose *Observations on a General Iron Rail-Way* appeared in five editions between 1820 and 1825, considerably expanded each time, argued for his proposed steam-driven railroad as follows: 'The exorbitant demands now made on the public, for conveyance of goods and persons by waggons and coaches, are caused principally, if not altogether, by the enormous expense of a stock of horses, the continual renewal of the stock, and the intolerable expense of their keep'.[9]

It is possible to see how advanced mechanization was in Britain at this time, in both theory and practice, when one consults a roughly contemporary French statement on the question of animal versus mechanical power. Pierre-Simon Girard, an engineer and member of the Académie des Sciences, who in 1819 had been given the task of planning and realizing a

8. Thomas Grahame, *A Treatise on Internal Intercourse and Communication in Civilised States* (London, 1834) p. vi.
9. Thomas Gray, *Observations* . . ., 3rd ed. (London, 1822), p. x.

street-lighting system for the city of Paris, ostensibly summarized the state of the English debate on horse-power versus steam power in an article published in 1827; in fact, his account, tinged with eighteenth-century physiocratic theory, projects French conditions onto England:

> The use of steam engines as locomotives on the railways is still a great open question in today's England. While one is willing to agree with the partisans of this solution that locomotives would be more economical than the use of horses, it is necessary to point out that the fuel on whose consumption these engines depend for the production of their motive power has to be extracted daily from natural deposits whose vast expanses nevertheless are not inexhaustible . . . The use of horses is not subject to similar hazards; the motive power horses are able to produce is fed by products of the soil that nature renews every year and will continue to reproduce in ever greater abundance as agriculture grows more advanced.[10]

The apprehension that coal resources would be exhausted one day, combined with the notion that organic horsepower is able to reproduce itself *ad infinitum*, reflected not only the physiocratic tradition that guided Girard's thinking, but also the economic realities of France during this period: specifically, the state of French coal production. During the first third of the nineteenth century, coal, in France, was *un produit révolutionnaire*.[11] While in England, coal production was sixteen million tons in 1816, thirty million tons in 1836, forty-four million tons in 1846, and fifty-seven million tons in 1851, French production figures were much lower: one million tons in 1820, two million tons in 1837, and five million tons in 1846.[12]

In addition, French production was not centered in one region, but was scattered throughout the country. Unlike the English, whose coal industry was centralized in a way that altered both landscape and consciousness, the French were unable to perceive coal as *the* endlessly available fuel. It was precisely because of the physical reality of the concentration of English

10. P. S. Girard, Foreword to the French edition of Friedrich von Gerstner's *Mémoire sur les grandes routes, les chemins de fer, et les canaux de navigation* (Paris, 1827), pp. cxxv–cxxvi.
11. C. Fohlen, in *Charbon et sciences humaines: Colloque international de l'Université de Lille en mai 1963* (Lille, 1963), p. 148.
12. Op. cit., pp. 141–2.

coal production, and their awareness of it, that the English were able to mechanize motive power with such ease.

The mechanization of overland traffic subjected it to the same degree of regularization that had already been firmly established in bourgeois self-discipline and in industrial production. Unlike traffic on the waterways,[13] land traffic had until then been the weakest link in the chain of capitalist emancipation from the limits of organic nature, because animal power — on which land traffic was based — cannot be intensified above a certain fairly low level. Yet one should not underestimate the efforts made in the decades before the advent of the railroads to increase the efficiency of land traffic within the framework of these narrow natural limits. These efforts did, in fact, introduce a trend that eventually made mechanization appear as the final logical step. According to Bagwell — who, interpreting the material available to him, saw the English 'transport revolution' as beginning as early as 1770 — traveling time between the most important cities was reduced by four-fifths between 1750 and 1830, and cut in half between 1770 and 1830.[14] The trip from London to Edinburgh, which in the 1750s still required ten days in the summer, took only forty-five and a half hours in 1836.[15] With the increase in traveling speed came increases in the number of traveled routes, in traffic intensity and in the number of transportation enterprises. In the ten most important English cities, there were eight times as many regular departures in 1830 as there had been in 1790; Bagwell thinks that the number of passengers was multiplied by a factor of fifteen, as some of them were carried 'outside' (i.e., on top of the coach) on regular runs.[16] Due to these improvements, the stagecoach surpassed the riding horse as the fastest mode of land transportation.[17] Karl Philipp Moritz gives us a vivid impression of that highly developed mode of passenger traffic in his *Reisen eines Deutschen in England* (*Travels of a German in England*). At this time, in the 1780s, the German

13. Traditionally, traffic on waterways has always been greater than overland traffic. From the early fifteenth century to the end of the nineteenth century, sailing-ship technology was sufficient for the transportation needs of capitalism in all its phases of expansion. Fifty years after the mechanization of land traffic by means of the railroad, sailing-ship technology (i.e., the clipper) still dominated ocean traffic.
14. Philip S. Bagwell, *The Transport Revolution from 1770* (London, 1974), p. 41.
15. Ibid., pp. 42, 43.
16. Ibid., p. 43.
17. Ibid., p. 49.

traveler mostly proceeded on foot. Moritz, who attempted to wander about England in this manner, found himself regarded as a curiosity. He noted with surprise that in England even the lower orders traveled by stagecoach.

Finally, the high degree of development that the coach system achieved can be seen in its economic concentration: of the 342 scheduled daily departures from London listed in John Bates' *Directory of Stage Coach Services* for 1836, 275 were run by three enterprises, the largest of which, owned by William James Chaplin, also had considerable interests in the catering business and employed a total of more than two thousand people and eighteen hundred horses. (Bagwell, p. 50).

One of the main arguments for replacing the horse teams with steam locomotives was presented by Nicholas Wood, author of the most authoritative technical work of his time on railroads: 'The greatest exertions have been used to accelerate the speed of the mails (which have hitherto been the quickest species of conveyance), without being able to exceed ten miles an hour; and that only with the exercise of such *destruction of animal power*, as no one can contemplate with feelings except of the most painful nature; while, upon the Liverpool Rail-way, an average rate of fifteen miles is kept up with the greatest ease'.[18] (Italics added.)

How long overdue the mechanically produced means of locomotion must have seemed to the progressive contemporary consciousness — and how hopelessly anachronistic the animal power still in use — can be seen in a text from 1825 that juxtaposes both forms of locomotion:

The animal advances not with a continued progressive motion, but with a sort of irregular hobbling, which raises and sinks its body at every alternate motion of the limbs. This is distinctly felt on horse-

18. Nicholas Wood, *A Practical Treatise on Rail-Roads, and Interior Communication in General*, 2nd ed. (London, 1832), p. xii. Within the mail system, there were attempts to increase physical capacity from the sixteenth century on: letters were no longer carried long distances by means of only one courier, but from one station to the next, 'with either changes of horses, or of couriers, *relays*, in any case, consisting of runners or riders or drivers'. (Sombart, op. cit., vol. 2, p. 382.) This subdivision of the formerly unified effort caused the process to become intensified, but the system remained subject to the limits of physical capacity, even though this was now the sum of the physical capacities of all the individual relays. This intensification also intensified costs, and thus only the mails employed this mode of transportation.

back, and it is the same when an animal draws a load. Even in walking and running one does not move regularly forward. The body is raised and depressed at every step of our progress; it is this incessant lifting of the mass which constitutes that drag on our motions which checks their speed, and confines it within such moderate limits. . . . With machinery this inconvenience is not felt; the locomotive engine rolls regularly and progressively along the smooth tracks of the way, wholly unimpeded by the speed of its own motions; and this, independent of its economy, is one of the great advantages it possesses over animal power.[19]

The mechanical motion generated by steam power is characterized by regularity, uniformity, unlimited duration and acceleration. 'No animal strength', says Gray, 'will be able to give that uniform and regular acceleration to our commercial intercourse which may be accomplished by railway'.[20]

As the motion of transportation was freed from its organic fetters by steam power, its relationship to the space it covered changed quite radically. Pre-industrial traffic is mimetic of natural phenomena. Ships drifted with water and wind currents, overland motion followed the natural irregularities of the landscape and was determined by the physical powers of the draught animals. Charles Babbage observed, concerning the eotechnical utilization of wind and water power: 'We merely make use of bodies in a state of motion; we change the directions of their movement, in order to render them subservient to our purposes, but we neither add to nor diminish the quantity of motion in existence'.[21]

The earliest perceptions of how steam power dissolved that mimetic relationship can be found in descriptions of the first steam-powered ships. An eyewitness to John Fitch's steamboat experiment in 1790 found it particularly remarkable that the boat proceeded in a straight line, instead of tacking, as one would expect, in the traditional eotechnically 'natural' manner of marine vessels.[22] Putting it differently, another account said of

19. James Adamson, *Sketches of Our Information as to Rail-Roads* (Newcastle, 1826), pp. 51–2.
20. Thomas Gray, *Observations* . . . (London, 1822), p. 39.
21. Charles Babbage, *On the Economy of Machinery and Manufacture* (Philadelphia, 1832), p. 27. An application to the motion of sailing ships, the text goes on to say, would mean that 'the quantity of motion given by them [the sails] is precisely the same as that which is destroyed in the atmosphere'.
22. Report in *New York Magazine* (1790), quoted in Seymour Dunbar, *A History of Travel in America*, 4 vols. (Indianapolis, 1915), vol. 1, pp. 256–7.

[9]

steam power that 'it *forces* the ships to traverse the ocean against wind and waves'.[23] (Italics added.)

Thus steam power appeared to be independent of outward nature and capable of prevailing against it — as artificial energy in opposition to natural forces. While this was first perceived in steamship traffic, it became even clearer only a little later, when animal power was abandoned in favor of mechanical power. As long as the conquest of space was tied to animal power, it had to proceed within the limits of the animals' physical capabilities. One way of gaining an immediate perception of the distance traveled was to observe the exhaustion of the draught animals. When they were over-taxed, it was seen as 'destruction of animal power'. Steam power, inexhaustible and capable of infinite acceleration, reversed the relationship between recalcitrant nature (i.e., spatial distance) and locomotive engine. Nature (i.e., spatial distance), which had caused the animal 'locomotive engines' to strain themselves to exhaustion, now succumbed to the new mechanical locomotive engine of the railroad that, in a frequently used metaphor, 'shoots right through like a bullet'. 'Annihilation of time and space' was the *topos* which the early nineteenth century used to describe the new situation into which the railroad placed natural space after depriving it of its hitherto absolute powers. Motion was no longer dependent on the conditions of natural space, but on a mechanical power that created its own new spatiality.

We have seen the power of steam suddenly dry up the great Atlantic ocean to less than half its breadth. . . . Our communication with India has received the same blessing. The Indian Ocean is not only infinitely smaller than it used to be, but the Indian mail, under the guidance of steam, has been granted almost a miraculous passage through the waters of the Red Sea. The Mediterranean, which is now only a week from us, has before our eyes shrunk into a lake; our British and Irish channels are scarcely broader than the old Firth of Forth; the Rhine, the Danube, the Thames, the Medway, the Ganges etc., have contracted their streams to infinitely less than half their lengths and breadths, and the great lakes of the world are rapidly drying into ponds![24]

23. W. Heimann, *Über Dampfmaschinen, Dampfwagen und Eisenbahnen* (Frankfurt, 1836), p. 2.
24. *Quarterly Review*, vol. 63 (1839), p. 23.

The shrinking of the natural world by means of mechanical transportation was perceived and evaluated in different ways, dependent on the evaluator's economic and ideological position: there was shrinkage as economic gain versus shrinkage as loss of experience. The representatives of industry and free enterprise saw transportation's release from nature's fetters as a gain: nature, in the form of distances that were hard to bridge, and exhaustible and unpredictable energy sources, had been an obstacle to the development of world trade. Mechanical energy rendered all transportation calculable. The promoters of the railroad regarded steam power's ability to do away with animal unreliability and unpredictability as its main asset. Here is Thomas Gray:

> The dangers to which the present coach system is obnoxious (such as the untractableness of horses, the imprudence of drivers, cruelty to animals, the ruggedness of roads, etc.), would not be encountered on the rail-way, whose solid basis and construction render it impossible for any vehicle to be upset or driven out of its course; and as the rail-way must also be perfectly level and smooth, no danger could be apprehended from the increased speed, for mechanic power is uniform and regular, whilst horse-power, as we all very well know, is quite the reverse.[25]

This rational and progressive evaluation was opposed by a contrary position, in which the loss of organic natural power was not seen as an elimination of interfering factors that have hitherto hindered the smooth conduct of business and transportation, but as the loss of a communicative relationship between man and nature. Thus for instance, Thomas De Quincey described the lost experience of coach travel:

> Seated in the old mail-coach, we needed no evidence out of ourselves to indicate the velocity. . . . The vital experience of the glad animal sensibilities made doubts impossible on the question of our speed; we heard our speed, we saw it, we felt it as a thrilling; and this speed was not the product of blind insensate agencies, that had no sympathy to give, but was incarnated in the fiery eyeballs of the noblest among brutes, in his dilated nostril, spasmodic muscles, and

25. Gray, op. cit., p. 55.

thunder-beating hoofs.[26]

We should not read that account of a past mode of travel merely as a reactionary-romantic tirade against the new technology. De Quincey described the disorientation experienced by the traveler when the traditional, 'natural' mode of travel, the one based on traditional technology, was superseded by a new travel technology. Contemporaries perceived the transition from coach to railroad technology as a decisively reduced expenditure of work or power: in the form of animal exhaustion, that expenditure had been immediately perceptible to the senses, and spatial distance had been experienced by means of sensory recognition of that physical exhaustion. As the sensory perception of exhaustion was lost, so was the perception of spatial distance. De Quincey's description of this process was echoed in numerous variations in contemporary literature and journalism, as in this anonymous polemic from the year 1839:

> When we are travelling by stage-coach at the rate of eight or ten miles an hour, we can understand the nature of the force which sets the vehicle in motion: we understand in a general way the nature of animal power: we see how soon it is exhausted; every successive hour do we watch the panting and reeking animals in their stalls, and, in the course of a day's journey, we can appreciate the enormous succession of efforts required to transport a loaded vehicle from London to a distant town.
>
> But, when proceeding on a journey by the rail-road, we are seldom allowed to get a sight of the wondrous power which draws us so rapidly along. The scene is altogether changed, there are no animals yoked to the car, to excite our pity by their apparently short, but really severe labour; we hear the steam gushing from the safety valve, while the machine is for a short time stationary; then we hear a number of rapid beatings: we feel that we are moving; the motion soon increases rapidly, and the journey which by the stage-coach is so tedious, is here, long before we are aware of it, at an end. The traveller then wonders not only at the rapidity of his journey, but often wishes to inspect and comprehend the means by which it was effected.[27]

26. Thomas de Quincey, *The Collected Writings*, ed. David Masson (London, 1897), vol. 13, pp. 283–4. (First published in 1849 in *Blackwood's Magazine*.)
27. *The Roads and Rail-Roads, Vehicles, and Modes of Travelling, of Ancient and Modern Countries* . . . (London, 1839), p. 279.

As the new technology terminated the original relationship between the pre-industrial traveler and his vehicle and its journey, the old technology was seen, nostalgically, as having more 'soul'. In addition to this sentimental line of thought there appeared another criticism of steam power that also had a high regard for the old technology but, while using the same arguments to be found in de Quincey and others, invested them with a modern content. This was accomplished by transferring the economically obsolete old technologies to a new realm, that of leisure and sports. What de Quincey deplored as a loss of sensory perception, others now attempted to reinstitutionalize. Thus, for instance, W. B. Adams' *Pleasure Carriages*, published in 1837, was the precursor of a literature of leisure and sports whose ever-increasing growth the century was to witness.[28] In this book, the use of horse-power was no longer treated nostalgically, but from a point of view that regarded the use of steam as merely unsportsmanlike:

> Steam is a mere labourer — a drudge who performs his work without speech or sign, with dogged perseverance but without emotion. . . . He may be personified when speaking *of* him; but no one pats his neck or speaks *to* him in a voice of encouragement. It is not so with a horse or horses. They are beautiful and intelligent animals, powerful yet docile; creatures that respond to kindness, and shrink from cruelty and injustice. The driver and owner can love them or feel proud of them; they step with grace, and can vary their form and movements in a thousand ways. They are creatures of individual impulses. . . . The man who rides a horse, feels a pleasure when the creature responds willingly to his purposes; and when he responds unwillingly, he feels a pride in the exercise of his power to compel him to obedience. Even when a horse is vicious, there is a pleasurable excitement in riding him. The rider's nerves are strung, his senses are quickened; eye, hand, and ear are alike on the alert; the

28. 'In the manual on the art of driving published by the president of the Four-in-Hand Driving and Coaching Club, which was revived in 1870 by the Duke of Beaufort, there is a chapter titled "The coaching revival" that deals exclusively with the club members' new practice of driving coaches on busy routes (e.g., to Brighton, Dover, Tunbridge Wells) and racing the railway trains to those destinations; this activity made the long-abandoned inns of the coaching era come alive again with the neighing of horses and the cracking of whips.' (P. D. Fischer, *Betrachtungen eines in Deutschland reisenden Deutschen* [Berlin, 1895], pp. 43–4. Fischer also mentions the following coaching titles published in the 1880s: Stanley Harris, *Old Coaching Days*; W. Outram Tristram, *Coaching Days and Coaching Ways*.)

[13]

blood rushes through the veins, and every faculty is aroused.[29]

The final fate of carriage-riding, the traditional mode of travel, was to become the amateur sport of the privileged classes. In everyday existence, the new technology took over. Only during a transitional period did the travelers who transferred from the stagecoach to the railway carriage experience a sense of loss due to the mechanization of travel; it did not take long for the industrialization of the means of transport to alter the consciousness of the passengers: they developed a new set of perceptions. The uniform speed of the motion generated by the steam engine no longer seemed unnatural when compared to the motion generated by animal power; rather, the reverse became the case. Mechanical uniformity became the 'natural' state of affairs, compared to which the 'nature' of draught animals appeared as dangerous and chaotic. An anonymous text from the year 1825 gives us an idea of the adaptation to this industrialization of travel. It discusses the 'sensitive or nervous man' who will find the new mechanical mode of transport more agreeable than the horse-drawn vehicle:

> It is reasonable to conclude, that the nervous man will ere long, take his place in a carriage, drawn or impelled by a Locomotive Engine, with more unconcern and with far better assurance of safety, than he now disposes of himself in one drawn by four horses of unequal powers and speed, endued with passions, that acknowledge no control but superior force, and each separately momentarily liable to all the calamities that flesh is heir to. Surely an inanimate power, that can be started, stopped, and guided at pleasure by the finger or foot of man, must promise greater personal security to the traveller than a power derivable from animal life, whose infirmities and passions require the constant exercise of other passions, united with muscular exertion to remedy and control them.[30]

The 'sensitive and nervous man', in whom those horses in front of the coach, tended to cause unhealthy excitement, was enabled to relax in the railway carriage, and to sit in it without moving a muscle, without 'exertion' or any 'other passions'.

29. W. B. Adams, *English Pleasure Carriages* (London, 1837), pp. 198–9.
30. *The Fingerpost; or, Direct Road from John O'Groat's to the Land's End*, 3rd ed. (London, 1825), pp. 24–5.

[14]

Despite the apparent smoothness of transition to industrialized travel, certain residues of anxiety remained. We get an inkling of this from the report written by Thomas Creevy, the Liberal politician, about a trip on Stephenson's locomotive in 1829: 'It is really flying, and it is impossible to divest yourself of the notion of instant death to all upon the least accident happening'.[31]

31. Jonn Gore, ed., *The Creevy Papers* (New York, 1963), p. 256.

[2]
The Machine Ensemble

Le chemin de fer et les chariots qu'il porte forme une sorte de machine complexe dont les parties ne sauraient être envisagées isolément.

[The railroad, and the carriages on it, make up a complex machine whose parts cannot be considered separately.]
— Anonymous, 1821

Like any other means of transportation, the railroad provided a medium for moving things from one place to another. Yet the precise way in which it accomplished this distinguished it from the other means of transportation.

Transportation on roads and canals, as developed in eighteenth-century England by private enterprise, made both a technical and an economic distinction between the *route* and the *means*. The capital investment companies that provided canals and turnpikes to be used upon payment of tolls did nothing further: they had nothing to do with the vehicles that were used on their routes. Anyone using one of these artificially created land routes or waterways did so with his own vehicle or hired an entrepreneur to transport the goods; that entrepreneur, in turn, operated quite independently from the canal or turnpike company. Route and means of transportation existed independently from one another, because individual movement of vehicles — their mutual flexibility in granting right-of-way, etc. — was technically possible.

The railways put an end to that liberal state of affairs. Route and vehicle became technically conjoined on the railroad: there was no leeway between the rails and the vehicle running on them, nor was it possible for one train to pull to one side when confronted by another. This was realized early on: all initial definitions of the railroad unanimously described it as a machine consisting of the rails *and* of the vehicles running on them. 'It is necessary . . . to insist that the railroad and its carriages be considered as one machine, or, as an indivisible entity,'[1] a French author stated in 1821. In 1839 Guillaume Tell Poussin went into somewhat greater detail:

> A railway is far from being the simple construct that a canal or a turnpike is: these have to fulfil quite limited objectives. A railway, on the contrary, is a construct that has to adjust to the eventual exigencies of a new engine, in which each day of experience may cause important new modifications. Consequently, in order for there to be harmony between the two quite distinct parts that a railway consists of, i.e., its rails and its engine, there has to be reciprocal interaction, so that the ameliorations of the one determines the improvements of the other. Thus it is evident that one cannot separate the increasing knowledge of steam engines from the construction of the railways.[2]

In an early phase of the railroad's technological evolution, the concept of 'one machine' appeared with particular clarity: the locomotive was not seen, as yet, as a self-contained, autonomous motive apparatus, but simply as a steam engine mounted on an undercarriage. Thus, a report in the *Bulletin de la société pour l'encouragement de l'industrie nationale* (1815) on the railways in the English coal-mining district says: 'New application of steam engines. For some time now, a steam engine has been mounted on wheels in Leeds, making it move on rails, by

1. Quoted in Peter J. Wexler, *La Formation du vocabulaire des chemins de fer en France, 1778–1842* (Geneva and Lille, 1955), p. 31.
2. G. T. Poussin, *Examen comparatif de la question des chemins de fer en 1839 en France et à l'étranger* (Paris, 1839), pp. xi–xii. English literature does, of course, offer corresponding definitions, e.g., Lardner (see n. 20 below). The French definitions are attractive in their clarity, which is based partly on the French consciousness of language, and partly on the fact that these definitions are, essentially, descriptions of something that was still unknown to the French reading audience in any immediate sense. Thus it is amusing to read a French report from England, written in 1820, that apparently corrects erroneous notions arising from the words *'chemin de fer'*: 'Il y en a qui croient que ces routes sont pavées avec des plaques de fer, mais ce n'est pas cela du tout, ce ne sont que des ornières en fer fondu'. ('There are those who believe that these are roads paved with sheets of iron, but that is not the case at all, it is merely a matter of cast-iron rails.') (Quoted in Wexler, op. cit., p. 44.)

[17]

means of a large cogwheel'.[3]

That steam engine mounted on an undercarriage did not connect with its rails by rolling on them but by means of interlocking cogs: it moved by propelling cogwheels along proportionately serrated rails. The latter appeared as horizontal cogwheels, providing counterparts to the engine's wheels. In their experimental phase, railways were constructed according to this technical principle; it is hard to imagine a more vivid demonstration of the railways *machine* character. In retrospect, in 1849, Dionysius Lardner described one of these creations, built by the mining engineer Blenkinsop: 'He obtained a patent, in 1811, for the application of a rack-rail. The railroad thus, instead of being composed of smooth bars of iron, presented a line of projecting teeth, like those of a cog-wheel, which stretched along the entire distance to be travelled. The wheels on which the engine rolled were furnished with corresponding teeth, which worked in the teeth of the railroad; and, in this way, produced a progressive motion in the carriage'.[4]

This curious, technically redundant form of construction also existed in a variant in which the driving wheel was a cog that connected with a cograil laid between the running rails. The engineers who designed mine railways adhered to this model for a surprisingly long time. Even the illustration that Thomas Gray provided in the fifth edition of his *Observations* in 1825 showed such a cogwheeled locomotive. The 'imaginary difficulty' (Lardner) in the minds of the early railway engineers was

3. In Wexler, p. 99. On pp. 107–8 Wexler notes how hesitantly the adjective *locomotif* becomes the noun *locomotive*. Generally, Wexler provides an excellent account of the railroad vocabulary's slow development from its initial 'descriptive period' to the later stage when it has become a new technical vocabulary (p. 128). The process can be demonstrated more easily in French than in English: in the latter, the development of a railway vocabulary took a much longer time. Yet it is possible to see the corresponding trend in English, as in the simplification of the initially descriptive term *iron rail-way* to *rail-way* and finally to *railway*.

4. D. Lardner, *The Steam Engine*, 3rd American ed. from 5th British ed. (Philadelphia, 1849), p. 161. Even Lardner, who sees the cogwheel episode as a historical mistake, based on the erroneous notion that smooth rails and wheels could not provide traction, is still able to comprehend without difficulty how it was possible to arrive at this erroneous conclusion on the basis of theories of physics derived from the tradition of Galileo and Newton. He explains the notion as follows: 'If the face of the wheel and the surface of the road were absolutely smooth and free from friction, so that the face of the wheel would slide without resistance upon the road, then the effect of the force thus applied would be merely to cause the wheel to turn around, the carriage being stationary, the surface of the wheel would slip or slide upon the road as the wheel is made to revolve.' (Op. cit., p. 160.)

the notion that smooth wheels could not provide traction on smooth rails. Until simple experience proved otherwise, smooth steel on smooth steel did not seem capable of sufficient adhesiveness. That such a notion seemed plausible even to engineers, and for a relatively long time, is instructive in a number of ways: it sheds light on the history of cultural and psychological perceptions of iron and steel, and points to a fundamental change in the history of the wheel. For the first time, the wheel was no longer set in motion by a power extraneous to itself — the draught animal — but was, to all appearances, propelling itself along.

The cogwheel episode now looks merely like a symbolically exaggerated demonstration of the concept of rail and carriage as *one* machine: it shows the esthetic exuberance of technology. The final standardized form of the railroad — smooth wheels on smooth rails — retains that concept of unity of parts, which became ever more important as the railroad was technologically perfected. Franz Reuleaux, who in his *Theoretische Kinematik* (1875) summed up the development of machinery in the nineteenth century, agreed with the early chroniclers of the railroad that the joining of rail and wheel was the decisive step '*that joined carriage and road into one machine*'.[5] (Italics in original; we will return to Reuleaux's theory of the machine later on in greater detail.)[6] He then described the development of the machine in the direction of increased performance, intensification, etc., in terms of an ever more precise interaction between its individual parts: 'During the last century we have gradually become used to understanding the wheel and its cogs as a unit, a whole, and thus to seeing those cog profiles in context. It is my conviction that, in only a few decades, all cogwheels will operate *without play*'.[7] (Italics added.) While Reuleaux was speaking about the cogwheel, he used it as a paradigm for *the* machine part in general. The disappearance of 'play' concerned all parts of the machine.

This tendency in machine development appeared early on in the railroad's continuous evolution toward ever greater speed,

---

5. Franz Reuleaux, *Theoretische Kinematik: Grundzüge einer Theorie des Maschinenwesens* (Brunswick, 1875), p. 231.
6. See the last few pages of Chapter 10 of the present work.
7. Reuleaux, op. cit., p. 234.

regularity, and uniformity. In *An Exposition of the Danger and Deficiencies of the Present Mode of Railway Construction*, published in 1846, we find a description that anticipates the prophecy made by Reuleaux thirty years later — or, to put it another way, the descriptions of the railroad in the text of 1846 parallel the theoretical formulations on the development of machines in general made by Reuleaux in 1875:

> The wheels, rails, and carriages are only parts of one great machine, on the proper adjustment of which, one to the other, entirely depends the perfect action of the whole. And as the velocity given to the moving parts increases, so does the necessity for perfect adjustment increase also, because the imperfect action, which, at moderate speed, would only cause a *jolt*, will, when moving at high velocity, gain sufficient force to cause an overthrow. Therefore, from this cause it becomes necessary, in order to secure safety when moving at great speed, to have the parts in contact adjusted to each other in such manner as at all times, and under varying circumstances, to preserve a true relationship one to the other, at the same time having a tendency to resist and counteract the impulses which would otherwise destroy their equilibrium, and endanger the safety of the moving body.[8]

The machine character of the railroad was dual: first, the steam engine (locomotive) generated uniform mechanical motion; secondly, that motion was transformed into movement through space by the combined machinery of wheel and rail.

We observed how the process of the mechanization of formerly organic motive powers by the steam engine was experienced as denaturalization and desensualization. Let us now see how the development of the railway completes the detachment from nature initiated by the discovery of steam power.

As it is the function of the rail to overcome natural resistances, or obstacles, it can be defined as a technical means to implement Newton's First Law of Dynamics, which states: 'Every body continues in its state of rest, or of uniform motion in a straight line, unless it is compelled to change that state by forces impressed upon it'.[9]

---

8. C. H. Greenhow, *An Exposition of the Danger and Deficiencies of the Present Mode of Railway Construction* (London, 1846), pp. 5–6.
9. The technical principle of the railroad is a practical demonstration of Newton's law of

The natural obstacles that are to be overcome by means of the rail are of two different kinds: first, the friction between wheel surface and road surface; secondly, the irregularity of the terrain. Friction may be called the microphysical resistance; the varying elevation of the land, the macrophysical. How does the rail deal with the microphysical resistance? Lardner provided a definition for the ideal (i.e., frictionless) road, acknowledging that it is directly derived from Newton: '*A perfect road should be smooth, level, hard, and straight.* Were it possible to construct a road between two places, absolutely smooth, absolutely level, absolutely hard, and absolutely straight, then a carriage put in motion from one end of this road would move to the other end without any tractive force at all, except so far as the resistance of the atmosphere would require it'.[10] (Italics in original.)

According to Lardner, the railway line was the optional approximation of that ideal road. Significantly, he based his argument on a brief delineation of traditional road-building technology. Only when the draught animals were replaced by mechanical motive power did it become possible to construct a road that possessed all four qualities — smoothness, hardness, levelness, and straightness: as long as road traffic relied on animal power, internal contradictions were inevitable. The smoothness and hardness of the road that the wheel required were directly opposed to the animals' technical demands, as their hooves could not get traction on a smooth and hard road; conversely, a road with a soft and uneven surface, ideal for hooves, did not meet the technical demands of the wheel. This contradiction was impossible to resolve as long as wheeled vehicles were pulled by draft animals. 'A road, then,' Lardner concluded, 'cannot be perfect, or even nearly perfect, for both purposes.' A 'compromise between the two principles is inevitable: a road that is as smooth and hard as possible, while being as soft and rough as is necessary for the horses' hooves'.[11]

---

motion; Newton's law, on the other hand, is based on the technical realities of its own time (i.e., shipbuilding, machine construction, and arms technology, especially ballistics), being, as it were, the theoretical sum of that technology. These connections are discussed brilliantly in B. Hessen's *The Social and Economic Roots of Newton's 'Principia'* (New York, 1971). (Originally an address to the International Congress of the History of Science and Technology in London in 1931.)

10. D. Lardner, *The Steam Engine, Steam Navigation, Roads and Railways*, 8th ed. (London, 1851), pp. 315–16.

11. Lardner, op. cit., pp. 339–40.

As the latter were replaced by the locomotive, the contradiction ceased to exist. Henceforth the four essentials of the mechanically perfect road could be realized without compromise. The railroad did this first and foremost by means of the rail, which was harder, smoother, more level, and straighter than any road before it. While this revolution in transportation technology took place in a location separate from the traditional road grid, it influenced the latter nevertheless. Serving the need for short-distance transportation not provided by the railroads, the old type of highway survived until the end of the nineteenth century; it became obsolete as the automobile began to mechanize road traffic, and as road-building technology made an effort to approximate the technical principles of the railroads. When road vehicles were no longer pulled by horses but propelled by the internal combustion engine, the roads they ran on tended to become as smooth, hard, level and straight as the rails. By the twentieth century, their surfaces were covered with asphalt and concrete, whereby they achieved the technical standards set by the railroads in the nineteenth century.

The rail's primary function, to minimize the resistance caused by friction, was complemented by its further function of leveling the irregularities of the terrain. To keep friction at a minimum, the rail must be smooth and hard, to achieve optimal performance with the least expenditure of energy, the rail must run a level and straight course. Before laying the track, considerable earth moving was necessary to lay a level and straight roadbed through uneven terrain. Nicholas Wood provided an illustration and description of this in the third edition of his standard technical work of 1838:

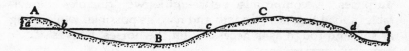

Let A, B, C, Fig. 1, represent a section or the outline of the country over which the railways is to pass, and a, b, c, d, e, the level at which the railway is to be formed. All those parts of the section which are above the line a, b, c, d, e, to the extent of the width required for the railway, will, therefore, require to be cut through, excavated, or levelled down; and those portions which are below that line, will require to be embanked or levelled up. The portions A and C, will, therefore, have to be cut down, and the portion B, raised up or embanked. The portions of railway, a b, and c d, of the section, are, consequently, called *excavations*, or *cuttings*; and the portions b c, d e, *embankments*, or *embanking*.[12] (Italics in original.)

Cuttings and embankments were the staple procedures of railroad construction. Greater irregularities of the terrain, such as valleys and mountains, were overcome by means of tunnels and viaducts.

The railroad, built thus across the terrain by means of cuttings, embankments, tunnels, and viaducts, made its mark on the European landscape from the 1850s on; it also made its mark on travelers' perceptions. The alienation from immediate, living nature that was initiated by the mechanization of motive power was increased as the railroad was constructed straight across the terrain, as if drawn with a ruler. The railroad was to the traditional highway as the steam engine was to the draught animal: in both cases, mechanical regularity triumphed over natural irregularity. The abandonment of animal power in favor of steam was experienced as the loss of sensorially perceptible animal power/exhaustion, i.e., as the loss of the sense of space and motion that was based on it. As the natural irregularities of the terrain that were perceptible on the old roads were replaced by the sharp linearity of the railroad, the traveler felt that he lost contact with the landscape, and surely experienced this most directly when going through a tunnel.

Early descriptions of journeys on the railroad noted that the railroad and the landscape through which it ran were in two separate worlds. Thus a report on a trip from Manchester to Liverpool in 1833: '. . . we enter the Olive Mount excavation. Here a passage for the railway has been effected through the solid rock by a cutting seventy feet deep and about fifteen wide. . . . Several bridges are thrown over to connect the opposite precipices, and appear to the eye, as we move along the depth below, like communications belonging to beings of another sphere'.[13]

Similarly, a description of a journey from London to Birming-

---

12. Nicholas Wood, *A Practical Treatise on Rail-Roads*, 3rd ed. (London, 1838), p. 136.
13. *The Railway Companion* (London, 1833), p. 40.

ham in 1839: 'As far as the eye can range, one immense chasm through the earth appears before the observer, and at intervals are bridges carrying roads across the railway at a frightful height. . . . The echoes in this place are very distinct, and whilst traversing its extent you seem shut out from all communication with the world'.[14]

The empirical reality that made the landscape seen from the train window appear to be 'another world' was the railroad itself, with its excavations, tunnels, etc. Yet the railroad was merely an expression of the rail's technological requirements, and the rail itself was a constituent part of the machine ensemble that was the system. It was, in other words, that machine ensemble that interjected itself between the traveler and the landscape. The traveler perceived the landscape as it was filtered through the machine ensemble.

That was the nature of the new perception of landscape and motion. If the material bases for the old perception of landscape and motion were the physical power of the draught animals, the road that followed the contours of the terrain, and the 'leeway' given to the vehicle on the road,[15] and if the old perception occurred via all these natural and only loosely connected elements of transportation technology, then the character of the new machine ensemble was one of tremendous technical discipline. To follow Reuleaux's argument, the appearance of the machine ensemble signalled the end of free play between the individual elements of machines in general. Compared to the old technology, the new appeared more derived, more unnatural, even more restrictive: this has been documented in contemporary literature and journalism. Yet it was not only the critical mind of the era that found it hard to accommodate itself to the new transportation technology. The railroad was such an entirely novel apparatus that even those who advocated its use

14. Thomas Roscoe, *The London and Birmingham Railway, With the Home and Country Scenes on Each Side of the Line* (London, 1839), pp. 67–8. The Liverpool–Manchester Act actually required the isolation of the railroad from the surrounding countryside, highways, etc., as Cohn points out while summarizing the edicts, 'a railway shall at no point intersect with another road, but shall proceed separately from all other thoroughfares by means of viaducts etc.' (Gustav Cohn, *Die Entwicklung der Eisenbahngesetzgebung in England, Untersuchungen über die englische Eisenbahnpolitik*, vol. 1 [Leipzig, 1874], p. 34.)

15. It is true that the highway and the vehicle moving on it also constitute a machine ensemble, because of their interrelationship. Yet that unity is, in practical terms, a very loose one, as the vehicle is individually manoeuverable and mobile on the road.

as a means of public transportation misunderstood it at first. They regarded it as a means like any other: they were aware of the peculiarity of rails but unable to recognize the consequences. It was obvious that an iron wheel running on an iron rail had less friction to contend with than a wheel on a highway, yet at first no one considered the possibility of constructing railroads independent from existing traditional roads. Thus, for instance, Richard Lovell Edgeworth — who in 1802, twenty years before Gray, published the first proposal to construct railways for public transport — saw the rail entirely in the context of the road, and thus proposed that the existing roads, more specifically, the ones with the heaviest volume of traffic, be furnished with rails. Here, the railroad was not seen as an autonomous traffic system, but merely as a highway provided with rails which essentially retained its traditional traffic pattern. The only change perceived was that friction was reduced. The vehicles remained individual road vehicles, but for the duration of their travel on the rails they had to be lifted onto an undercarriage that is fitted to the rails:

> Now to accommodate coaches and chaises, etc., to these rail-ways, I would have them carried, wheels and all, in cradles or platforms, *which should have wheels adapted to the rail-ways.* By these means no alteration would be necessary in any of the carriages commonly used; but the horses of any coach or chaise might, as soon as they had got out of town, walk up an inclined plane into the cradle or platform, and draw their respective carriages after them: the horses should then walk out at the farthest end of the platform, upon the road belonging to the rail-ways. They would then draw the chaise not upon its own wheels, but upon the wheels of the platform or cradle in which the *chaise* should be detained.[16] (Italics in original.)

A little later, in the same text, Edgeworth stressed once more the autonomy retained by the private vehicles using the rails: 'The chief convenience of this project arises from the mode of receiving and transporting on rail-ways every carriage now in use *without any change in their structure* so that a traveller may quit and resume the common road at pleasure'.[17] (Italics in

16. William Nicholson, *Journal of Natural Philosophy, Chemistry, and the Arts* (London, 1802), p. 222.
17. Op. cit., p. 223.

original.)

While Edgeworth still saw his 'rail-way', quite naively, as a potential extension of the common road, he was, however, aware of the rail's tendency to restrict the free and individual maneuvering of vehicles. This gave rise to his suggestion that four separate railways be constructed on a road, two in either direction, and in each pair, one for coaches, one for vehicles carrying goods. That first premonition of a reorganization of traffic according to the technology of the rail was developed further twenty years later in Gray's proposal for a *national* system of railways. Gray still thought in terms of the categories of individual traffic, but his railways were to constitute a traffic system independent from the existing highways.[18] Gray quite clearly demonstrates the ever-more acute perception of the inherent contradiction between the rail and individual traffic, a contradiction that remained unresolved until the late 1830s. While the technical concept of the rail did not tolerate individual traffic, the economic thinking of the time could conceive of nothing *but* such individual traffic. As long as the contradiction remained unresolved, the only way in which both conditions could be satisfied was to multiply the number of parallel railways. Between Edgeworth's time and Gray's, their number had already grown: 'In order to establish a general iron rail-way, it will be necessary to lay down two or three rail-ways for the ascending, and an equal number for the descending vehicles. In the immediate neighbourhood of London the traffic might demand six rail-ways'.[19]

In the writings of Edgeworth and Gray, the conflict between the rail and individual traffic appeared merely in the form of proposals and projections for ways of organizing railways for public transportation; however, the actual practice of such transportation, as it became a reality in the 1820s, became more and more seriously impeded by that conflict.

In 1855, Lardner retrospectively described the economic views

18. The very first edition of Gray's *Observations* (1820) contains a map of England, Scotland and Wales, on which the national railroad network has been drawn in as a series of *straight* connecting lines between the major cities. In the subsequent editions we find an increasingly strong emphasis on the idea that this would have to be a transportation network of an entirely novel kind. Thus, for instance, in the fifth edition, Gray speaks of the 'absolute necessity of an entirely new system of national intercourse'. (p. 1.)
19. Gray, 5th ed. (London, 1825), p. 12.

of the early period, when the railroad was regarded simply as a means of transportation similar to canal and turnpike, to be used by individual vehicle owners upon the payment of tolls:

> It was expected that the public should be admitted to exercise the business of carriers upon them [the rails], subject to certain specified regulations and by-laws. It soon became apparent, however, that this new means of transport was attended with qualities which must exclude every indiscriminate exercise of the carrying business. A railway, *like a vast machine*, the wheels of which are all connected with each other, and whose movement requires a certain harmony, can not be worked by a number of independent agents. Such a system would speedily be attended with self-destruction. The organization of a railway requires unity of direction and harmony of movement, which can only be attained by the combination of the entire carrying business with the general administration of the road.[20](Italics in original.)

It took a while before the technological necessity of the railroad companies' monopoly on transportation (i.e., the management of both rails and carriages under one supervisory agency) prevailed against the liberal view that was based on principles applicable to canals and turnpikes. As late as 1838, there were private vehicles on the Liverpool–Manchester line.[21] W. T. Jackman enumerates the following reasons for the termination of such individualism in transportation, which was occurring despite the fact that 'laissez-faire doctrines were so predominant in every other aspect of the national life':

(1) Dangers caused by non-coordination of trains of vehicles traveling on the line.

(2) The absence of technically necessary facilities along the line (coal and water depots).

20. D. Lardner, *Railway Economy* (London, 1851), pp. 421–2.
21. W. T. Jackman, *The Development of Transportation in Modern England* (1st ed., 1916; repr. London, 1962), p. 573. Jackman deals with the entire complex on pp. 572–9. Cohn quotes the clause of the Liverpool–Manchester Act which guarantees free access to all vehicles: 'All persons shall have free liberty to use with carriages all roads, ways and passages for the purpose of conveying goods or passengers or cattle' (op. cit., p. 36). Cohn continues: 'For this to be possible, the carriages used by the freight entrepreneurs have to conform to those regulations that the railroad company deems practicable and advertises in every station. Furthermore, the owners of adjoining property receive the right to construct branch lines to the Liverpool–Manchester line' (op. cit., pp. 36–7).

(3) Negligible profits for the private transport entrepreneurs.

(4) The disregard evinced by those entrepreneurs and private users of the line towards the railroad's technical regulations.[22]

Jackman describes the end of individual rail traffic:

Soon it became evident to the railway companies that, with due regard to the efficiency of their line and to the public convenience and safety, they could not allow rival parties to run engines and carriages on the same line; and it was eventually acknowledged that these lines of communication must be placed under undivided control and authority. Accordingly, a Parliamentary Committee of 1839 urged the necessity of prohibiting, as far as locomotive power was concerned, the rivalry of competing parties on the same line of railway; and the Committee of 1840 decided that railway companies using locomotive power possessed a particular monopoly for the conveyance of passengers, from the nature of their business.[23]

Thus, finally, after many vain efforts to accommodate the new transport technology to juridical concepts appropriate to the old, the inherent character of that new technology prevailed even in the juridical realm. The railroad as a machine ensemble received its legal and politico-economic sanction in the form of the transport monopoly.

The process by which the institutions accommodated themselves to the railroad as a machine ensemble did not end with the acceptance of the transport monopoly. The chaos caused by individual traffic on the rail lines, now terminated by the monopoly, repeated itself on a higher level. In England (although not in Belgium or France) the railroad system grew without central planning, on a purely private-enterprise basis. The railway network grew denser through the construction of more and more lines, but never became a unified entity: it remained merely the sum of numerous local and regional lines that operated independently from each other. Technologically, it was a national transportation grid, providing fast and comfortable

22. Op. cit., pp. 573–4.
23. Op. cit., p. 574; see also Cohn, p. 45.

access to all its parts; but as an organization, based on private enterprise, it was a multitude of individual lines, isolated, working without coordination, or even working against each other. While objectively the expansion of the system should facilitate travel, in fact it increased the difficulties involved in changing trains and in transferring goods from one line to another, by creating impediments such as uncoordinated schedules and stations located at long distances from one another.

The unification of the railway network proceeded just as slowly and reluctantly as did the development of the transport monopoly. Finally, in 1842 the English railway companies created a cooperative and coordinating authority to deal with traffic moving along more than one line — i.e., through traffic, as distinct from merely local and regional traffic.[24] This through traffic was becoming more and more important to the national economy.

Thus the railroad as a machine ensemble finally became institutionalized even in this respect, despite the resistance offered by the economic thought of the period, which was based on the principle of competition. The machine ensemble, consisting of wheel and rail, railroad and carriage, expanded into a unified railway system, which appeared as one great machine covering the land.[25]

In order to guarantee the proper functioning of this machine, juridical and politico-economic regulations had to be revised, but technological improvements proved equally necessary. The most important technological addition to the railways was the electrically operated telegraph system.

While this telegraph system had been technically perfected at the beginning of the nineteenth century, before the advent of the railroad it did not, at first, find any practical application; there was no part for it to play. That changed with the coming of

---

24. The institution was the Railway Clearing House, based on the Clearing House of English Banks. The best description of its genesis and function can be found in Philip S. Bagwell, *The Railway Clearing House in the British Economy, 1842–1922* (London, 1968).
25. The notion of the railroad as a great machine spread out over the land is implicit in the early definitions of the railroad as a machine ensemble. There is a vivid example of it in Governor Everett's speech at the opening of the Boston–Albany Line (quoted in J. S. Buckingham, *The Eastern and Western States of America* [London, 1842], vol. 1, p. 51): 'Let us contemplate the entire railroad, with its cars and engines, as one vast machine! What a portent of art! its fixed portion a hundred miles long; its moveable portion flying across the State like a weaver's shuttle'.

the railways, on which a signaling system played a vital part from the very beginning. The machine ensemble, whose parts had to be minutely adjusted to each other, must not fall prey to catastrophes. Contemporary illustrations demonstrate the tense watchfulness that characterized early journeys on the railroad. On each carriage of the train we see one, two, sometimes three persons, whose sole task it is to scan the line ahead for obstacles, approaching trains, etc. The first optical and acoustical signals that were devised to assist in this activity soon proved insufficient in dark, foggy or noisy conditions and, of course, when going through tunnels.

Tunnel passages provided the telegraph with its first practical application.[26] The system devised for its use (first in tunnels, later all along the line), the 'space interval system', consisted of a division of the entire line into separate 'blocks', each served by a telegraph transmitter. This transmitter signalled to the block ahead when the line was clear; the engine-driver then received an optical signal that told him to go ahead. The system relieved the engine-driver from any remaining obligation to exercise his personal powers of perception and judgement on the conditions that prevailed around him and his train: all he needed to do was to follow the signals given by a distant telegraph center. Because a train runs on a predetermined line an engine-driver could never aspire to the social role of a 'captain on dry land': the electric telegraph confirmed his true status, that of an industrial worker, an operator of a machine. The telegraph became an integral element of the machine ensemble; Max Maria von Weber, a philosophically-minded railroad expert and son of the well-known composer, observed that without the telegraph the railway would be like an organism without a nervous system: '. . . as the muscle of a human body without the nerve flashing through it would be a mere lifeless hunk of flesh, so would the flying muscles that Watt's and Stephenson's inventions have lent to humanity be only half as capable of winging their way, if they were not animated by the guiding thought imperiously flashing through the nerves of the telegraph wires'.[27]

26. Cooke and Wheatstone introduced it from Germany to England in the early 1830s. (Karl Zetsche, *Geschichte der elektrischen Telegraphie* [Berlin, 1877], p. 157.)
27. In Dolf Sternberger, *Panorama, oder Ansichten vom 19. Jahrhundert*, 3rd ed. (Hamburg, 1955); transl. as *Panorama of the Nineteenth Century* (Oxford and New York, 1978). The

However, the electric telegraph did not gain such tremendous significance solely for its effect on the actual running of the machine ensemble. Its visual imagery became a major emblem of railway travel: the outer world beyond the compartment window was mediated to the traveler by the telegraph poles and wires which flashed by — no longer did he see only the landscape through which he journeyed, but also, continuously, the poles and wires that belong to the railroad as intimately as the rails themselves do. The landscape appeared *behind* the telegraph poles and wires; it was seen *through* them. As we noted earlier, the rail traveler's perceptions were changed by the intervention of the machine ensemble between him and the landscape; there was a material demonstration of that intervention in those poles and wires, which were a part of the machine ensemble. They interposed themselves, both physically and metaphorically, between the traveler and the landscape.[28] To use Dolf Sternberger's term, the resulting perception was 'panoramic'. Verlaine, in the seventh poem of his cycle *La Bonne Chanson*, describes it with technical precision. The hurtling railroad train appears as the very motion of writing and the telegraph poles and wires are the calligraphic instruments with which the new perception inscribes the panoramic landscape upon the real one:

> *Le paysage dans le cadre des portières*
> *Court furieusement, et des plaines entières*
> *Avec de l'eau, des blés, des arbres et du ciel*
> *Vont s'engouffrant parmi le tourbillon cruel*

---

passage comes from the posthumously published volume *Vom rollenden Flügelrade* (1882). The phrase 'flying muscles' refers to the railroad's trademark, or symbol, the winged wheel. Sternberger quotes the passage while discussing the mutual influence exercised by technological and organic metaphors in the nineteenth century.

28. A prosaic footnote to the poetic perception of telegraph poles can be found in an anonymous work of 1848, *Railway Appliances in the Nineteenth Century; or, The Rail, Steam, and Electricity* (London, 1848), p. 32. It is a proposal to determine the speed of the train (which could not yet be determined directly due to lack of technical 'instinct') by means of close observation of the telegraph poles, i.e., by measuring the time that the train needs to pass from one pole to the next. 'These [the poles] are generally erected about sixty yards apart, or thirty in the mile, so that the speed of the train is easily found by counting the number of poles passed in a minute and multiplying by two, which, of course, gives the rate per hour'. Thus the telegraph poles act as a kind of gauge for determining an element of the journey, i.e., velocity, that can no longer be experienced in an immediate way. This is a factor that contributes to the traveler's alienation from the landscape.

Où tombent les poteaux minces du télégraphe
Dont les fils ont l'allure étrange d'un paraphe.

(The scene behind the carriage window-panes
Goes flitting past in furious flight; whole plains
With streams and harvest-fields and trees and blue
Are swallowed by the whirlpool, whereinto
The telegraph's slim pillars topple o'er,
Whose wires look strangely like a music-score.)[29]

29. Paul Verlaine, *Oeuvres poétiques complètes* (Paris, 1951), p. 106. The cycle 'La bonne chanson' was written in the winter of 1869/70; transl. Gertrude Hall, in *Baudelaire, Rimbaud, Verlaine: Selected Verse and Prose Poems*, (New York, 1947).

[3]
Railroad Space
and Railroad Time

Economically, the railways' operation . . . causes distances to
diminish . . . Lille suddenly finds itself transported to Louvres;
Calais to Pontoise; le Havre to Poissy; Rouen to Sèvres or to
Asnières; Reims to Pantin; Strasbourg to Meaux; Lyon to a place
half-way between Melun and Corbeil; Marseilles to Nemours;
Perpignan to Pithiviers; Bordeaux to Chartres or to Étampes;
Nantes to Arpajon, etc.
— Constantin Pecqueur, 1839

'Annihilation of space and time' was the early-nineteenth-
century characterization of the effect of railroad travel. The
concept was based on the speed that the new means of transport
was able to achieve. A given spatial distance, traditionally covered in a fixed amount of travel time, could suddenly be dealt
with in a fraction of that time; to put it another way, the same
amount of time permitted one to cover the old spatial distance
many times over. In terms of transport economics, this meant a
shrinking of space: 'Distances practically diminish in the exact
ratio of the speed of personal locomotion', Lardner says in his
Railway Economy.[1]

The average traveling speed of the early railways in England
was twenty to thirty miles an hour, or roughly three times the

1. D. Lardner, *Railway Economy* (London, 1850), p. 35.

speed previously achieved by the stagecoaches.[2] Thus, any given distance was covered in one-third of the customary time: temporally, that distance shrank to one-third of its former length. In early-nineteenth-century writings the temporal diminution is expressed mostly in terms of a shrinking of space. An article published in the *Quarterly Review* in 1839 speaks of 'the gradual annihilation, approaching almost to the final extinction, of that space and of those distances which have hitherto been supposed unalterably to separate the various nations of the globe', and continues:

> For instance, supposing that railroads, even at our present simmering rate of travelling, were to be suddenly established all over England, the whole population of the country would, speaking metaphorically, at once advance *en masse*, and place their chairs nearer to the fireside of their metropolis by two-thirds of the time which now separates them from it; they would also sit nearer to one another by two-thirds of the time which now respectively alienates them. If the rate were to be sufficiently accelerated, this process would be repeated; our harbours, our dock-yards, our towns, the whole of our rural population, would again not only draw nearer to each other by two-thirds, but all would proportionally approach the national hearth. As distances were thus annihilated, the surface of our country would, as it were, shrivel in size until it became not much bigger than one immense city.[3]

The image of a temporal shrinkage seen as a spatial one appeared in an even more extravagant guise in the work of Constantin Pecqueur, the economist and Saint-Simonian, whose *Economie sociale* received a prize from the Institut de France in 1838. Here, the temporally shrunk transport space is a new geography of France, a geography based on the new conditions of speed, a condensed geography, as it were. The cities of France approached each other while simultaneously advancing on Paris. These changes in location, enumerated in

2. According to H. G. Lewin, *The Railway Mania and its Aftermath, 1845–52* (London, 1936), the average speed, up to 1845, was 'between 20 and 30 miles per hour' (p. 95). The Great Western Express, the fastest English train, reached a speed of 46 mph. Lardner says the speed of the stagecoaches was a little less than 8 mph (*Railway Economy*, p. 36), whereas Lewin claims that the fastest coaches achieved 10 mph. The actual speed of English trains in the 1840s, i.e., their top speed, was, according to Lardner, frequently 60 to 70 mph (*Railway Economy*, p. 170).
3. *Quarterly Review*, vol. 63 (1839), p. 22.

the epigraph to this chapter, are summarized in Pecqueur's statement that it had become possible to see 'the new France as fitting into the space of the *old* Île-de-France, or its equivalent'.

The diminution of transport distances seemed to create a new, reduced, geography, yet it did not actually alter the size of the spaces between the points connected by the new mode of transport. 'Yet by a sort of miracle,' says the *Quarterly Review* article, after describing the shrinking process, 'every man's field would be found not only *where* it always was, but *as large* as ever it was'. Pecqueur expressed the same notion in literary hyperbole: the diminished transport geography of France contained the true geography of France within it in a condensed form: 'Each bit of terrain, each field on this surface would still remain intact; so would every house in a village, the village itself, or the town; every territory with its village in the center would remain a province; on the map of the imagination, all of these would finally be reproduced and reduced down to the infinitely small! As for Louvres, or Pontoise, or Chartres, or Arpajon, etc., it is obvious that they will just get lost in some street of Paris or its suburbs'.[4]

The notion that a French town could fit into a Paris street demonstrates that the alteration of spatial relationships by the speed of the railway train was not simply a process that diminished space, but that it was a dual one: space was both diminished *and* expanded. The dialectic of this process states that this diminution of space (i.e., the shrinking of transport time) caused an expansion of transport space by incorporating new areas into the transport network. The nation's contraction into a metropolis, as described in the *Quarterly Review*, conversely appeared as an expansion of the metropolis: by establishing transport lines to ever more outlying areas, the metropolis tended to incorporate the entire nation. Thus the epoch of the suburbs, of the amoebic proliferation of the formerly contained cities into the surrounding countryside, began with the railroads. This is Lardner in 1851:

> It is not now unusual for persons whose place of business is in the centre of the capital, to reside with their families at a distance of from

4. Constantin Pecqueur, *Économie sociale* (Paris, 1839), vol. 1, p. 26.

fifteen to twenty miles from that centre. Nevertheless, they are able to arrive at their respective shops, counting-houses, or offices, at an early hour of the morning, and to return without inconvenience to their residence at the usual time in the evening. Hence in all directions round the metropolis in which railways are extended, habitations are multiplied, and a considerable part of the former population of London has been diffused in these quarters.[5]

The notion that the railroad annihilated space and time was not related to that expansion of space that resulted from the incorporation of new spaces into the transport network. What was experienced as being annihilated was the traditional space –time continuum which characterized the old transport technology. Organically embedded in nature as it was, that technology, in its mimetic relationship to the space traversed, permitted the traveler to perceive that space as a living entity. What Bergson called the *durée* (duration, the time spent getting from one place to another on a road) is not an objective mathematical unit, but a subjective perception of space–time. The dependence of this perception on transport technology illustrates Durkheim's notion that a society's space–time perceptions are a function of its social rhythm and its territory.[6] 'What is decisive', says Erwin Straus, discussing the psychology of distances, 'is not the objectively measured distance, but the relation of such distance to potentiality.'[7] Transport technology is the material base of potentiality, and equally the material base of the traveler's space–time perception. If an essential element of a given sociocultural space–time continuum undergoes change, this will affect the entire structure; our perception of space–time will also lose its accustomed orientation. Sorokin, following Durkheim, distinguishes between sociocultural and physico-mathematical notions of space–time, and has described the hypothetical effects of a sudden replacement of customary sociocultural time measures with purely mathematical ones: 'If we try to replace sociocultural time by a purely quantitative time, time becomes devitalized. *It loses its reality, and we find ourselves in an exceedingly difficult position in our efforts to orient ourselves in the time process, to*

5. Op. cit., p. 36.
6. Émile Durkheim, *The Elementary Forms of the Religious Life* (Glencoe, Ill., 1947), pp. 10–11, 440.
7. Erwin Straus, *The Primary World of the Senses* (New York and London, 1963), p. 385.

find out "where we are" and where are the other social phenomena on "the bridge of time"'.[8] (Italics in original.)

Thus, the idea that the railroad annihilated space and time must be seen as the reaction of perceptive powers that, formed by a certain transport technology, find suddenly that technology has been replaced by an entirely new one. Compared to the eotechnical space–time relationship, the one created by the railroad appears abstract and disorientating, because the railroad — in realizing Newton's mechanics — negated all that characterized eotechnical traffic; the railroad did not appear embedded in the space of the landscape the way coach and highway are, but seemed to strike its way through it.

Heinrich Heine captured the disorientation experienced by the traditional space–time consciousness when confronted by the new technology; apropos the opening of railway lines from Paris to Rouen and Orléans in 1843, he wrote of the 'tremendous foreboding such as we always feel when there comes an enormous, an unheard-of event whose consequences are imponderable and incalculable', and called the railroad a 'providential event', comparable to the inventions of gunpowder and printing, 'which swings mankind in a new direction, and changes the color and shape of life'. Heine continues in this vein:

> What changes must now occur, in our way of looking at things, in our notions! Even the elementary concepts of time and space have begun to vacillate. Space is killed by the railways, and we are left with time alone. . . . Now you can travel to Orléans in four and a half hours, and it takes no longer to get to Rouen. Just imagine what will happen when the lines to Belgium and Germany are completed and connected up with their railways! I feel as if the mountains and forests of all countries were advancing on Paris. Even now, I can smell the German linden trees; the North Sea's breakers are rolling against my door.[9]

We have now clearly stated the two contradictory sides of the same process: on one hand, the railroad opened up new spaces that were not as easily accessible before; on the other, it did so by destroying space, namely the space between points. That in-between, or travel space, which it was possible to 'savor'

---

8. Pitrim A. Sorokin, *Sociocultural Causality, Space, and Time* (Durham, NC, 1943), p. 197.
9. Heine, *Lutezia*, pt 2, lvii, Elster ed., vol. 6, p. 360.

while using the slow, work-intensive eotechnical form of transport, disappeared on the railroads. The railroad knows only points of departure and destination. 'They [the railways] only serve the points of departure, the way-stations, and the terminals, which are mostly at great distances from each other', said a French author in 1840, 'they are of no use whatsoever for the intervening spaces, which they traverse with disdain and provide only with a useless spectacle'.[10]

As the space between the points — the traditional traveling space — was destroyed, those points moved into each other's immediate vicinity: one might say that they collided. They lost their old sense of local identity, formerly determined by the spaces between them. The isolation of localities, which was created by spatial distance, was the very essence of their identity, their self-assured and complacent individuality. Heine's vision of the North Sea breaking on his doorstep in Paris was tinged with 'tremendous foreboding' because both localities — Paris and the North Sea — were still presented in their mutually isolated state, 'worlds apart': thus their collision appeared unfathomable. Thirty years later, as an interlocking network of railroad lines connected all of Europe, that kind of consciousness was no longer realistic. Regardless of their geographical remoteness, the regions appeared as close and as easily accessible as the railways had made them. One generation after Heine, the more privileged inhabitants of Paris had the option of letting themselves be transported, in a matter of hours, to a region that was as distant from their city as Heine's North Sea. The Mediterranean does not extend its shores right up to Parisian thresholds, but it could be reached so much more quickly than before that the journey there was no longer experienced as such. The Parisians who migrated south in the winter saw nothing but blue skies and the sea. As Mallarmé wrote in the winter of 1874/5, in *La Dernière Mode*, the journal he edited, they are 'calm, self-absorbed people, paying no attention to the invisible landscapes of the journey. To leave Paris and to get to where the sky is clear, that is their desire'.[11] They were no longer travelers — rather, as Ruskin puts it, they were human parcels who dis-

10. Charles Dunoyer, *Esprit et méthodes comparés de l'Angleterre et de la France dans les entreprises de travaux publics et en particulier des chemins de fer* (Paris, 1840), p. 104.
11. Stéphane Mallarmé, *Oeuvres complètes*, Pléiade ed. (Paris, 1970), p. 843.

patched themselves to their destination by means of the railway, arriving as they left, untouched by the space traversed.

Even though the railroad was incapable of bringing the remote regions physically to Paris, the speedy and comfortable accessibility of those regions created a consciousness of distance that approximated to Heine's vision of space, but without the sense of foreboding. The region that could be reached by train from Paris realized itself for the Parisians by means of the train. It then appeared as the product or appendage of the railroad, as in a phrase of Mallarmé's: 'Normandy, which, like Brittany, is part of the Western Railway'.[12]

But if Normandy and Brittany, being its destinations, were part of the Western Railway, then the point of departure of that same railway, the station in Paris, became the entrance to those regions. This was a common enough notion in the nineteenth century: it is to be found in every one of Baedeker's travel guides that recommends a certain railroad station as the point of departure for each excursion.

The identification of the railroad station with the traveler's destination, and the relative insignificance of the journey itself, were expressed by Mallarmé in *La Dernière Mode*, under the heading *Gazette et Programme de la Quinzaine*; the following subheadings represented equally important institutions for entertainment: *Les Librairies, Les Théâtres, Les Gares* (the last sometimes replaced by *Les Voyages*). Thus a railroad journey appeared in no way different from a visit to the theater or the library — the purchase of a train ticket was equivalent to that of a theater ticket.

A generation after Mallarmé, Marcel Proust, in *A la Recherche du temps perdu*, discussed the difference between a journey by train and one in a motorcar:

> The journey was one that would now be made, probably, in a motor-car, which would be supposed to render it more interesting. We shall see too that, accomplished in such a way, it would even be in a sense more genuine, since one would be following more clearly, in a closer intimacy, the various contours by which the surface of the earth is wrinkled. But after all, the special attraction of the journey lies not in our being able to alight at places on the way and to stop

12. Op. cit., p. 774.

altogether as soon as we grow tired, but in its making the difference between departure and arrival not as imperceptible but as intense as possible, so that we are conscious of it in its totality, intact, as it existed in our mind when imagination bore us from the place in which we were living right to the very heart of a place we longed to see, in a single sweep which seemed miraculous to us not so much because it covered a certain distance as because it united two distinct individualities of the world, took us from one name to another name; and this difference is accentuated (more than in a form of locomotion in which, since one can stop and alight where one chooses, there can scarcely be said to be any point of arrival) by the mysterious opera-tion- that is performed in those peculiar places, railway stations, which do not constitute, so to speak, a part of the surrounding town but contain the essence of its personality just as upon their sign-boards they bear its painted name.[13]

The fate wrought upon the outlaying regions by the railroads affected goods even sooner: as long as production and con-sumption were strictly regional — which they were until the beginning of modern transportation — goods remained part of the local identity of their place of production. Their route of circulation was to be perceived at a glance. Only when modern transportation created a definite spatial distance between the place of production and the place of consumption did the goods become uprooted commodities. In *Grundrisse*, Marx makes an observation about the relation between spatial distance and the nature of commodities; it tells us a good deal about how modern transportation has affected our perception of goods: 'This lo-cational movement — the bringing of the product to the market, which is a necessary condition of its circulation, except when the point of production is itself a market — could more precisely be regarded as the transformation of the product *into a commodity*'.[14] (Italics in original.)

With the spatial distance that the product covered on its way from its place of production to the market, it also lost its local identity, its spatial presence. Its concretely sensual properties, which were experienced at the place of production as a result of

---

13. *Remembrance of Things Past*, vol. II, *Within a Budding Grove*, I; transl. by C. K. Scott Moncrieff (New York, 1934, pp. 489–90).
14. Karl Marx, *Grundrisse, Foundations of the Critique of Political Economy* (London, 1973), p. 534.

the labor process (or, in the case of the fruits of the land, as a result of natural growth), appeared quite different in the distant market-place. There the product, now a commodity, could realize its economic value and simultaneously gain new qualities as an object of consumption. No longer was it seen in the context of the original locality of its place of production but in the new locality of the market-place: cherries offered for sale in the Paris market were seen as products of that market, just as Normandy seemed to be a product of the railroad that takes you there. Pecqueur touches on the notion of the unity of the realization of economic value and the biological process, using the example of the ripening of fruit: 'For instance, economically speaking, and for the sake of freshness and price, the cherries of Montmorency really ripen on the uncultivated summits of the Quartier Lafayette; the roses of Fontenay burst into bloom and fragrance in the flower beds of the Jardin du Luxembourg; the peaches of Montreuil in the Parc de Monceaux, and the grapes of Fontainebleau, too, ripen on some hill closer to Paris than the one where the Surênes is still greening'.[15]

The regions, joined to each other and to the metropolis by the railways, and the goods that are torn out of their local relation by modern transportation, shared the fate of losing their inherited place, their traditional spatial–temporal presence or, as Walter Benjamin sums it up in one word, their 'aura'.

The detaching of the remote region from its original isolation, its opening-up by the railroad, can well be defined as the 'loss of its aura', as Benjamin characterizes the aura and its loss in his essay 'The Work of Art in the Age of Mechanical Reproduction'. The notions of spatial–temporal presence and distance were integral parts of Benjamin's concept of the aura. He defined the 'aura of natural objects' as 'the unique phenomenon of a distance, however close it may be'.[16] The aura of a work of art is 'its unique existence at the place where it happens to be'.[17] This spatial–temporal singularity, this 'happening-but-once-ness', this *genuineness* of the object, is, according to Benjamin, destroyed by reproduction. 'The situations into which the product of mechanical reproduction can be brought may not touch the

15. Op. cit., pp. 34–5.
16. Walter Benjamin, *Illuminations*, (New York, 1973), p. 222.
17. Ibid., p. 220.

actual work of art, yet the quality of its presence is always depreciated.'[18] It is tempting to apply this statement to the outlying regions that were made accessible by the railroad: while being opened up to tourism, they remained, initially at least, untouched in their physical actuality, but their easy, comfortable, and inexpensive accessibility robbed them of their previous value as remote and out-of-the-way places. 'The staple of the district is, in fact, its beauty and its character of seclusion and retirement', Wordsworth wrote in 1844, defending the Lake District against the intrusion of the railways.[19] The devaluation of outlying regions by their exploitation for mass tourism, by means of the railroad in the nineteenth century and air traffic in the twentieth, is a familiar occurrence. As soon as the railroad reached the seaside towns of southern England that had been strongholds of the aristocracy far into the nineteenth century, the middle classes took them over. Then the aristocracy retired to remote localities such as Scotland, Ireland, and the Lake District.[20] Contemporary air-line tourism is engaged in further devaluation of formerly exclusive, very remote regions.

The destruction of aura by means of reproduction, of which Benjamin speaks, is an expression of the same trend that brought the masses 'closer' to the outlying regions in the nineteenth century: 'The desire of contemporary masses to bring things "closer" spatially and humanly . . . is just as ardent as their bent toward overcoming the uniqueness of every reality by accepting its reproduction'.[21] The remote regions were made available to the masses by means of tourism: this was merely a prelude, a preparation for making any unique thing available by means of reproduction. When spatial distance is no longer experienced, the differences between original and reproduction diminish. In the filmic perception — i.e., the perception of *montage*, the juxtaposition of the most disparate images into one unit — the new reality of annihilated in-between spaces finds its clearest expression: the film brings things closer to the viewer as well as closer together.

The regions lost their temporal identity in an entirely concrete

18. Ibid., p. 221.
19. William Wordsworth, *The Prose Works*, ed. A. B. Grosart, (London, 1876, vol. 2), p. 326.
20. J. A. R. Pimplott, *The Englishman's Holiday* (London, 1947), p. 118.
21. Benjamin, ibid., p. 223.

sense: the railroads deprived them of their local time. As long as they remained isolated from each other, they had their individual times: London time ran four minutes ahead of time in Reading, seven minutes and thirty seconds ahead of Cirencester time, fourteen minutes ahead of Bridgwater time.[22] This patchwork of varying local times was no problem as long as traffic between the places was so slow that the slight temporal differences really did not matter; but the temporal foreshortening of the distances that was effected by the trains forced the differing local times to confront each other. Under traditional circumstances, a supra-regional schedule would be impossible: times of departure and arrival are valid only for the place whose local time is being used. For the next station, with its own time, that previous time is no longer valid. Regular traffic needs standardized time; this is analogous to the way in which the machine ensemble constituted by rail and carriage undermined individual traffic and brought about the transportation monopoly.

In the 1840s, the individual English railway companies proceeded to standardize time, but did not coordinate their efforts; each company instituted a new time on its own line. The process was so novel that it was repeated daily, in the most cumbersome manner, as Bagwell describes, apropos of the Grand Junction Company's procedure: 'Each morning an Admiralty messenger carried a watch bearing the correct time to the guard on the down Irish Mail leaving Euston for Holyhead. On arrival at Holyhead the time was passed on to officials on the Kingston boat who carried it over to Dublin. On the return mail to Euston the watch was carried back to the Admiralty messenger at Euston once more'.[23]

When, after the establishment of the Railway Clearing House, the companies decided to cooperate and form a national railroad network, Greenwich Time was introduced as the standard time, valid on all the lines.[24] Yet railroad time was not accepted as

22. Philip S. Bagwell, *The Transportation Revolution from 1770* (London, 1974), p. 124.
23. Op. cit., p. 125.
24. Greenwich time is the time kept at the Royal Observatory in Greenwich, founded in 1675. 'The precise standardization of time measurement dates from the foundation of the Royal Observatory in 1675' according to G. J. Whittow, *The Nature of Time* (London, 1972). Like the later standard time, the original Greenwich time was created to meet the needs of expanding traffic, i.e., shipping, in the seventeenth century. Vessels carried Greenwich time with them on their chronometers, as it was necessary for orientation and navigation. However, it was not used as a generalized norm for the division of the

anything but schedule time until late in the century. As the rail network grew denser, incorporating more and more regions, the retention of local times became untenable: in 1880, railroad time became general standard time in England. In Germany, official recognition came in 1893; as early as 1884, an international conference on time standards, held in Washington, DC, divided the world into time zones.

In the United States, the process was more complicated, as there was no cooperation whatsoever between the private railroad companies. Each company had its own time, in most cases the local time of the company's headquarters. In stations used by several different lines there were clocks showing different times: three of these in Buffalo, six in Pittsburgh.[25] In 1889, the United States was divided into four time zones, essentially unchanged to this day; officially, at first, the times within the zones were regarded only as railroad time; in practice, these became regional standard times, although they were not given legal recognition until 1918.

---

day: Greenwich time was still restricted to the walls of the cabinet that contained the chronometer during the voyage.

25. John Stover, *American Railroads* (Chicago, 1961), p. 157.

Excursus
The Space of Glass Architecture

The railroad reorganized space. In architecture, a similar reorganization occurred with the introduction of glass and steel as new building materials. The railroad machine ensemble multiplied speed and capacity of traffic; steel and glass multiplied the capacity of roofed structures. Both the railroad and the glass buildings were direct expressions of the multiplied productivity brought about by the industrial revolution. The railroad brought new quantities of goods into circulation; the edifices of glass architecture — railroad stations, market halls, exhibition palaces, arcades — served as places of transit and storage. The spatial capacity of glass architecture stands in a similar relation to the capacity of traditional architecture as the railroad's capacity stands to that of preindustrial transportation. This is due to the greater strength and resistance to stress characteristic of steel, the necessary complement to glass, compared to the previously utilized building materials. According to Alfred Gotthold Meyer, steel, in terms of stress resistance, is forty times as strong as stone, ten times as strong as wood.[1] The combination of steel as the carrier and glass as the filler led to a reappraisal of all previously recognized architectural principles; Meyer expresses it as follows:

(1) *The reappraisal of strength and mass.* By means of mathematical

1. Alfred Gotthold Meyer, *Eisenbauten: Ihre Geschichte und Ästhetik* (Eßlingen, 1907), p. 11.

[45]

calculation, it is possible to determine the statistically possible minimum of material required for a given structure, using a material that has hitherto unheard-of powers of resistance. The opposing forces are rationally divided into vectors of push and pull and then dealt with by appropriately formed cross sections. The result is strength without mass.

(2) *The reappraisal of spatial boundaries.* The wall masses shrink to thin boundary surfaces. The contained space no longer functions in terms of walls and vaults: it stands on its own, and does so inside as well as outside, without intermediaries.

(3) *The reappraisal of light and shadow.* New purposes demand maximal interior light: thus we get the glass roof, and with it, a diffuse light without contrast, lacking plastic definition of form, but also lacking painterly indefiniteness.

(4) To greater extent than with other building materials, the effective form of glass and steel architecture is based primarily on the structure itself, with its ubiquitous logical pattern of girders: The essential thing is now *the line*, not the self-contained mass.[2] (Italics in original.)

To sum up: it was the very nature of glass architecture that put an end to traditional architecture and its inevitable contrasts of light and shadow. As Meyer says, glass architecture creates a 'light-space'. 'The striving for lightness', he writes, 'is one of the main motivating forces in the developmental history of interior space. In the walls erected by stone or wood architecture, it could express itself only by breaking through the surfaces, in order to provide light for the interior; there was a conflict between light and shadow, between light and dark. It is, primarily, that contrast that gives us our sense of interior space and that gives a building its character, inside as well as outside.'[3]

The Crystal Palace, erected for the Great Exhibition in London in 1851, was the first true large-scale realization of glass and steel architecture; it caused perceptual shocks similar to those experienced by the first railway travelers. 'The enormous areas of glass introduced into the vaulting', Giedion says, describing contemporary reaction, 'almost blinded contemporary spectators, who were unaccustomed to the amount of light that was admitted.'[4]

2. Op. cit., p. 184.
3. Op. cit., p. 64.
4. Siegfried Giedion, *Space, Time and Architecture* (Cambridge, Mass., 1962), p. 255.

In his report on the 1851 Great Exhibition, Lothar Bucher — an emigré after the German Revolution of 1848, and later a collaborator of Bismarck — gave a vivid picture of the dazzling effect of ferro-vitreous architecture on the customary patterns of light and shadow perception:

We see a fine network of symmetrical lines that does not, however, provide any clues whereby one could estimate its distance from the eye or the actual size of the mesh. The side walls stand too far apart to be taken in at a glance, and instead of meeting a facing wall, the eye moves upward over an endless perspective, or one whose end appears diffuse and blue. We do not know whether that mesh hovers a hundred or a thousand feet above us, or whether the ceiling is flat or formed by a number of small parallel ceilings; this is due to the total absence of shadows, which normally aid the psyche in comprehending the impression received by the optical nerve. If we let our gaze slowly move downward again, it encounters the filigreed girders, painted blue, far apart from each other at first, then moving ever closer, then superimposed on each other, then interrupted by a shining band of light, and finally dissolving in a remote background in which everything corporeal, even the lines themselves, disappears and only the color remains. Looking at the side walls, we orient ourselves, by seeking out, from among the profusion of carpets, tapestries, animal skins, mirrors, and a thousand other draperies, a single uncovered pillar — so slender that it does not seem to be able to hold up any weight, but is there only to satisfy the eye's need to recognize a support; we can estimate its height by comparing it to some person passing by, and by observing a second and a third one above it.[5]

The impression of glass architecture can be summed up in one word: evanescence. The uniform quality of the light and the absence of light–shadow contrasts disorientated perceptual faculties used to those contrasts, just as the railroad's increased speed disorientated the traditional perception of space. The motion of the railway, proceeding uniformly and in a straight line, was experienced as abstract, *pure* motion, dissociated from the space in which it occured. Analogously, the space of ferro-vitreous architecture appeared as pure and abstract light-space,

5. Lothar Bucher, *Literaturhistorische Skizzen aus der Industrieausstellung aller Völker* (Frankfurt, 1851), pp. 10–11 (also quoted by Meyer and Giedion).

dissociated from all customary architectural form, a space without qualities and contrasts. Richard Lucae described the space of the Crystal Palace as an 'artificially created environment' that 'no longer is a space', and continues with an elegant simile:

> As in a crystal, there no longer is any true interior or exterior. We have been separated from nature, but we hardly feel it. The barrier erected between us and the landscape is almost ethereal. If we imagine that air can be poured like a liquid, then it has, here, achieved a solid form, after the removal of the mold into which it was poured. We find ourselves within a cut-out segment of atmosphere. . . . It is, in my opinion, extraordinarily difficult to arrive at a clear perception of the effect of form and scale in this incorporeal space.[6]

In dissociating light and atmosphere from the context of the natural overall atmosphere by means of 'an almost ethereal' barrier, ferro-vitreous architecture created a novel condition. Light and atmosphere were perceived as independent qualities, no longer subject to the rules of the natural world in which they had hitherto manifested themselves. This process was comparable to the experience of pure speed on the railroad, that is, speed perceived as an independent quality because it is divorced from the organic base of horse-power. (At the beginning of the twentieth century, the human voice was subjected to that same process of dissociation from its natural habitat, its natural condition, by the microphone and the radio.)[7]

Considering the newly gained independence of light from nature and the dissolution of corporeality that characterize Bucher's and Lucae's perceptions of the Crystal Palace, one might call their descriptions 'Impressionist'. Max Raphael's definition of the Impressionists' method of painting corresponds, in detail, to their perceptions of the inner space of the Crystal Palace: 'A dissolution of the object, in its closed form as well as in its inherent significance within the atmosphere; a cancellation of

6. Richard Lucae, 'Über die Macht des Raumes in der Architektur', *Zeitschrift für Bauwessen*, vol. 19 (1869), p. 303. A similar comment was made by the French architect Boileau in regard to the Galerie des Machines of the Paris World Expo of 1878: 'The spectator is not aware of the weight of the transparent surfaces. These surfaces are to him air and light, that is to say, an imponderable fluidity'. (Quoted in Giedion, op. cit., p. 265.)
7. I owe this realization to Hans-Thies Lehmann, who applies the thought successfully to this analysis of the early poetry of Bertolt Brecht.

the material concepts, e.g., the local color, the line of three-dimensional form, in favor of a relationship with light; an emphasis on appearance that simultaneously removes it into distance; the removal of space from the realm of visual representation'.[8] Siegfried Giedion[9] understands the effect of the Crystal Palace on its contemporaries as objectively Impressionist in intention, and makes a connection between Turner's painterly objectives and those of the architect of the Crystal Palace; that seems far-fetched, but it does seem justifiable to view Impressionism as a codification of a certain nineteenth-century perception of an evanescence whose most powerful material manifestations are the railroad and ferro-vitreous architecture.[10]

This digression on the novel spatiality of that architecture would not be complete without a reference to the developments that led to its demise. The Crystal Palace was the culmination and termination of ferro-vitreous architectural functionalism: it was followed, in the latter half of the century, by restorative developments. Ferro-vitreous methods of construction were relegated to tasks of roofing and dome-building. Builders reverted to the erection of massive and pompous stone fronts: these covered up the ferro-vitreous constructions, which could not be abandoned entirely owing to the lighting requirements of large interior spaces.

By the turn of the century, as it became possible to generate inexpensive artificial electric light by industrial means, ferro-vitreous architecture became redundant. The need for large structures for the display, storage, and merchandising of commodities remained, but the dependence on natural light disappeared. The ferrous mode of construction, which remained necessary for the stability of large rooms and buildings, detached itself from the vitreous aspect and took the form of steel

---

8. Max Raphael, *Von Monet zu Picasso* (Munich, 1913), p. 59.
9. Giedion says that Turner's painting *Simplon Pass*: '. . . uses a . . . humid atmosphere to dematerialize landscape and dissolve it into infinity. The Crystal Palace realizes the same intention through the agency of transparent glass surfaces and iron structural members. In the Turner picture the means employed are less abstract, but an equivalent insubstantial and hovering effect is produced'. (Op. cit., p. 253.)
10. The general economic base for this evanescence of perception is the fact that less and less labor (i.e. value) was invested in the individual product. Natural organic materials were increasingly replaced by synthetic surrogates; mass-produced objects were given built-in obsolescence; and 'surface finish' was emphasized.

skeletons for edifices that were once again constructed in the traditional massive materials.

Artificial electric light as a mass phenomenon originated and achieved its most extended potential in the United States of Edison's day. It was another giant step in the direction of independence from nature. Although ferro-vitreous architecture was an initial development in that same direction, it was still dependent upon and orientated toward nature, in that it attempted to maximize the use of natural light. The new, artificially lighted type of enclosed space required the very opposite — the minimization of glass windows. No longer was daylight an exploitable raw material but an uncertain factor that should be eliminated, as Matthew Luckiesh points out in his work *The Lighting Art*, published in 1917: 'Natural light does not possess the potentiality that artificial light does because it is generally less readily controlled and adapted to the problems'.[11] Windows were not only sources of irregular, unreliable and difficult-to-control natural light, they also presented problems of expenditure. Luckiesh: 'The cost of natural light for indoor illumination is considerable because of the floor and wall area that has to be sacrificed for window space; in addition there are various minor factors which increase the cost of natural light indoors'.[12]

The solution that determined the future development of commercial building spaces was artificial light, i.e., the production of the same amount of light that filled the inner space of vitreous architecture by technical means. 'In considering future applications of artificial daylight it is well to note that even when natural daylight is available *it cannot be brought into interiors without cost*. The construction of the daylight entrance is more expensive than ordinary roofing and blank walls.'[13]

In less than a century, the problem of lighting underwent two revolutionary transformations. In the first half of the nineteenth century, ferro-vitreous architecture dissolved the elements of traditional architecture in order to gain natural light. As a result of the development of artificial light, this was followed by a

---

11. M. Luckiesh, *The Lighting Art* (New York and London, 1917), p. 210. Luckiesh was still aware that the price paid for such controlability is monotony: 'In fact, the most striking feature of daylight is its variability and, although this is often annoying, the lack of monotony is one of the attractive features of daylight'.
12. Op. cit., p. 3.
13. Op. cit., p. 85.

movement in the opposite direction, by a closing-off of interior spaces against uncontrollable daylight, a tendency leading to the elimination of windows and glass buildings.[14]

This second turn did not have anything like the effect on contemporary consciousness and perception that the 'light-space' of glass architecture had. It is not difficult to see why this was so: glass architecture had dissolved the traditional forms because it fulfilled a dual function — it was architecture as well as lighting technology and a technical and architectural surrogate for the artificial light that was not yet available. It prepared the way for artificial lighting by making the natural light appear artificial — a process comparable to the development of the water wheel which initially received its regular water supply by means of a steam-powered water pump before it was replaced by the steam engine.

14. However, such radical changes took place only in the USA. A German engineering text (Hefele, *Das Fabrik-Oberlicht* [Berlin, 1931]) presented a critical view of American efforts to eliminate the use of daylight in buildings. This argument is an excellent example of how the different developmental stages of any given industry (e.g., its degree of productivity) influence the engineering consciousness. In the Germany of 1931 an engineer could still make a case for the use of daylight because the German electrical industry was not yet as productive and dominant as the American; because artificial light had not yet been made available *en masse* and cheaply; and because there were traditional and cultural reasons for using daylight.

[4]
Panoramic Travel

Dreamlike traveling on the railroad. The towns which I pass
between Philadelphia and New York make no distinct
impression. They are like pictures on a wall. The more, that you
can read all the way in a car a French novel.
— Emerson, *Journals*, 7 February 1843

In Goethe's journal on his trip to Switzerland in 1797, there is
the following entry:

> Left Frankfurt shortly after 7:00 A.M. On the Sachsenhausen moun-
> tain, many well-kept vineyards; foggy, cloudy, pleasant weather.
> The highway pavement has been improved with limestone. Woods
> in back of the watch-tower. A man climbing up the great tall beech
> trees with a rope and iron cleats on his shoes. What a village! A
> deadfall by the road, from the hills by Langen. *Sprendlingen*. Basalt in
> the pavement and on the highway up to Langen; the surface must
> break very often on this plateau, as near Frankfurt. Sandy, fertile, flat
> land; a lot of agriculture, but meagre . . .[1]

As Goethe told Eckermann, this journal was 'merely jotted
down as given by the moment'. Thus it is no poetic text, but a
description of a journey by coach in the late eighteenth century,
a record of impressions received on that journey. Goethe's trip
from Frankfurt to Heidelberg consisted of a continuous se-

---

1. *Werke*, East Berlin ed., vol. 15, pp. 348 ff.; the complete journal of the Swiss journey in
Werke, Sophia ed., vol. 2, sec. 3.

quence of impressions that demonstrate how intense was the experience of traversed space. Not only the villages and towns on the way are noted, not only the formations of the terrain, but even details of the material consistency of the pavement of the highway are incorporated into his perceptions.

The railway put an end to this intensity of travel, which had reached its peak in the eighteenth century and had found its cultural expression in the genre of the 'novel of travels'. The speed and mathematical directness with which the railroad proceeds through the terrain destroy the close relationship between the traveler and the traveled space. The space of *landscape* becomes, to apply Erwin Straus' concept, *geographical* space. 'In a landscape', says Straus, 'we always get to one place from another place; each location is determined only by its relation to the neighboring place within the circle of visibility. But geographical space is closed, and is therefore in its entire structure transparent. Every place in such a space is determined by its position with respect to the whole and ultimately by its relation to the null point of the coordinate system by which this space obtains its order. Geographical space is systematized.'[2] Straus sees the railroad as the essential agent of the transformation of landscape into geographical space:

> The modern forms of traveling in which intervening spaces are, as it were, skipped over or even slept through, strikingly illustrate the systematically closed and constructed character of the geographical space in which we live as human beings. Before the advent of the railroad, geographical connections evolved, for the traveler, from the change in landscape. True, today the traveler also goes from place to place. But now we can get on a French train in the morning, and then, after twelve hours on the train (which is really being nowhere), we can get out in Rome. The old form of traveling provided for a more and better balanced relationship between landscape and geography.[3]

The nineteenth century found a fitting metaphor for this loss of continuity: repeatedly, the train was described as a projectile. First, the projectile metaphor was used to emphasize the train's

2. Erwin Straus, op. cit., p. 319.
3. Op. cit., p. 320.

speed, as in Lardner: a train moving at seventy-five miles an hour 'would have a velocity only four times less than a cannon ball'.[4] Then, as Greenhow points out, there is the cumulative power and impact that turns a speeding train into a missile: 'When a body is moving at very high velocity, it then, to all intents and purposes, becomes a projectile, and is subject to the laws attending projectiles'.[5] In 1889, after the complete cultural assimilation of the railroad, the projectile metaphor was still quite attractive. 'Seventy-five miles an hour', says a technical text published in that year, 'is one hundred and ten feet a second, and the energy of four hundred tons moving at that rate is nearly twice as great as that of a 2,000-pound shot fired from a 100-ton Armstrong gun.'[6]

The train was experienced as a projectile, and traveling on it, as being shot through the landscape — thus losing control of one's senses. 'In travelling on most of the railways . . .', says an anonymous author of the year 1844, 'the face of nature, the beautiful prospects of hill and dale, are lost or distorted to our view. The alternation of high and low ground, the healthful breeze, and all those exhilarating associations connected with "the Road", are lost or changed to doleful cuttings, dismal tunnels, and the noxious effluvia of the screaming engine.'[7] Thus the rails, cuttings, and tunnels appeared as the barrel through which the projectile of the train passes. The traveler who sat inside that projectile ceased to be a traveler and became, as noted in a popular metaphor of the century, a mere parcel.[8] 'It matters not whether you have eyes or are asleep or blind, intelligent or dull', said Ruskin, 'all that you can know, at best, of the country you pass is its geological structure and general

---

4. D. Lardner, *Railway Economy*, p. 179.
5. C. H. Greenhow, *An Exposition of the Danger and Deficiencies of the Present Mode of Railway Construction* (London, 1846), p. 6.
6. H. G. Prout, 'Safety in Railroad Travel', in *The American Railway*, ed. T. M. Cooley (New York, 1889), p. 187.
7. *Horse-Power Applied to Railways At Higher Rates of Speed than by Ordinary Draught* (London, 1844), p. 48.
8. 'It [the railway] transmutes a man from a traveller into a living parcel.' (Ruskin, *The Complete Works*, vol. 8, p. 159.) Manfred Riedel provides the two following quotes from lesser authors: for Ida Hahn-Hahn, the traveler 'demotes himself to a parcel of goods and relinquishes his senses, his independence' (Manfred Riedel, 'Vom Biedermeier zum Maschinenzeitalter', *Archiv für Kulturgeschichte*, vol. 43, (1961), fascicle 1, p. 119); and, according to Joseph Maria von Radowitz, 'for the duration of such transportation one ceases to be a person and becomes an object, a piece of freight'. (Op. cit., p. 120.)

clothing.'[9]

This loss of landscape affected all the senses. Realizing New-ton's mechanics in the realm of transportation, the railroad created conditions that also 'mechanized' the traveler's percep-tions. According to Newton, 'size, shape, quantity, and motion' are the only qualities that can be objectively perceived in the physical world. Indeed, those became the only qualities that the railroad traveler was able to observe in the landscape he traveled through. Smells and sounds, not to mention the synesthetic perceptions that were part of travel in Goethe's time simply disappeared.

The change effected in the traveler's relationship to the land-scape became most evident in regard to his sense of sight: visual perception is diminished by velocity. George Stephenson tes-tified to this in a statement given at a parliamentary hearing on safety problems on the railways in 1841: when asked for his estimation of the engine-driver's ability to see obstacles, he replied: 'If his attention is drawn to any object before he arrives at the place, he may have a pretty correct view of it; but if he only turns himself round as he is passing, he will see it very imperfectly'.[10]

Unlike the driver, the travelers had a very limited chance to look ahead: thus all they saw was an evanescent landscape. All early descriptions of railroad travel testify to the difficulty of recognizing any but the broadest outlines of the traversed land-scape. Victor Hugo described the view from a train window in a letter dated 22 August 1837: 'The flowers by the side of the road are no longer flowers but flecks, or rather streaks, of red or white; there are no longer any points, everything becomes a streak; the grainfields are great shocks of yellow hair; fields of alfalfa, long green tresses; the towns, the steeples, and the trees perform a crazy mingling dance on the horizon; from time to time, a shadow, a shape, a spectre appears and disappears with

9. Ruskin, vol. 36, p. 62; this is essentially echoed by a French medical author: 'He [the traveler] hardly knows the names of the principal cities through which he passes, and only recognizes them, if at all, by the steeples of the best-known cathedrals which appear like trees by some faraway road'. (A. Aulagnier, *L'Union médicale de la Gironde* [Bordeaux, 1857], p. 525.)
10. Great Britain, *Parliamentary Papers*, 'Report from the Select Committee on Railways', vol. 5 of the section 'Transport and Communications' (repr. ed., Shannon, Ireland, 1968), p. 125.

lightning speed behind the window: it's a railway guard'.[11] And Jacob Burckhardt wrote in 1840: 'It is no longer possible to really distinguish the objects closest to one — trees, shacks, and such: as soon as one turns to take a look at them, they already are long gone'.[12] In a text from 1838 we find the statement that it is impossible to 'recognize a person standing by the road while driving past him' at the 'greatest speed',[13] which prompted the following advice: 'He who has good eyesight . . . does well to acquire the habit of observing from a certain distance everything that attracts his attention while traveling: given some power of observation, he will not miss anything at all, not even during the stage of utmost velocity'.[14]

The recommendation to look at things 'from a certain distance' does not seem entirely realistic, in view of the traveler's situation in the train compartment: enclosed in it, the traveler has no way of distancing himself from the objects — all he can do is to ignore them and the portions of the landscape that are closest to him, and to direct his gaze on the more distant objects that seem to pass by more slowly. If he does not modify his old way of observing things while traveling — if he still tries to perceive proximity and distance in equal measure — the result, as noted in 1862 by *The Lancet*, a medical journal, is fatigue:

> The rapidity and variety of the impressions necessarily fatigue both the eye and the brain. The constantly varying distance at which the objects are placed involves an incessant shifting of the adaptive apparatus by which they are focused upon the retina; and the mental effort by which the brain takes cognizance of them is scarcely productive of cerebral wear because it is unconscious; for no fact in physiology is more clearly established than that excessive functional activity always implies destruction of material and organic change of substance.[15]

Increased velocity calls forth a greater number of visual impressions for the sense of sight to deal with. This multiplication

11. Quoted in Baroli, *Le Train dans la Littérature Française*, Paris, 1964, p. 58.
12. From Manfred Riedel, op. cit., p. 112.
13. G. Muhl, *Die westeuropäischen Eisenbahnen in ihrer Gegenwart und Zukunft* (Karlsruhe, 1838), p. 18.
14. Op. cit., p. 19.
15. *The Influence of Railway Travelling on Public Health*, (London, 1862), p. 44 (is a compendium of articles previously published in *The Lancet*).

of visual impressions is an aspect of the process peculiar to modern times that Georg Simmel has called the development of urban perception. He characterizes it as an *'intensification of nervous stimulation* which results from the swift and uninterrupted change of outer and inner stimuli'.[16] (Italics in original.) 'Lasting impressions', Simmel says, 'impressions which take a regular and habitual course and show regular and habitual contrasts — all these use up, so to speak, less consciousness than does the rapid crowding of changing images, the sharp discontinuity in the grasp of a single glance and the unexpectedness of onrushing impressions.'

The difference between the quality of stimuli in the metropolis and those of railroad travel need not concern us here: what is decisive is the quantitative increase of impressions that the perceptual apparatus has to receive and to process. Contemporary texts that compare the new travel experience with the traditional one demonstrate how that stimulus increase produced by increased velocity is experienced as stressful. The speed causes objects to escape from one's gaze, but one nevertheless keeps on trying to grasp them. This is implied in Eichendorff: 'These travels by steam keep on shaking the world — in which there really is nothing left but railway stations — like a kaleidoscope, incessantly, the landscapes speeding by in everchanging grimaces even before one has been able to perceive any genuine traits of physiognomy; the flying salon presents one with ever new coteries, even before one has been able to really deal with the old ones'.[17]

John Ruskin, whose dislike of the railways created the most sensitive descriptions of the peculiar traits of pre-industrial travel, proposed an almost mathematical negative correlation between the number of objects that are perceived in a given period of time and the quality of that perception: 'I say, first, to be content with as little change as possible. If the attention is awake, and the feelings in proper train, a turn of a country road, with a cottage beside it, which we have not seen before, is as much as we need for refreshment; if we hurry past it, and take two cottages at a time, it is already too much; hence to any

16. *The Sociology of Georg Simmel*, ed. Kurt M. Wolff (Glencoe, Ill., 1950), p. 410.
17. Joseph von Eichendorff, *Werke* (Munich, 1970), vol. 2, p. 895.

person who has all his senses about him, a quiet walk along not more than ten or twelve miles of road a day, is the most amusing of all travelling; and all travelling becomes dull in exact proportion to its rapidity'.[18]

That final statement — traveling becomes dull in exact proportion to its rapidity — represents the evaluation of railroad travel made by all those nineteenth-century travelers who were still accustomed to pre-industrial travel and thus not able to develop modes of perception appropriate to the new form of transportation. Dullness and boredom resulted from attempts to carry the perceptual apparatus of traditional travel, with its intense appreciation of landscape, over to the railway. The inability to acquire a mode of perception adequate to technological travel crossed all political, ideological, and esthetic lines, and appeared among the most disparate personalities of the nineteenth century. Flaubert wrote to a friend in 1864: 'I get so bored on the train that I am about to howl with tedium after five minutes of it. One might think that it's a dog someone has forgotten in the compartment; not at all, it is M. Flaubert, groaning'.[19] Before a railway journey, Flaubert stayed up all night in order to be able to sleep through the journey and not experience it at all: he could do nothing with the vista offered to him by the compartment window.[20] The most diverse sources provide any number of similar complaints. To indicate the width of the spectrum, and its independence from attitudes based on *Weltanschauung*, let us examine one more piece of evidence: the report of a railroad journey in the United States by the politically liberal German-American Francis J. Lieber in 1834:

From Albany to Schenectady, you travel by rail-road; and the least

18. Ruskin, vol. 5, p. 370. Elsewhere, Ruskin speaks of the travelers 'who once in their necessarily prolonged travel were subjected to an influence, from the silent sky and slumbering fields, more effectual than known or confessed', (Vol. 8, p. 246.)
19. *Correspondence* (Paris, 1929), vol. 5, pp. 153–4.
20. Op. cit., letter dated 30 October 1873, quoted in Baroli, *Le Train*, p. 201. People slept in their train compartments not only out of boredom; an equally strong motivation was the need to escape from the tiring influx of stimuli by means of sleep: 'There are people, hurried by their business, who . . . in the course of one day have to cast their eyes upon the panoramas of several hundreds of places. They arrive at their destination overwhelmed by a previously unknown fatigue. Just ask these victims of velocity to tell you about the locations they have traveled through, to describe the perspectives whose rapid images have imprinted themselves, one after another, on the mirror of their brain. They will not be able to answer you. The agitated mind has called sleep to its rescue, to put an end to its overexcitation'. (Gustave Claudin, *Paris* [Paris, 1867], pp. 71–2.)

exciting of all traveling, it seems to me, is decidedly locomotion by steam on a rail-road. The traveler, whose train of ideas is always influenced by the manner in which he proceeds, thinks in a steam car of nothing else but the place of his destination, for the very reason that he is moving so quickly. Pent up in a narrow space, rolling along on an even plain which seldom offers any objects of curiosity, and which, when it does, you pass by with such rapidity, that your attention is never fixed; together with a number of people who have all the same object in view, and think like you of nothing else, but when they shall arrive at the journey's end — thus situated, *you find nothing to entertain or divert you*, except now and then a spark flying into the window of the car. . . . There is no common conversation, no rondolaugh, nothing but a dead calm, interrupted from time to time, only by some passenger pulling out his watch and uttering a sound of impatience. . . .[21] (Italics in original.)

While the consciousness molded by traditional travel found itself in a mounting crisis, another kind of perception started to develope, one which did not try to fight the effects of the new technology of travel but, on the contrary, assimilated them entirely. For such a pair of eyes staring out of the compartment window, all the things that the old consciousness experienced as losses became sources of enrichment. The velocity and linearity with which the train traversed the landscape did not destroy it — not at all; only under such conditions was it possible to fully appreciate that landscape. Thus, a description of a trip from Manchester to Liverpool in the year 1830:

The passenger by this new line of route having to traverse the deepest recesses where the natural surface of the ground is the *highest*, and being mounted on the loftiest ridges and highest embankments, riding above the tops of the trees, and overlooking the surrounding country, where the natural surface of the ground is the *lowest* — this peculiarity and this variety being occasioned by that essential requisite in a well-constructed Railway — a level line — imposing the necessity of cutting through the high lands and embanking across the low; thus in effect, presenting to the traveller all the variety of mountain and ravine in pleasing succession, whilst in reality he is moving almost on a level plane and while the natural face of the country scarcely exhibits even those slight undulations which

21. Francis Lieber, *The Stranger in America* (London, 1834), vol. 2, pp. 1–2.

are necessary to relieve it from tameness and insipidity.[22]

That is not a picturesque landscape destroyed by the railroad; on the contrary, it is an intrinsically monotonous landscape brought into an esthetically pleasing perspective by the railroad. The railroad has created a new landscape. The velocity that atomized the objects of Ruskin's perception, and thus deprived them of their contemplative value, became a stimulus for the new perception. It is the velocity that made the objects of the visible world attractive. Let us compare the following passage with Ruskin's comments, and we shall see how differently velocity and evanescence can be experienced during the same period of time: 'The beauties of England', an American traveler wrote in 1853, 'being those of a dream, should be as fleeting':

> They never appear so charming as when dashing on after a locomotive at forty miles an hour. Nothing by the way requires study, or demands meditation, and though objects immediately at hand seem tearing wildly by, yet the distant fields and scattered trees, are not so bent on eluding observation, but dwell long enough in the eye to leave their undying impression. Every thing is so quiet, so fresh, so full of home, and destitute of prominent objects to detain the eye, or distract the attention from the charming whole, that I love to dream through these placid beauties whilst sailing in the air, quick, as if astride a tornado.[23]

To Benjamin Gastineau, whose newspaper essays on travel were collected in 1861 in book form as *La Vie en chemin de fer*, the motion of the train through the landscape appeared as the motion of the landscape itself. The railroad choreographed the landscape. The motion of the train shrank space, and thus displayed in immediate succession objects and pieces of scenery that in their original spatiality belonged to separate realms. The traveler who gazed through the compartment window at such successive scenes, acquired a novel ability that Gastineau calls 'la philosophie synthétique du coup d'oeil' ('the synthetic philosophy of the glance'). It was the ability to perceive the discrete, as

22. Henry Booth, *An Account of the Liverpool and Manchester Railway* (Liverpool, 1830), pp. 47–8.
23. Matthew E. Ward, *English Items; or, Microcosmic Views of England and Englishmen* (New York, 1853), pp. 71–2.

it rolls past the window, indiscriminately. The scenery that the railroad presents in rapid motion appeared in Gastineau's text as a panorama, without being explicitly referred to as such:

> Devouring distance at the rate of fifteen leagues an hour, the steam engine, that powerful stage manager, throws the switches, changes the decor, and shifts the point of view every moment; in quick succession it presents the astonished traveler with happy scenes, sad scenes, burlesque interludes, brilliant fireworks, all visions that disappear as soon as they are seen; it sets in motion nature clad in all its light and dark costumes, showing us skeletons and lovers, clouds and rays of light, happy vistas and sombre views, nuptials, baptisms, and cemeteries.[24]

In another, roughly contemporary, French text we find all three essential characteristics of the panorama described. Jules Clarétie, a Parisian journalist and publicist, characterized the view from the train window as an evanescent landscape whose rapid motion made it possible to grasp the whole, to get an overview; defining the process, he made specific use of the concept of panorama: 'In a few hours, it [the railway] shows you all of France, and before your eyes it unrolls its infinite panorama, a vast succession of charming tableaux, of novel surprises. Of a landscape it shows you only the great outlines, being an artist versed in the ways of the masters. Don't ask it for details, but for the living whole. Then, after having charmed you thus with its painterly skills, it suddenly stops and quite simply lets you get off where you wanted to go'.[25]

What, exactly, did this new perception that we are referring to as 'panoramic' consist of? Dolf Sternberger uses this concept of the panorama and the panoramic to describe European modes of perception in the nineteenth century — the tendency to see the discrete indiscriminately. 'The views from the windows of Europe', Sternberger says, 'have entirely lost their dimension of depth and have become mere particles of one and the same panoramic world that stretches all around and is, at each and every point, merely a painted surface.'[26] In Sternberger's view,

24. Benjamin Gastineau, *La Vie en chemin de fer* (Paris, 1861), p. 31.
25. Jules Clarétie, *Voyages d'un parisien* (Paris, 1865), p. 4.
26. Dolf Sternberger, *Panorama, oder Ansichten vom 19. Jahrhundert*, 3rd ed. (Hamburg, 1955), p. 57.

modern transportation, the railroad first and foremost, is the main cause for such panoramization of the world: 'The railroad transformed the world of lands and seas into a panorama that could be experienced. Not only did it join previously distant localities by eliminating all resistance, difference, and adventure from the journey: now that traveling had become so comfortable and common, it turned the travelers' eyes outward and offered them the opulent nourishment of ever changing images that were the only possible thing that could be experienced during the journey'.[27]

What the opening of major railroads provided in reality — the easy accessibility of distant places — was attempted in illusion, in the decades immediately preceding that opening, by the 'panoramic' and 'dioramic' shows and gadgets. These were designed to provide, by showing views of distant landscapes, cities, and exotic scenes, 'a substitute for those still expensive and onerous journeys'.[28] A newspaper of the year 1843 described the Parisian public 'reclining on well-upholstered seats and letting the five continents roll by at its pleasure without having to leave the city and without having to risk bad weather, thirst, hunger, cold, heat, or any danger whatsoever'.[29] That the diorama fad died out in Paris around 1840,[30] more or less at the same time that the first great railways were opened (lines from Paris to Orléans and Rouen appearing in 1843) would seem corroborative evidence for the presumed connection. The simultaneous rise of photography provides more support for the thesis. According to Buddemeier, the public became fascinated, at first:

Not by the taking of a picture of any specific object, but by the way in which any random object could be made to appear on the photographic plate. This was something of such unheard-of novelty that the photographer was delighted by each and every shot he took, and it awakened unknown and overwhelming emotions in him, as Gaudin points out. . . . Indeed, the question arises: why did the exact

27. Op. cit., p. 50.
28. Hans Buddemeier, *Panorama, Diorama, Photographie: Entstehung und Wirkung neuer Medien im 19. Jahrhundert (Origin and Effect of New Media in the Nineteenth Century)* Munich, 1970, p. 41.
29. Ibid., p. 45.
30. Ibid., p. 48.

repetition of reality excite people more than the reality itself? Gaudin hints at an answer: he describes how intensely the first photographs were scrutinized, and what people were mostly looking for. For instance: looking at a picture of the building across the street from one's own window, one first started counting the roof shingles and the bricks out of which the chimney was constructed. It was a delight to be able to observe how the mason had applied the mortar between the individual stones. Similar instances occur in other texts dealing with photographs. Tiny, until then unnoticed details are stressed continuously: paving stones, scattered leaves, the shape of a branch, the traces of rain on the wall.[31]

Thus the intensive experience of the sensuous world, terminated by the industrial revolution, underwent a resurrection in the new institution of photography. Since immediacy, close-ups and foreground had been lost in reality, they appeared particularly attractive in the new medium.

Sternberger observes that the vistas seen from Europe's windows had lost their dimension of depth; this happened first with the vistas seen from the train compartment window. There the depth perception of pre-industrial consciousness was, literally, lost: velocity blurs all foreground objects, which means that there no longer is a foreground — exactly the range in which most of the experience of pre-industrial travel was located. The foreground enabled the traveler to relate to the landscape through which he was moving. He saw himself as part of the foreground, and that perception *joined* him to the landscape, included him in it, regardless of all further distant views that the landscape presented. Now velocity dissolved the foreground, and the traveler lost that aspect. He was removed from that 'total space' which combined proximity and distance: he became separated from the landscape he saw by what Richard Lucae, speaking of ferro-vitreous architecture, has called an 'almost immaterial barrier'. The glass separated the interior space of the Crystal Palace from the natural space outside without actually changing the atmospheric quality of the latter in any visible manner, just as the train's speed separated the traveler from the space that he had previously been a part of. As the traveler stepped out of that space, it became a stage setting, or a series of

31. Ibid., p. 78.

such pictures or scenes created by the continuously changing perspective. Panoramic perception, in contrast to traditional perception, no longer belonged to the same space as the perceived objects: the traveler saw the objects, landscapes, etc. *through* the apparatus which moved him through the world. That machine and the motion it created became integrated into his visual perception: thus he could only see things in motion. That mobility of vision — for a traditionally orientated sensorium, such as Ruskin's, an agent for the dissolution of reality — became a prerequisite for the 'normality' of panoramic vision. This vision no longer experienced evanescence: evanescent reality had become the new reality.

While the railroad caused the foreground to disappear, it also replaced looking at the landscape with a new practice that had not existed previously. Reading while traveling became almost obligatory. The dissolution of reality and its resurrection as panorama thus became agents for the total emancipation from the traversed landscape: the traveler's gaze could then move into an imaginary surrogate landscape, that of his book. By the mid-nineteenth century, reading while traveling had become an established custom. The following observation is found in the minutes of an 1860 congress of French physicians: 'Practically everybody passes the time reading while traveling on the train. This is so common that one rarely sees members of a certain social class embark on a journey without first purchasing the means by which they can enjoy this pastime'.[32]

The idea of reading while traveling on trains is as old as the railroad itself. An article in the *Quarterly Review* of 1830 noted that the journey is 'so easy, that a passenger might read a newspaper with perfect comfort'.[33] A German text of 1833 made a connection between the dissolution of the outer world by means of velocity, and the opportunity to compensate for this by developing an activity within the train compartment that will engage one's attention. Lips spoke of 'a speed at which the objects outside rush past the eye without color or contour, and thus cannot be recognized anymore', and continued: 'And yet, the motion of such a steam-car is so imperceptible, smooth, and

32. *Congrès médical de France, troisième session tenue à Bordeaux* (Paris, 1866), p. 828.
33. *Quarterly Review*, vol. 42 (1830), p. 384.

comfortable, that it is not only possible to *read* but even to *write* in it with the greatest ease; thus, a great number of people, such as scholars, officials, merchants, etc., need no longer rest or interrupt their regular routine while traveling, but can pursue it while sitting in the steam-car'.[34] (Italics in original.)

In the late 1840s, English booksellers established stalls in railway stations, as well as a peculiar kind of lending library, to meet the general demand for things to read while traveling. John W. Dodds describes this development:

> The development of railways encouraged the sale of books of all kinds. Until 1848 no systematic attempt had been made to supply passengers with either books or papers at the railway stations. In that year W. H. Smith got the exclusive right to sell books and papers on the Birmingham Railway. His first bookstall was at Euston Station. Shortly he had the franchise for the entire London and Northwestern System. By 1849, the station library at Paddington terminus contained one thousand volumes, chiefly works of fiction. Here, for the charge of one penny, a passenger had free access to the use of the library while waiting for trains, and for slightly more could take a volume with him on his journey, turning it in at his destination. To meet this new demand Routledge launched his *Railway Library* — novels by Cooper, James, Hawthorne, James Grant, Dumas, and others. Murray advertised his 'Literature for the Rail — works of sound information and innocent amusement'.[35]

In 1852 Louis Hachette emulated the English model in France: in a communication to the French railroad companies he proposed a 'large-scale operation of bookselling that apart from its advantages for the companies would also be both useful and pleasing to the public'. The monotony and boredom of travel by rail, mentioned in so many contemporary descriptions, reappears here as a commercial argument for the establishment of railroad bookstalls:

> The traveler finds himself condemned to idleness as soon as he enters the carriage. The monotony of the trip soon takes effect: boredom arrives, and, what is worse, impatience engulfs the unfor-

34. Michael Alexander Lips, *Die Unanwendbarkeit der englischen Eisenbahnen auf Deutschland und deren Ersatz durch Dampffuhrwerk auf verbesserten Chausseen* . . . (Marburg, 1833), p. 4.
35. John W. Dodds, *The Age of Paradox* (New York and Toronto, 1952), p. 374.

tunate traveler, pulled along by the machine like a piece of baggage.... L. Hachette and Company have come up with an idea for turning the enforced leisure and the boredom of a long trip to the enjoyment and instruction of all. They have thought of establishing a railway library that will provide only interesting volumes in a handy format and at a moderate price.[36]

Only two years after the opening of the first railway bookstall in France, of whose income the rail companies received 30 per cent, Hachette operated sixty branches in the whole of France. In 1864, the income exceeded for the first time one million francs, and the sale of books was still greater than that of newspapers. A little later that ratio is reversed: in 1866 the income from the sale of newspapers was 969,000 francs, that from the sale of books, 527,000 francs.[37]

A glance at the offerings of the English and French railway bookstalls shows that the reading public was almost exclusively bourgeois. An English survey of 1851 showed that, in contrast to the supply of trashy mass literature in the regular bookstores, the railway bookstalls and lending libraries in London carried highly respectable non-fiction, fiction, travel guides, etc.[38] Hachette's catalogue had the following categories: travel guides, books about travel, French literature, classics, agriculture and industry, children's books.[39]

Reading while traveling was an exclusively bourgeois occupation. The lower classes who used the railroad did not read, not only because they could not afford to but also because they had no desire to do so. Their traveling situation was quite different from that of the more privileged strata. The carriages of the third and fourth class were not divided into compartments: they had no formal resemblance to the traditional means of travel, while the compartments of the first and second class did. The lower classes, who really joined the ranks of travelers only after the advent of the railroad, were unencumbered by memories of previous forms of travel: thus the new forms were not as strange to them as they were to those classes who had to abandon their private coaches for the train. The primitive,

36. Jean Mistler, *La Librairie Hachette de 1826 à nos jours* (Paris, 1964), p. 123.
37. Op. cit., p. 299.
38. Dodds, pp. 374–5.
39. Mistler, p. 124.

spacious third- and fourth-class carriages into which the proletarian traveling public was crowded characteristically promoted
continuous communication: in the compartments of the bourgeois first- and second-class carriages, such communication had
died out, at least by the end of the nineteenth century. 'How
often . . . I have . . ., while traveling alone or with people with
whom it was impossible to start a conversation, envied the
travelers of the third and fourth class, from whose heavily
populated carriages merry conversation and laughter rang all
the way into the boredom of my isolation cell', says P. D.
Fischer.[40]

The emergence of the habit of reading while traveling was not
only a result of the dissolution and panoramization of the
outside landscape due to velocity, but also a result of the
situation inside the train compartment. The railroad disrupted
the travelers' relationships to each other as it disrupted their
relationship to the traversed landscape. Constantin Pecqueur
explains the phenomenon of dissolution, dispersal, and triviali-
zation of perception and communication, by the greater number
of objects and persons with which the travelers' power of
attention (which have remained constant) were forced to deal:

In these great halls, and in the cheerful caravans of the trains and
steamships, one's affections tend to go out to a greater number of
objects and individuals, and consequently become less intense or
durable in each case. This encourages inconstancy and creates excitement over variety; life and affections are seen to lose in depth what
they gain in range; the social and general sentiments, on the other
hand, find this to be a most pleasing state; while the private sentiments, the familial ones, would seem to suffer from it.[41]

Travelers of the eighteenth century, prior to the railroads,
formed small groups that, for the duration of the journey, were
characterized by intensive conversation and interaction: the
travel novels of the period testify to this quite eloquently. The
travelers in the train compartment did not know what to do with
each other, and reading became a surrogate for the communication that no longer took place. This connection between

---

40. P. D. Fischer, *Betrachtungen eines in Deutschland reisenden Deutschen* (Berlin, 1895), p. 31.
41. Constantine Pecqueur, *Économie Sociale*, vol. 1, p. 349.

reading and the alienation of railroad travelers from one another was made by all authors dealing with the subject of travel reading. It appears in the following contribution to the medical congress of 1866, in which travel reading is cited as the general and sole activity of travelers:

> Nowadays one travels so fast and sees, if the journey is of any duration, such a succession of new faces, that one frequently arrives at the destination without having said a single word. Conversation no longer takes place except among people who know each other, at least not beyond the exchange of mere generalities; any attempt to go beyond these often lapses due to the indifference of some travelers. Thus one might say that the railroads have in this respect, too, completely changed our habits. Whenever, in the past, one knew that one was going to pass several hours, sometimes several days, in the company of others, one tried to establish a rapport with one's companions that often lasted beyond the duration of the journey. Today we no longer think about anything but the impatiently awaited and soon reached destination. The traveler one takes one's leave from may get off at the next station where he will be replaced by another. Thus reading becomes a necessity.[42]

The effects of reading while traveling were discussed generally in medical circles in the 1860s. The debate as to whether it was harmful or beneficial related the practice to the special stresses put on the optical sense by rail travel, and to visual perception in general. According to one side of the argument, reading while traveling was harmful to the eye because 'when the traveler sets himself to read, he imposes yet further labour on the eye in tracing the shifting characters of his book or newspaper, and also on the brain'.[43] The traveler who *concentrated* on his reading behaved in just as old-fashioned a manner as the traveler who, accustomed to the pace of the stagecoach,

---

42. Op. cit., p. 830.
43. *The Influence of Railway Travelling on Public Health*, p. 44. A French author even posited a connection between mental affliction and travel reading, claiming that the latter caused a 'congestion of the retina': 'An eminent Parisian alienist, with whom I recently discussed this pernicious influence of reading while traveling on trains, told me that he not only admitted it to be true, but that an English physician, the head of a great private hospital, had told him that he had treated several patients suffering from general paralysis whose initial phenomenon, or determining cause, had been cerebral congestion brought about by those conditions that I have described.' (Legrand, de Saulle, in *Bulletin de la Societé de Médecine pratique*, (1863), p. 9.)

attempted to fix his stare on the objects flitting past the compartment window. In both cases, the result was exhaustion of the senses and of the mind. To adapt to the conditions of rail travel, a process of deconcentration, or dispersal of attention, took place in reading as well as in the traveler's perception of the landscape outside: Hachette's rising sales of newspapers and falling sales of books attest to that. The afore-mentioned contribution to the medical congress of 1866 stated that travel reading may have had deleterious effects on eyesight, but adds that it would be impossible to curtail it: 'Nevertheless, no matter what one says or does, reading will remain the most natural occupation of railway travelers, in this new form of locomotion that has so profoundly altered the traveler's relations to each other'.[44]

44. Op. cit., p. 830.

[5]
The Compartment

Cette boite ambulante où j'ai dû me cloîtrer. Je n'en puis plus sortir,
mais nul n'y peut entrer.

[This ambulatory box in which I have had to enclose myself:/I
can't get out of it, but nothing can come in, either.]

— Eugène Manuel, 1881

To adherents of progressive thought in the first half of the
nineteenth century, the railroad appeared as the technical guarantor of democracy, harmony between nations, peace and progress.
According to them, the railroad brought people together both
spatially and socially. This current of European thought found
its most emphatic expression in the followers of Saint-Simon:
the intellectual generation that appeared on the French political
and economic stage around 1825, the year Saint-Simon died,
projected all the egalitarian hopes left unfulfilled by Revolution
and Empire onto industry and its spectacular spearhead, the
railroad: to them it was the material force that would realize the
equality and fraternity of 1789 more effectively than any merely
formal political emancipation.

Pecqueur formulated the belief that the railroad, as a part of
industry, works for human emancipation:

> The communal journeys on trains and steamships, and the great
> gatherings of workers in the factories, inspire, to a great degree, the
> sentiment and habits of equality and liberty. By causing all classes of
> society to travel together and thus juxtaposing them into a kind of

[70]

living mosaic of all the fortunes, positions, characters, manners, customs, and modes of dress that each and every nation has to offer, the railroads quite prodigiously advance the reign of truly fraternal social relations and do more for the sentiments of equality than the most exalted sermons of the tribunes of democracy. To thus foreshorten for everyone the distances that separate localities from each other, is to equally diminish the distances that separate men from one another.[1]

If Pecqueur was convinced that trains and steamers 'truly are the chariots of equality, freedom, and civilization', he did, on the other hand, recognize the possibility that old privileges and inequalities might reappear in the creations of industry, even though their essential nature was egalitarian and democratic. The equality and democracy of industry in general and the railroad in particular had to be safeguarded by 'a certain degree of preexisting equality between the diverse classes or races that constitute the nation: without this, we might end up creating subdivisions in the railway carriages and thus a separation and distinction between social and economic ranks analogous to *stagecoaches, private vehicles for rent,* and *livery stable'*.[2] (Italics in original.)

Pecqueur regarded the division of rail carriages into classes as a baleful possibility. At the time of the writing of his *Economie sociale* that division did not exist in France, simply because the railroads had not instituted a passenger service. Until the early 1840s, apart from one short line, the railroad existed in France only in the form of descriptions of the railways in England and Belgium. In those two countries, however, the railways' division into classes was a fact from the start. Yet the progressives of the early nineteenth century, especially the Saint-Simonian proponents of industry, paid hardly any attention to that fact, being dazzled by the overwhelming fascination exerted by steam power. In the face of the unheard-of energy and productivity made possible by the railroad, the traditional social privileges seemed to be so hopelessly outdated that it appeared hardly worthwhile to deal with them. Even though Pecqueur did not entirely discount the possibility of a survival of inequality, he

1. *Économie sociale*, vol. 1, pp. 335–6.
2. Op. cit., p. 338.

regarded the ultimate victory of equality based on technology as certain. The travelers in a train, he argued, are all equal because they find themselves in a situation of technological equality: 'It is the *same convoy*, the *same power* that carries the great and the small, the rich and the poor; thus, the railroads most generally provide a continuous lesson in equality and fraternity'.[3] (Italics in original.)

But the continuing history of the railroad, manifesting separation of classes even on French trains, exploded (along with many other Saint-Simonian hopes) the notion that social equality would result from the technically equal situation of the travelers. Yet that history had shown that Pecqueur's idea had a core of truth in it, although it was very different from what Pecqueur believed. The fact that the members of different classes traveled on the same train, moved by the same power, did not render them social equals, but it was ever present in their minds. Travel by rail, being pulled by the power of steam, was experienced as participation in an industrial process. For the lower classes this experience was quite immediate: in England they were transported in open boxcars on freight trains, up to the 1840s. They were regarded not as recipients of passenger service but as freight goods. The Gladstone Act of 1844 required the carriages of the third and fourth class to be covered, yet they still looked more like covered boxcars than passenger cars. The traveling situation of the more privileged classes was entirely different: their carriages looked like coaches mounted on rails. Not only was this design forgetful of the industrial origin and nature of the railroad, it was a literal attempt to repress awareness of them. The compartment, an almost unaltered version of the coach chamber, was designed to reassure the first-class traveler (and, to a lesser degree, the second-class traveler as well) that he was still moving along just as he did in his coach, only at less expense and greater speed. Its effect was the exact opposite of the one desired. Precisely because the compartment was so closely linked to traditional pre-industrial travel — imbued with its spirit as it were — the new industrial mode of transportation was experienced as even more traumatic. Bourgeois first-class travelers complained that they no longer felt like travelers but like

3. Op. cit., p. 338.

mere parcels: this rendered their subjective experience of travel just as industrial as was the objective experience of the lower classes. Yet the bourgeois experience was only subjective to the extent that it actually occured in a well-upholstered and outfitted compartment instead of the boxcar-like traveling space of the lower classes: it was equally objective in its realization that the traveler was the object of an industrial process — all the upholstery in the world could not make him forget it.

The End of Conversation while Traveling

Transplanted from the coach to the railroad train, the compartment lost some of its functions. What was functional in the time of pre-industrial travel now became redundant. The essential social function of the coach chamber arose out of its form, namely, the seating arrangement: in the U-shaped coach chamber the travelers faced each other, and such an arrangement encouraged conversation while traveling. The historical genesis of the coach as a means of travel justified the classification of that communicative form of seating as a specifically bourgeois idea; a brief digression should make this clear.

In the Middle Ages, people traveled almost exclusively on foot or on horseback, depending on their class. The custom of traveling in coaches arose at the beginning of the Early Modern period, concurrently with a great number of other practices that arose from the processes of defeudalization and urbanization of Western European life. Thus Werner Sombart describes the origin of coach travel:

> In the course of the sixteenth century, presumably due to the improvement of the roads, travel by horse-drawn carriage became more common. True, we encounter the merchants of the sixteenth with increasing frequency in their 'coaches': but as late as in the mid-seventeenth century we find resistance against coach travel on the grounds that it is detrimental to the welfare of the nation — it makes the people too soft, it ruins horse-breeding, etc. By the end of the seventeenth century travel by coach had finally established itself as equally acceptable as travel on horseback.[4]

4. *Moderner Kapitalismus*, vol. 2, p. 262.

According to Jackman,[5] the coach found its first mass propagation at the beginning of the seventeeth century in and around London — a region where Europe's urbanization had progressed farthest.

The form and seating arrangement of the coach harks back to another specifically urban vehicle for the transportation of individuals, the sedan chair.[6] One might say that the coach consists of two frontally joined sedan chairs. The creation of this curious arrangement during the same period that saw the rise of other bourgeois institutions of communication, such as coffee-houses, clubs, newspapers, and theaters, indicates that the coach must be seen as part of that larger configuration.

Travel in the coach was characterized not only by the travelers' intensive relationship to the world outside, the traversed landscape, but also by their lively communication with each other. Coach travelers were talkative folk, providing material for numerous novels published in the eighteenth and early nineteenth centuries. The railroad put an end to all that. As a Frenchman reminisced in 1857: 'In the coach, conversation got off to an easy start after a few moments of preliminary study of one's companions; at the moment of parting, one oftentimes regretted the brevity of the journey, having almost made friends. How different it is on the train. . . !'[7]

The face-to-face arrangement that had once institutionalized an existing need for communication now became unbearable because there no longer was a reason for such communication. The seating in the railroad compartment forced the travelers into a relationship based no longer on living need but an embarrassment. Georg Simmel's explanation of the way in which modern perception both orientates itself and is disorientated by the optical sense refers to modern transportation as one of the agents of that development:

Generally speaking, what we *see* of a person is interpreted by what

---

5. Op. cit., pp. 110ff.
6. G. A. Thrupp, *The History of Coaches* (London, 1877), p. 48: 'Sedan chairs came into fashion in England in 1634, and were in general use by the middle of the century. The alteration in the form of the coach, from the long barge shape of Charles I's time to that of Charles II was, no doubt, suggested by the shape of the sedan chair, in London as well as in Germany.'
7. *L'Union médicale de Gironde* (Bordeaux, 1857), pp. 524–5.

we *hear* of him, the reverse being a much rarer case. Therefore one who sees without hearing is far more confused, undecided, upset than one who hears without seeing. This must have an important bearing on the sociology of the big city. Compared to the traffic in the small town, the traffic in the city creates an infinitely greater proportion of cases of seeing rather than hearing others; this is so not only because a great proportion of encounters on a small-town street involve either acquaintances with whom we exchange a few words or those whose appearance allows us to reproduce their entire personality, not only the visible part, but, above all, because of the fact of public transportation in the big city. *Before the development of buses, trains and streetcars in the nineteenth century, people were quite unable to look at each other for minutes or hours at a time, or to be forced to do so, without talking to each other.* Modern traffic increasingly reduces the majority of sensory relations between human beings to mere sight, and this must create entirely new premises for their general sociological feelings.[8] (Italics in long passage added.)

What Simmel describes as a feeling of being confused, undecided, and upset may be described simply as the embarrassment of people facing each other in silence in the train compartment. As we have seen, the perusal of reading matter is an attempt to replace the coversation that is no longer possible. Fixing one's eyes on a book or a newspaper, one is able to avoid the stare of the person sitting across the aisle. The embarrassing nature of this silent situation remains largely unconscious: any insight into it will therefore appear only in hidden terms, hinted at 'between the lines'. We find one example of such hidden implication in M. M. von Weber's railroad handbook of 1857, in

8. Georg Simmel, *Soziologie* (Leipzig, 1908), pp. 650–1. This passage is partially quoted in Walter Benjamin, 'On Some Motifs in Baudelaire', in *Illuminations*, ed. Hannah Arendt, transl. Harry Zohn (New York, 1969), p. 191. Erving Goffman defines visual contact between persons unknown to each other as a disruption of the 'territory of the self', i.e., one's 'personal space'. Goffman proceeds, interestingly enough, to give an example of a situation on a train journey: 'This is nicely illustrated in Eastern seaboard parlor cars designed with a wide, longitudinal aisle and single seats at intervals on either side, the seats arranged to swivel. When there is crowding, travelers maximize their "comfort" by turning their seats to exactly that direction that will allow the eyes, when oriented in the direction of the trunk, to gaze upon the least amount of passenger flesh. . . . In ordinary railway or bus seating in America, passengers who feel overcrowded may be able to send their eyes out the window, thereby vicariously extending their personal space'. (*Relations in Public* [New York, 1972], p. 30.) It would obviously be useful to know if and to what extent average 'personal space' has changed in the last 150 years, i.e., whether it has grown larger or smaller. It would be equally interesting to determine the national and cultural differences between Europe and the United States with regard to 'personal space'.

which the author considered the pros and cons of the European compartment versus the American car. (The American standard carriage differs, as we shall see in the next chapter, from the European in that the seats have not been arranged in compartments and facing each other, but in a long car and facing one way.) Weber believed that the American type would be unsuitable for European conditions. He championed the compartment system and then stated that he felt a particular fondness for the half compartments (*bâtard-coupés*) 'which, placed at both ends of the car, have the advantage that *the passengers have no one facing them*, while being able to look outside through the windows that open out to three sides of the compartment'.[9]

One of the few open criticisms of the compartmental seating arrangement can be found in an 1838 issue of the *Railway Times*. A letter to the editor, signed with irony 'An Enemy to Imprisonment for Debt and in Travelling', suggests an alternative:

> With reference to the interior arrangement of Railway Carriages . . ., I beg to suggest . . . to the public, whether their comfort could not be promoted, by having some of them, in each train, fitted up, so that the passengers should sit back to back, and look out upon the country, from a range of windows the whole length of the carriage. By this plan, a man going to and from Southampton or Bristol might, by taking opposite sides of the carriage, on each journey, see all the country within view of both sides of the road; and, surely, *this would be pleasanter than a three or four hours' study of physiognomy at a stretch, for want of any better occupation.*[10] (Italics added.)

Only the privileged classes underwent this experience of no longer speaking to each other and being increasingly embarrassed by their companions. In the carriages of the third and fourth class, which mostly had not been divided into compartments but consisted of one large space, there was neither embarrassed silence nor general perusal of reading matter. On the contrary, the sounds emanating from these carriages could be overheard in the compartments of the privileged: 'merry conversation and laughter rang all the way into the boredom of my isolation cell', remarks P. D. Fischer in a previously quoted

9. Max Maria von Weber, *Schule des Eisenbahnwesens* (Leipzig, 1857), p. 178.
10. *The Railway Times*, vol. 1 (1838), p. 46.

passage. The French novelist Alphonse Daudet gave his impression of the lively goings-on in the proletarian carriages in the following vivid sketch that is reminiscent of Honoré Daumier's caricatures of train scenes: 'I'll never forget my trip to Paris in a third-class carriage . . . in the midst of drunken sailors singing, big fat peasants sleeping with their mouths open like those of dead fish, little old ladies with their baskets, children, fleas, wet-nurses, the whole paraphernalia of the carriage of the poor with its odor of pipe smoke, brandy, garlic sausage and wet straw. I think I'm still there'.[11]

Isolation

There were occasions when the first-class traveler found himself untrammelled by the displeasing presence of fellow travelers. Being alone in the compartment was an ambivalent situation. This solitude could be experienced as a state of satisfaction, of safety, of happiness. 'Alone in the compartment', said Taine in his *Carnet de voyage*, 'I have spent three of the sweetest hours I have experienced in a long time.'[12] Another passage in the *Carnet* gives concreteness to this state of serenity: 'I was alone in my carriage . . . the wheels rolled on indefatigably, with a uniform noise like that of a prolonged roaring note played on an organ. All mundane and social ideas faded from my mind. No longer did I see anything but the sun and the countryside, in bloom, smiling, all green and with a greenness so various and illuminated by that gentle rain of warm beams that caressed it'.[13]

It is tempting to give a psychoanalytic explanation for that pleasurable feeling of self-forgetfulness which was brought on by the isolation of the ego in the compartment and the powerful mechanical motion of the train. Freud and Karl Abraham have indicated the connection between mechanical agitation and sexual arousal and have called the railroad the most powerful agent of that arousal.[14] The joy of riding trains found its counterpart,

11. 'La petite chose' (1866), quoted in Baroli, p. 151.
12. Ibid., p. 153.
13. Ibid., p. 152.
14. Freud: 'The shaking produced by driving in carriages and later by railway-travel exercises such a fascinating effect upon older children that every boy, at any rate, has at one time or other in his life wanted to be an engine driver or a coachman. It is a puzzling

as soon as there is repression, in what Freud termed 'fear of trains', Karl Abraham interprets the fear experienced by neurotics in the face of accelerating or uncontrollable motion as the fear of their own sexuality going out of control: 'Their fear is related to the danger of finding themselves in a kind of unstoppable motion that they can no longer control. The same patients generally exhibit fear of locomotion in any vehicle they cannot bring to a halt themselves at any time'.[15]

The travelers themselves experienced that fear of the independence of their own sexuality as a fear of derailment. The fear of derailment was ever present on train journeys in the early days. The greater the ease and speed with which the train 'flew' (a typical nineteenth-century term for rail travel)[16] the more acute the fear of catastrophe became: we have already quoted Thomas Creevy's statement made in 1829, that the railroad journey was 'really flying, and it is impossible to divest yourself of the notion of instant death to all upon the least accident happening'. A German text of 1845 speaks of 'a certain constriction of the spirit that never quite leaves one no matter how comfortable the rail journeys have become'. It was the fear of derailment, of catastrophe, of 'not being able to influence the motion of the carriages in any way'.[17]

The fear of derailment was in fact a feeling of impotence due to one's being confined in a fast-moving piece of machinery without being able to influence it in the least. The isolation of the compartment that enclosed the passenger intensified this

---

fact that boys take such an extraordinarily intense interest in things connected with railways, and, at the age at which the production of phantasies is most active (shortly before puberty), use those things as the nucleus of a symbolism that is peculiarly sexual. A compulsive link of this kind between railway-travel and sexuality is clearly derived from the pleasurable character of the sensations of movement. In the event of repression, which turns so many childish preferences into their opposite, these same individuals, when they are adolescents or adults, will react to rocking or swinging with a feeling of nausea, will be terribly exhausted by a railway journey, or will be subject to attacks of anxiety on the journey and will protect themselves against a repetition of the painful experience by a dread of railway-travel'. Sigmund Freud, *The Complete Psychological Work*, op. cit., vol. 7, p. 202.

15. *Psychoanalytische Studien*, vol. 2, p. 102.
16. The flying metaphor has received its pictorial expression in the symbol of the winged wheel, adopted by numerous European railway companies as their trademark. The descriptions of rail travel in terms of 'flying' are too copious to enable one to make a sensible selection.
17. *Zeitung für Eisenbahnwesen, Dampfschiffahrt und Maschinenkunde*, vol. 1 (1845), pp. 114–15.

feeling of helpless passivity. While the compartment facilitated the pleasurable experience of mechanical motion, it became, in equal measure, a locus of trauma. Its enclosed nature hid whatever happened in it from outside glances: once the traveler had seated himself in it, he was alone with himself or with fellow travelers for the duration of the journey, or at least for the time taken to travel from one station to the next. There were no channels of communication to the outside world, and there were actual risks involved in that. Peter Lecount, an English engineer, wrote in 1839: 'In road travelling, a passenger suddenly taken ill, or from any other cause, has nothing to do but to put his head out of the coach window and make his wants known; the coach can be stopped, and he can receive the necessary assistance. But how different is the case in railway travelling! There, unless he has by accident a seat just under the guard, he might exert his voice in vain and could by no possibility receive the least help if he was dying; in fact, the more he wanted it, the less able he would be to endeavour to obtain it'.[18]

The compartment's total optical and acoustical isolation from the rest of the train and its inaccessibility during the journey (until the 1860s, even the compartments of express trains could be entered only from outside: there was no communication between them) caused the travelers' interrelationships to change from mere embarrassment at silence to fear of potential mutual threat. The train compartment became a scene of crime — a crime that could take place unheard and unseen by the travelers in adjoining compartments. This novel danger captivated the nineteenth-century imagination: 'The loudest screams are swallowed up by the roar of the rapidly revolving wheels, and murder, or violence worse than murder, may go on to the accompaniment of a train flying along at sixty miles an hour. When it stops in due course, and not till then, the ticket collector coming up may find a second-class carriage converted into a "shambles". We are not romancing'.[19]

---

18. Peter Lecount, *A Practical Treatise on Railways, Explaining Their Construction and Management* (Edinburgh, 1839), p. 196.
19. 'The Globe' (1863), quoted in Ivor Smullen, *Taken for a Ride* (London, 1968), p. 131.

Drama in the Compartment

In the issue of the *Annales d'Hygiène Publique* of January 1861, we find the headline 'Dangers Run by Travelers on Trains' and the following description:

> On the sixth of December last year, the train from Mulhouse entered the Paris station at a quarter past three in the morning. The passengers made haste to leave their compartments; as the door of one of them remained closed, a railway employee went to open it. How great was his surprise when he perceived the shape of a man lying between the seats! He then asked the man to get out, but received no answer. He found it difficult to see clearly in the uncertain light of the fixture in the compartment that was further dimmed by the black silk shade designed to make it more agreeable; he reached out, and upon withdrawing his hand, found it covered in blood. He notified the stationmaster and the police commissioner, and it was soon ascertained that the man was nothing but a cadaver bathed in a pool of blood.[20]

The dead man was Chief Justice Poinsot. The ensuing investigation revealed that he shared his compartment with a single fellow passenger, his murderer. No trace of the latter was found. The case aroused unusual interest. 'The painful interest excited in Paris by the dreadful death of M. Poinsot has been extraordinarily great', *Galignani's Messenger*, an English-language newspaper published in Paris, reported on 9 December, 'and a certain feeling of uneasiness has arisen at the idea of the extreme facility with which the crime appears to have been perpetrated.'

'What is so strange, so inexplicable', said an article in the *Journal des Débats* of 8 December that expressed the general public's fearful interest in the case, 'is that the travelers who were in the compartment next to M. Poinsot's had not heard a single shot: without being able to affirm this in any certain manner, they thought that they had heard a shout, but only one.'

In the days following the discovery of the crime, the columnists of the Parisian press published pieces whose satirical

20. *Annales d'hygiène publique et de médecine légale*, vol. 15 (1861), p. 224.

surface was a transparent attempt to conceal the deeper fears that this murder had stirred. In the *Figaro* of 20 December we find this suggestion: 'In every well-arranged train we find a carriage reserved for smokers and another one for ladies who desire to travel by themselves. Why not provide a carriage with the legend: *compartment reserved for assassins*? But we know those gentlemen well: they are perhaps too shy to want to attract attention'. (Italics in original.)

On 25 December *Figaro* published a satirical description of the atmosphere of anxiety that pervaded railroad travel:

M. Poinsot's assassination still has the privilege of being a matter of concern to the public. . . . There is a great deal of egotism in that general preoccupation. Everyone feels menaced in his mortal condition as a traveler. For the employees of the railroad, the affair has become a comedy. We now see well-known millionaires boarding third-class carriages. Others have started traveling in the company of their valet, their coachman, and their cook. Those whom fortune has not blessed with such accessories remain prey to terrible perplexities.

This was followed by a satirical demonstration of such perplexities, a fictitious dialogue between two unaccompanied passengers in one compartment:

Not too long ago, the train from Brussels carried to Paris, in a compartment of the first class, two voyagers who were hermetically sealed in their topcoats and scarves. After a very defiant study of their respective physiognomies, one of the two passengers decided to speak to his traveling companion.

'Monsieur', he said, 'one really is lucky to find an honest man traveling first-class these days. I congratulate myself on the stroke of luck that has joined us here, seeing as I might have fallen upon a villain. By the way, I am a cautious man. I do not carry any money, nor a watch, nor any jewelry. I'm wearing an old pair of trousers in order not to excite anyone's greed; and as for my topcoat, a rag-dealer refused to give me forty sous for it. Besides, anyone who dares to attack me will find himself out of luck. I have here a Catalan dagger, two saddle pistols, and a revolver that has as many barrels as one of M. Alexandre's organs has pipes. In this game bag I carry bullets and gunpowder. I have more than a hundred and ten shots that I can fire before surrendering. . . .'

[81]

'Well, that's just like me, Monsieur', replied the other traveler. 'I've been pretending to sleep, just pretending. But I'm never more formidable than when I seem to be snoring. You see, I know how to take care of myself. . . . I can take you into my confidence, since you seem to be such an honest man. At the very moment when some scoundrel thinks he can assassinate me, I can riddle his chest with holes. . . .'

'By what means, Monsieur?'

'Look, Monsieur, it's very simple. I told M. Godillot of the travelers' outfitters to make me a breastplate armored with thirty bayonet points. See, it's very ingenious. . . . I only have to embrace my adversary heartily in order to turn him into a sieve'.

Reassured by their reciprocal confidences the two travelers fell asleep with one eye open, clutching their pistols.

A look at entirely non-satirical official reports and technical works that appeared a few years later demonstrates how realistic that satirical sketch of the new attitudes of first-class passengers toward one another was. When another compartment murder occurred in England in 1864, it received both official and satirical comment. A series of *Punch* cartoons dealt with the mutual distrust of first-class passengers, and an official report described the same phenomenon as follows: 'There has been, indeed, a panic amongst railway passengers. Ladies, unable, of course, to discriminate at the moment between those whom they should avoid and those who should be their protectors, shun all alike; and gentlemen passengers, as well as railway officers of all classes, constantly refuse to travel singly with a stranger of the weaker sex, under the belief that it is only common prudence to avoid in this manner all risk of being accused, for purposes of extortion, of insult, or assault'.[21]

The above is from the report prepared by a committee of experts for the House of Commons in 1865: the committee's task was to find out what technical possibilities there were for the creation of means of communication between train compartments, so that further compartment murders could be averted. Similar deliberations took place in France and Germany. The feverish search for ways to end the isolation of the compartment was based on the nightmarish vision of the compartment as

21. 'Report of Captain Tyler', House of Commons, *Sessional Papers*, vol. 50 (1865), p. 6. An entire series of *Punch* cartoons renders similar situations.

such being a provocation to murder.[22] That fantasy recurs even in purely technical dissertations, such as *Le matériel roulant de chemins de fer au point de vue du comfort et de la sécurité des voyageurs* (*The rolling stock of the railroads from the point of view of the passengers' comfort and security*) by Ernest Dapples: 'If one is not alone in the compartment, one has one or several fellow passengers on the journey. If there is only one of them, and this is often impossible to avoid . . ., one may be exposed, by that solitary fellow passenger, to all kinds of disagreeable things, possibly even robbery and murder, as has been shown, unfortunately, by certain well-known events'.[23]

As late as 1870 we find this in the *Handbuch für spezielle Eisenbahntechnik* (*Handbook for special railway technology*): 'The passenger is so pleased when he finds a vacant compartment; but he is not so fortunate when he acquires a fellow passenger who robs him in his sleep, or perhaps even murders him, and then ejects his body from the compartment piecemeal, without attracting the train personnel's attention'.[24]

The Compartment as a Problem

After the Poinsot murder in France in 1860 and the Briggs murder in England in 1864, two traumatic experiences for Europeans, the search was begun for ways to end the isolation of the compartment. That only two cases of murder, occurring four years apart and in two different countries, were able to trigger a collective psychosis tells us as much about the compartment's significance for the nineteenth-century European psyche as does the fact that it took so long to become conscious of the compartment's dysfunctionality. The surprising aspect of the history of the train compartment is, indeed, that it remained unchanged for so long, and that it has, in fact, survived to the present day in modified form, despite the drawbacks that were so plain from the very beginning. While the railroad itself was

---

22. Baroli points to the murder in Gide's 'Les Caves du Vatican', where 'isolation in the compartment almost provokes the crime'. (Baroli, p. 450).
23. Ernest Dapples, *Le matériel roulant . . .* (Lausanne, 1866), p. 8.
24. Heusinger von Waldegg, ed., *Handbuch für spezielle Eisenbahn-Technik* (Leipzig, 1870), vol. 2, p. 298.

recognized to be fundamentally different from the highway from the very beginning,[25] the form of the passenger carriage moving on it was kept strictly imitative of the traditional form of the coach. As far as I know, in Europe there were no attempts to create a passenger car that would be compatible in its form with the modern technology of the railroad — i.e., one that would no longer have anything to do with the coach-derived compartment. The closest thing to such a Utopian carriage is a proposal published by the Scots journalist MacLaren in 1825. It appears to be entirely free of any formal reminiscences of the stagecoach: MacLaren proposed a ship-like space, 'a form analogous to that of the steam-boat and track boat would be the best'. Nevertheless, another arrangement slipped in covertly and it can be easily recognized as the familiar compartment system: 'It might, for instance, consist of a gallery seven feet high, eight wide, and one hundred feet in length, *formed into ten separate chambers* ten feet long each, connected with each other by joints working horizontally, to allow the train to bend where the road turned. A narrow covered footway, suspended on the outside over the wheels on one side, would serve as a common means of communication for the whole'.[26] (Italics added.) Thus we get, on the one hand, the idea of a large room on wheels, a ship on land as it were (not long after, a similar proposal was made in America),[27] and, on the other, the subdivision of that large room into a row of smaller, compartment like spaces. Admittedly, these had the advantage of being connected with each other — an innovation predictive of the one realized forty years later.

MacLaren's proposal remained on paper. The carriage consisting of a series of unconnected compartments — as it had been first introduced on the Manchester–Liverpool line — remained, in spite of all obvious shortcomings and dangers, the European standard for half a century thereafter. This persistent survival of an impractical form appears even less explicable

25. This has to be qualified: initial attempts were made to transfer the principle of individual traffic to the railroads, before the transportation monopolies became established. Yet the contemporary realization that the railroad differed from the old highways is reflected in the fact that the Canal Acts, not the Turnpike Acts, were chosen as the organizational model for railroad law.
26. Charles MacLaren, *Railways Compared with Canals and Common Roads* . . . (Edinburgh, 1825), pp. 45–6.
27. Morgan in *The American Traveller*, vol. 4 (1829), no. 83. We will also deal with the subject extensively in the next chapter of the present work.

considering that Europe became cognizant, around 1840, of a technically functional type of carriage — the American car. This type had all the advantages its European counterpart lacks. Due to the open spatial arrangements, problems such as heating and toilets,[28] insurmountable in the compartment system, were easily solved; nor did the traveler in the American car fear for his life, being at all times in communication with a great number of other passengers.

In the public discussion to which the compartment system became subjected in the 1860s, the American car appeared as an alternative. With a few marginal exceptions, [29] the European rail companies rejected its adoption. The psychology of the European traveling public was an important reason for this: the English and French commissions appointed to study the problems of the compartment all agreed that the European rail passenger actually *wished* to be left alone while traveling. 'The passengers', Dapples said in summing up the French Commission's report, 'would complain if they were obliged to spend a long time in public carriages, subjected to all the noises, vulnerable to all eyes and all ears. . . .'[30]

The proposals for ways to improve communication between the compartments that come up in the 1860s, in the wake of the Poinsot and Briggs murder cases, all took the 'desire to be left alone' into account. In them, the compartment remained essentially unchanged. There was talk of various alarm systems which would enable passengers to transmit calls of help when they found themselves in acute danger: these included a speaking tube running the entire length of the train; a cord that could be pulled to activate an alarm bell; an arrangement of mirrors that enabled the train personnel to see into the compartments; and an electric alarm system. The French commission, ap-

---

28. For a long time, toilets did not exist on trains. As soon as the train was in motion, the travelers had to curb their bladders. As soon as it pulled into a station, they could race each other to the facilities. Perdonnet's handbook (*Traité élémentaire des chemins de fer* [Paris, 1855–6], vol. 2, p. 34) states that 'especially on the arrival platforms we have to install urinals of large dimensions'. Commenting on the later on-train toilets, Waldegg's handbook says that these 'have the drawback that the traveler using them has to remain in them from one station to the next, and this, at least in the case of express trains, can be a more or less unpleasant experience'. (*Handbuch für spezielle Eisenbahn-Technik*, vol. 2, p. 342.)

29. In Württemberg, in Switzerland and in Austria, on short-distance lines there was a kind of overland bus traffic.

30. Dapples, op. cit., p. 11.

pointed in 1861 after the Poinsot murder, suggested that the simplest and most effective solution would be to open up small peephole windows in the dividing walls between compartments:

> The dormer window placed in the upper part of the compartment wall offers, in its modest way, some of the advantages of communication between the compartments. In certain cases it could be of useful assistance to the passengers, inspire a healthy fear in wrongdoers, and thus be a material and moral deterrent. It has no detrimental effect whatever on the comfort or privacy of the passengers, as these would always be at liberty to cover it up should they think this advisable. It could also be introduced at very small expense. It does not transmit, from one compartment to the next, words spoken by the travellers, nor draughts, nor tobacco smoke.[31]

This peephole was actually introduced on numerous lines, and it soon became a subject of caricature.[32] It assuaged the immediate cause of the compartment controversy, i.e., the fear of murder. It did not, however, solve the problem of actual physical communication; for that, mobility between compartments and carriages would be absolutely necessary. (This mobility was also a prerequisite for toilets, heating installations, dining and sleeping cars, and ticket control during the journey.)

The most primitive form of physical communication between the compartments was a footboard mounted on the outside of the carriage and running its entire length. The French commission recommended this, in addition to the peephole, for general adoption. The peephole facilitated optical communication between adjoining compartments; the footboard was designed to enable the train personnel to gain access to the compartments during the journey. Passengers, obviously, were not supposed to avail themselves of the daredevil contraption which caused numerous deaths every year.

Effective, safe and comfortable communication between compartments and carriages could be established only by means of a passageway in the interior of the carriage: this meant at least

---

31. 'Report of Captain Tyler', p. 12.
32. In England, these were soon called 'Muller's Windows', after the name of Brigg's murderer. See cartoons in *Punch*, e.g., issue of 25 November 1865.

partial adoption of the American system. At the beginning of the 1860s, the Swiss Northeast Line introduced a type of carriage that represented a first step in that direction. The carriage remained divided into compartments, but these were connected by means of doors in the dividing partitions. The arrangement did, however, meet with the same line of criticism that prevented the introduction of the American system. It was said that the compartment's privacy and quiet was disturbed by the traffic through it. Heusinger von Waldegg, the man who finally came up with the definitive solution to the compartment problem, summarized that criticism:

> As essential as are the advantages gained by these various means of intercommunication, it cannot be denied that the main argument against the American system, that of the continuous disturbance of the travelers due to the passage through the middle, was not resolved even in the compartmental arrangement of the first and second class, and that such disturbance is most annoying to travelers, particularly in the night-time. The only way to avoid it would be to either provide sliding doors or curtains between the two sides of the compartment and the passageway, or to move the latter . . . to the side of the carriage.[33]

Heusinger von Waldegg's solution was to move the corridor to one side and to separate it from the compartments by sliding doors. Now the compartments could no longer be entered from the outside but only indirectly, through the corridor. The carriage had entrances at both ends, similar to the American system. This remains the current arrangement of European passenger carriages. The compartment has been preserved as an intimate, enclosed traveling space. Intercommunication does not take place by movement *through* but *past* the compartment. The side corridor is not regarded as part of the actual traveling space: it is merely a compromise with technical necessity to establish communication; it is not an offshoot of the compartment but of the footboard. This became apparent from the first publication of Waldegg's proposal.[34] For the European public, the essential

---

33. *Handbuch . . .*, vol. 2, p. 303.
34. Initially, Waldegg did not discuss a side corridor, but a gallery mounted on the *outside* of the carriage. (*Zeitung des Vereins Deutscher Eisenbahn-Verwaltungen*, No. 25 (1863), p. 354.)

traveling space was and is the compartment: in order to preserve its quiet and isolation, experienced as both pleasurable and frightening, the nineteenth century had to come up with Von Waldegg's monstrous spatial design. The entirely different development of the railroad and the railroad carriage in the United States demonstrates to what a great degree the compartment is an expression of European traditions and class relationships, and how far it is from being the 'natural' form of railroad travel.

[6]
The American Railroad

Un train de chemin de fer est dans ce pays-là considéré comme une voiture ordinaire. On est habitué à s'en garder comme nous nous gardons d'un cabriolet qui passe dans la rue.

[In that country, a railroad train is just another vehicle. People are accustomed to watch out for it the way we watch out so as not to be knocked over by a buggy in the street.]
— French travel account, 1848

The history of the railroad in the United States differs from its history in Europe in that the American railroad was not the industrial successor to a fully-fledged pre-industrial transportation system: in America, the railroad served to open up, for the first time, vast regions of previously unsettled wilderness. 'With the construction of railroads, American culture *began* what European culture completed with them', says Max Maria von Weber; '*before* the humble footpath, before the cattle road, the railroad stretched itself through the wild savannah and primeval forest. In *Europe*, the railroad system *facilitates* traffic; in America, it creates it.'[1] (Italics in original.)

That difference has to do with the specific nature of the industrial revolution in America, where it did not begin with manufacturing, but with agriculture and transportation. In England the transport revolution was a consequence of the prior development of industrial production, and of the textile industry, first and foremost. The prime mover in the construction of

1. *Vom rollenden Flügelrade* (Berlin, 1882), p. 66.

the first railroad between Manchester and Liverpool was the increased need for transportation between Liverpool, the main cotton port, and Manchester, the main center of the textile industry. In England, the increased productivity of the transport system was felt throughout the entire economy and gave it a tremendous boost, but this does not alter the initial order of events — first came the industrial revolution in manufacturing, then the transport revolution.[2]

Weber has indicated the reason for the reversal of that order in the United States. The first prerequisite for opening up the wilderness to civilization and economic utilization was the creation of an effective transport system. W. W. Rostow has said of the American railroad system between 1850 and 1875 that it was 'the instrument for launching the American industrial revolution';[3] this is true from the very beginning, and applies equally to the railroad's predecessor, the river steamboat, and to the mechanization of agriculture.

In order to understand the American relationship to machinery, mechanization and industrialization, one must bear in mind the initial application of machinery in transportation and agriculture. While Europe experienced mechanization and industrialization as largely destructive, replacing as they did a highly developed artisan culture and an equally highly developed travel culture, the case of America is the exact opposite. At the beginning of the nineteenth century, when steam power was first introduced, there was no developed American culture of artisanship or of travel. The American situation was characterized by enormous and practically worthless (because unutilized) natural resources on the one hand and a chronic shortage of labor on the other. As it did not cause unemployment, every form of mechanization was experienced as creative. The mech-

2. 'The revolution in the mode of production of industry and agriculture specifically required another revolution in the general conditions of the social production process, i.e., in the means of communication and transportation.' (Marx, *Capital*, pp. 404–5.)
3. *The Process of Economic Growth* (New York, 1962), p. 262. George R. Taylor: 'The American economy of the early nineteenth century might best be described as extractive-commercial in character. It is true that the beginnings of industrial growth were already discernible. But in this land of continental expanses only revolutionary developments in the techniques of transportation and communication would make possible that almost explosive rush of industrial expansion which characterized the later decades of the century.' (*The Transportation Revolution, 1815–1860* [New York, 1968], p. 3.)

anization of transportation was not seen, as in Europe, as the destruction of a traditional culture, but as a means of gaining a new civilization from a hitherto worthless (because inaccessible) wilderness. As the transport system did not merely take over pre-existing traffic but opened up new territories for traffic, it appeared productive to a degree unimaginable to Europeans. This productivity found its clearest expression in the policy of land grants.[4] The mechanized transportation system became, as it were, a producer of territories, in the same way that mechanized agriculture became a producer of goods. Since American history really began with the industrial revolution (all else being colonial pre-history), that revolution is a constituent part of American national and cultural identity to a far greater degree than it is in Europe. Steam power was perceived as a guarantor of national unity,[5] since the latter was as impossible without it as would be the extraction of wealth from the vast, seemingly endless land by means of mechanized transportation, agriculture, and industry.

In the United States the industrial revolution was seen as a natural development, not only because it appeared right at the beginning of American history, but also because it happened first in agriculture and transportation, and was thus related directly to nature. The main instruments of American industry in the early-nineteenth century were not machines in factories, as in England, but river steamboats, railroad trains, sawmills, harvesting combines. This immediate relation with (or embed-

4. 'The lands were unoccupied, and so valueless. By the building of the railroads a market would be created, and by the doubling of the price of the sections reserved the government would be reimbursed for the amount given away. The grant would therefore assume the nature of a commission from the government to the railroads as agents for placing the unoccupied lands upon the market.' (*Railroad Promotion and Capitalization in the United States* [1st ed., 1909; rep. ed., New York, 1966], p. 246.)

5. Henry Nash Smith, *Virgin Land* (Cambridge, Mass., 1973), pp. 158, 162. A typical example can be found in Charles Fraser's article 'The moral influence of steam' (*Hunt's Merchant Magazine*, vol. 14 [1846], p. 509): 'Without the steamboat, ages might have passed without such a development of her [America's] resources as is now exhibited. The enterprises and industry of the West would have been unrewarded; the progress of civilization would have been slow; the trees of the forest would have still overshadowed the sites of flourishing villages; silence and solitude would have prevailed, where now the busy hum of men resounds, and the inheritance of the hardy pioneer would have been ignorance and barbarism'. Henry Adams: ' . . . while the United States were commercial allies of England, and needed steam neither for mines nor for manufactures, but their need was still extreme. Every American knew that if steam could be successfully applied to navigation, it must produce an immediate increase of wealth'. (*History of the United States* [1st ed., 1891–6; rep. ed., New York, 1962], vol. 1, p. 66.)

ding in) nature provided the material base for the American notion, classically described by Leo Marx, of machinery and industry as forces that do not destroy nature but actually realize its potential by cultivating it. Paraphrasing Emerson, Marx says that the industrial revolution appeared as a 'railway journey in the direction of nature'.[6]

In nineteenth-century American thought, the machine appeared to be closely linked to nature and simultaneously, the American landscape was seen as closely linked to the machine.[7] The material foundation for those perceptions lay in the peculiarity of American economic life in the nineteenth century; Habakkuk has formulated this as the 'substitution of natural resources for capital'.[8] The shortage of capital and labor in the United States led to new forms of raw material production, to an uninhibited exploitation of seemingly inexhaustible natural resources; the lack of restraint was merely a form and expression of the low investment of capital and shortage of labor. The application of the same principle to transportation led to entirely different results: here, there was no unrestrained exploitation of nature, but a practically mimetic utilization of the existing natural routes, i.e., the waterways. 'The inland routes which required the least capital to utilize in a primitive way were the rivers', explained Cleveland and Powell,[9] discussing early transportation in the United States, which was indeed based almost exclusively on the natural waterways. The motivation to utilize the waterways was the same one that led to extensive and heedless exploitation of resources ('substitution of natural resources for capital'). The results differed: the first left nature intact, the second led to its destruction. In both cases, however, nature was experienced at a closer range and with greater immediacy than in Europe. The history of American transportation in general and of its railroads in particular can only be understood in terms of an immediate relationship to nature which is not aesthetic but economic.

---

6. *The Machine in the Garden* (London, Oxford and New York, 1972), p. 238.
7. Leo Marx, op. cit., especially chap. 5.
8. H. J. Habakkuk, *American and British Technology in the Nineteenth Century* (Cambridge, 1967), p. 32.
9. *Railroad Promotion and Capitalization* (New York, 1909), p. 28.

Transportation Before the Railroad

At the beginning of the nineteenth century, the United States did not possess a network of roads and highways comparable to those of Europe. Only in New England and between the cities of Boston, New York, Philadelphia, Baltimore and Washington was there a genuine highway system traveled by regular stage-coach traffic. In the rest of the country, the roads were 'unbelievably poor',[10] being of merely local importance, and functioning as service connections to the waterways. The latter constituted the essential transportation system. Settlement proceeded along the natural waterways,[11] and these were, long into the nineteenth century, the main routes of traffic for goods as well as persons. We can still note to what an extent water traffic has

10. G. R. Taylor, op. cit., pp. 15–16.
11. In the colonial period, settlement occurred along the Atlantic Coast and the nearby river estuaries. 'A study of the spread of settlement up to 1775 shows that the immigrant population ran up the river valleys as far as the fall-line, and there generally stopped.' (Balthasar Henry Meyer, ed., *History of Transportation in the United States before 1860* [1st ed., 1917; rep. ed., Washington, DC, 1948] p. 4.) After the waterways that connected directly with the Atlantic had been opened, the settlement expanded by leaps and bounds: big pockets appeared by the Great Lakes and in the Ohio Valley, and these were no longer directly connected to the ocean. That connection was then created either artificially (Erie Canal — Great Lakes) or by using natural detours (Ohio River — Mississippi River — Gulf of Mexico — Atlantic Ocean). The same process repeated itself on a grand scale in California, where settlement began along the Pacific Coast, and traffic proceeded mainly via Cape Horn or the Isthmus of Panama until the completion of the trans-continental railroad. The development of settlement and transportation in the US was not unique in its initial reliance on waterways — in fact, colonization always begins from these — but it was unique in terms of the brief and concentrated span of time in which that settlement took place. The settlement of Europe also began by the water (Mediterranean Sea, great rivers), but in the course of the millennia an infrastructure of European overland routes developed which obscured the initial pattern of aquatic connections. In the US the foreshortening of that process to less than a century leads to a prolongation in consciousness of the initial settlement and traffic phase (i.e., the one based on waterways): in other words, American traffic consciousness in the nineteenth century still bore the imprint of the categories established by the waterways. We find a good example of this in Henry Nash Smith's discussion of the plan for a trans-continental waterway connection proposed by Thomas Hart Benton as late as 1846, after the railroad had been firmly established as a means of overland transportation in the US: 'The reason why Benton showed such a monumental inability to understand the revolution in transport that was under way was that he thought in terms of a tradition, a century of preoccupation with the network of natural waterways overspreading the Mississippi Valley'. (*Virgin Land*, pp. 30–1.) One of the essential differences between the European railway and the American railroad is that they establish connections of a different nature. In Europe, these connections were mainly between cities; in America, the railroad connected entire areas of settlement that could previously be reached only by means of great detours on the natural waterways. Thus the American railroad first appeared as a complement to the waterway network. The first explicit recognition of this appears in an article in the *North American Review* in 1829 dealing with the projected Baltimore and Ohio Railroad: 'Not only do our great rivers

shaped th   American consciousness of transportation in the
commor   nerican usage of the verb 'to ship' for all forms of
transport,   'hether on dry land or across water.[12] In marked
contrast to _urope, the abundance of waterways made it possible for them to gain paramount importance. Contemporary
travel journals testified to this as, for example, G. T. Poussin, in
1836: 'One of the most curious circumstances is, no doubt, the
abundance of its [America's] vast and navigable rivers, its great
bays, straits, and lakes, all of which contribute to a coherent
interior navigation system incomparable to that of any other
continent'.[13] Thus passenger travel used these waterways in the
absence of highways. From the eighteenth century on (at the
latest), the dominant form of travel in Europe was over land, by
stagecoach·or on horseback; Kitchener's *The Traveller's Oracle*, an
English handbook of 1827, lists travel on foot, on horseback and
by coach with no mention of travel by water, this apparently
being seen strictly as a form of transoceanic travel. The American situation was exactly the reverse; one traveled by water
wherever possible. Thus, for instance, the Englishman W. Bul-
lock, who traveled through the United States from south to
north using only the waterways, wrote in 1827: 'On my return
from Mexico to England, in the spring of the present year, I was
induced, by the representation of an American friend, to pass
through the United States by way of New Orleans, up the
Mississippi and Ohio, by Lake Erie, the Falls of Niagara, the Erie
Canal, and Hudson River, to New York . . .; nearly the whole

---

and lakes already afford to the vast surface which they drain, an extensive carriage of
their products to some market or other, but it is found that, by means of the frequent
connection of their headstreams, this advantage may be very greatly increased and
diffused'. (Pp. 166–7.) The customary notion that the American railroads struck straight
out into the wilderness is not entirely correct; they were, indeed, built through extensive wilderness areas, but in order to reach another, already existing, region of settlement that could previously be reached only by water.

12. C. W. Ernst, 'Boston and Transportation' (*Proceedings of the Bostonian Society* [January,
1888], pp. 22–3, cites a few more concepts borrowed from nautical terminology. See also
the concept of 'land navigation', a term which Daniel Webster coined for the railroad
(*The Writings and Speeches* [Boston, 1903], vol. 4, p. 113).

13. G. T. Poussin, *Amerikanische Eisenbahnen* (Regensburg, 1837), p. 13. David Stevenson
provides a typical example of the European travelers' astonishment at finding a waterway culture of almost maritime dimensions in the middle of the continent. He describes
the view of the Ohio River at Pittsburgh: 'Here, in the very heart of the continent of
North America, the appearance of a large shipping port, containing a fleet of thirty or
forty steamers moored in the river, cannot fail to surprise him' (*Sketch of the Civil
Engineering of North America* [London, 1838], p. 76).

journey being now performed by commodious steam and tow boats on the rivers, lakes and canals in the interior of the states'.[14]

The technical innovation that enabled water traffic to gain such prominence was the river steamboat. Henry Adams called it 'the most efficient instrument yet conceived for developing such a country'.[15] The development of the American riverboat may be called the first transport revolution, even preceding the railroad. Only by means of steam power did the Mississippi and Ohio rivers become navigable in both directions. Freight rates were reduced to such a degree that the railroad, when it appeared later, did not provide further economy but merely extended freight traffic into regions that were not accessible to waterways.[16] The great numbers of riverboats also indicate their importance: until the mid-nineteenth century, the tonnage of riverboats navigating on the 'Western Waters' (the Mississippi and the Ohio) alone was equal to that of the entire British steamship fleet traveling the high seas.[17] Louis C. Hunter, the historiographer of the American river steamboat, sums up its importance as follows: 'The steamboat was not America's first contribution to the technology of the Industrial Revolution, but in scale and complexity of mechanisms as well as in range of social and economic influence it was in many ways the most notable achievement of our industrial infancy. Before the railroad age it was the chief technological means by which the wilderness was conquered and the frontier advanced, and the principal instrument by which steam power was introduced and spread in the United States'.[18]

The Construction of the Railroad

The American railroad continued what the river steamboat began. This applies, as we shall see, even to the design of its carriages

14. 'A Sketch of a Journey through the Western States of North America' (1827), quoted in Reuben Gold Thwaites, ed., *Early Western Travels, 1748–1846* (Cleveland, 1905), vol. 19.
15. *History of the United States*, vol. 9, p. 173.
16. J. Mark and G. Walton, 'Steamboats and the Great Productivity Surge in River Productivity', *Journal of Economic History*, vol. 32 (1972), pp. 619–40.
17. Louis C. Hunter, *Steamboats on the Western Rivers* (New York, 1969), p. 33.
18. Ibid., p. 61.

and, in equal degree, to the design of the railroad lines themselves. In England such a line was built to be as straight as possible, partly because railroad technology favored this, partly for economic reasons. Labor was cheap and land expensive. Thus it paid to construct tunnels, embankments and cuttings in order to make the rails proceed in a straight line, at a minimum of land cost. The diametrically opposed American conditions produced opposite results. Labor was expensive, land practically worthless. In accordance with the principle of 'substitution of natural resources for capital', the American railroad did not proceed in a straight line through natural obstacles, but ran around them like a river. An article published in 1858 in the *Atlantic Monthly* observed that the English railroad engineer 'defies all opposition from river and mountain, maintains his line straight and level, fights Nature at every point, cares neither for height nor depth, rock nor torrent. . . . On the other hand, the American engineer, always respectful (though none the less determined) in the presence of natural obstacles to his progress, bows politely to the opposing mountain-range . . . '.[19] The American engineer proceeded in this manner not so much out of a respect for nature as out of the wish to build the line as cheaply as possible. As Von Gerstner, one of the first European railroad experts to visit America in the 1830s, noted, 'a great deal of earthwork is avoided' by building the line around natural obstacles. Indeed, the cost per mile of the American lines was only a fraction of that of the English, even though the rails were imported from England at considerable expense. According to Von Gerstner, the building of one mile of American railroad cost only one-tenth of what it would in England;[20] according to a report presented to the House of Commons in 1857, the cost was roughly a third — and this would seem closer to the truth.[21]

19. *Atlantic Monthly*, vol. 2 (1858), pp. 644–5.
20. Franz Anton Ritter von Gerstner, *Berichte aus den Vereinigten Staaten von Nord-Amerika, ihrer Eisenbahnen, Dampfschiffahrten, Banken, und andere öffentliche Unternehmungen* (Leipzig, 1839), pp. 15, 60. The figures relate to the Liverpool–Manchester Line and include not only the actual expenditure for constructing the line itself, but also expenditures for buildings, rolling stock, and administration.
21. Captain Douglas Galton's 'Report to the Lords of the Committee of Privy Council for Trade on the Railways of the United States' (London, 1857; p. 11), gives £10,000 to £12,000 versus £35,000. Towards the end of the century, Arthur T. Hadley quotes the following figures: $204,000 per mile in England versus $61,000 in the US (*Railroad Transportation* [New York and London, 1897], p. 260.)

All European observers noted how the American railroad lines proceeded by curves rather than straight lines: from the very beginning, this was the main characteristic of American railroads. As early as 1827, when the first reports of the English railroad experiments inspired the proposal for the first American railroad (the Baltimore and Ohio), one of its promoters, Minus Ward, stated that the English innovation would have to be modified to suit American conditions: among other things, he mentioned 'the necessity of departing from the transatlantic system of straight rail-roads'.[22] In a survey report for the Baltimore and Ohio Company, S. H. Long concluded in 1830 that the English mode of construction would be uneconomical in American circumstances. He expressed his preference for a line with numerous curves, justifying it by the observation 'that . . . the expense of avoiding a hill or valley, by a prolongation of the route, in a manner to maintain a uniformity in its vertical direction, is less than that of *cutting* and *filling*'.[23] (Italics in

22. Minus Ward, *Remarks, Propositions and Calculations, Relative to a Rail-Road and Locomotive Engines . . . from Baltimore to the Ohio River* (Baltimore, 1827), pp. iv–v.

23. Stephen H. Long, 'On the Principles Which Should Govern the Location and Construction of Rail-Roads', *Journal of the Franklin Institute*, vol. 6 (1830), p. 183. The construction of curving stretches of rail, an adaptation to natural obstacles, merely presented a possibility of capital savings. As European experts unanimously noted, and American engineers openly admitted, the railroads were built as cheaply as possible, i.e., in a very primitive manner. This was justified by the initial necessity to establish transport connections, which could be improved later on. Galton: ' . . . as in a new country it is impossible to foresee at the opening of a railway where the main centres of traffic will eventually be, it would have been a mere waste to invest more capital in the construction of a railway than would render it efficient for the work immediately before it'. (Op. cit., p. 10.) This 'predisposition toward impermanence' (Marvin Fisher, *Workshops in the Wilderness* [New York, 1967], p. 71) was a characteristic trait of American industrial development and one that was recognized early on. 'At first view, one is struck with the temporary and apparently unfinished state of many of the American works', observed David Stevenson in 1838, 'and is very apt, before inquiring into the subject to impute to want of ability what turns out, on investigation, to be a judicious and ingenious arrangement to suit the circumstances of a new climate . . .'. (*Sketches of Civil Engineering of North America* [London, 1838], p. 192) In the US, industrial machinery was exploited according to the same principle, 'substitution of nature for capital', as were natural resources. It was constructed inexpensively, quickly, and in accordance with the latest technological developments; later it was scrapped with equal speed. Habakkuk says that 'American manufacturers were readier than the English to scrap existing equipment and replace it by new, and they therefore had more opportunities of taking advantage of technological progress and acquiring know-how'; his remark that 'the English inclination was to repair rather than to scrap' indicates that America's and England's differing attitudes towards machinery may be explained, not only by the obvious economic motivations, but also in terms of differing traditions: on the one hand, Europe's still-active heritage of careful craftsmanship; on the other, the American vision of an infinitely disposable nature, which even included the machines. (Habakkuk, pp. 56ff.)

original.) To what extent the curving route appeared to be both economical and sensible to the American engineers can be realized from their incomprehension of the English mode of construction. Thus an American text of 1844 fails to grasp the reason for the English engineer's method: 'To approximate to an air-line and a dead level . . ., recourse has been had to cuts, embankments, and tunnels, involving great expense and an immense annual outlay for repairs, which might have been easily avoided by waving the line, increasing the gradients, and conforming to the surface of the country'.[24]

In this somewhat condescending evaluation, tinged with pity, the American commentator showed his ignorance of the fact that the English straight-line manner of construction was based not on esthetics but on purely technical considerations. The rigid axles of the English rolling stock required a line that was as straight as possible: English rolling-stock would inevitably derail in the attempt to take a sharp curve.

Let us now look at the reason why the American railroads with their abundance of curving lines did not have that technical problem.

The New Type of Carriage

In rigid-axle construction, the sharper the curves of a railroad line, the closer together the axles of a carriage need to be placed to avoid derailment. From a technical viewpoint, the frequently curving American route would require so short a distance be-tween the axles that an economically-sized carriage would be an utter impossibility. Thus the innovation of the curving route required a complementary technological innovation, that of a carriage capable of dealing with those curves. The mechanical solution of the problem required a synthesis of contradictory requirements: both rigidity and mobility of the individual axle, and simultaneity of a long and a short distance between the axles. In 1834, Ross Winans provided the solution in his pa-tented invention, which became the basis for the development of the specifically American type of railroad car: Winans sug-

24. Elias Derby, *Two Months Abroad* (Boston, 1844), p. 8.

gested a new design for the undercarriage — the 'bogie'. It fulfilled the seemingly contradictory requirements. Two rigid axles were combined in an undercarriage, with an extremely short distance between them: this guaranteed that wheels and rails would remain parallel even on the sharpest curve. Mobility was added to this rigid component by attaching it to the body of the car by means of a swivelling pivot. One of these double-axled bogies was at each end of the car. In his patent application Winans said: 'I construct two bearing carriages, each with four wheels, which are to sustain the body of the passenger or other car, by placing one of them at or near each end of it. . . . The two wheels on either side of these carriages are to be placed very near to each other: the spaces between their flanges need to be no greater than is necessary to prevent their contact with each other'.[25]

This constituted a breakthrough from the earlier prevalent principle of technical unity between undercarriage and car body. That unity was dissolved into two mutually independent technical complexes, an achievement that coincided, more or less, with Colt's and Whitney's development of the technology of inter-changeable parts.

Technically emancipated from the rails, the car was now capable of being extended in length, virtually *ad infinitum*. Winans modestly proposed cars that would be only twice as large: 'The body of the passenger or other car I make is double the ordinary length of those which run on four wheels, and capable of carrying double their load'.

This is an elegant example of the thesis that a technological innovation becomes a historically significant one only when there is an actual economic demand for it: Winan's bearing carriage was, in fact, the *second* discovery of the same idea that had been developed twenty years earlier in England. In 1812 William Chapman had patented the same technical principle of a four-wheeled bearing carriage in England.[26] No real need for it then existed because the straight line appeared as 'natural' and economically sensible to the English — due to high real estate

---

25. 'Letters Patent of Ross Winans' (1 October 1834), Library of the Association of American Railroads, Washington DC.
26. C. F. Dendy Marshall, *A History of Railway Locomotives down to the Year 1831* (London, 1953), pp. 62ff.

costs and low wages, and also the Newtonian tradition — as the curving track seemed in the United States.[27]

The timing of Winans' patent and its quick adoption by the American lines in the 1830s and early 1840s is revealing. At first, at the beginning of the 1830s, the compartment design of the English railroad had been adopted along with the rest of the technology. As the curving tracks of America demanded an extremely short distance between axles, it was found to be impossible to place three compartments in a series on one bearing carriage: there was room for only one.[28] This cultural lag between the already-Americanized (curving) mode of construction of the road and the still-European type of car lasted for a few years. Only after the bogie had solved the technical problem of how to build a car suited to the American routes was it possible to develop an entirely new *form* of car.

That form, the long car without compartments, quite devoid of reminiscences of the stagecoach, became the standard in America from the 1840s on. A report on the American railroads, commissioned by and presented to the British House of Commons in 1857, contains the following description:

> The bodies of the passenger cars are from thirty to forty-five, and even sixty, feet in length. . . . On lines of four feet eight and one half inches gauge the cars are about nine feet, and on the New York and Erie, ten feet wide, and from six feet to seven feet six inches high. . . . The interior of the car forms a large room, with a passage, of from one foot nine inches to two feet wide, down the centre, upon each side of which cross seats are arranged. These seats are intended for two passengers each; they are from three feet three inches to three feet six inches long, about one foot six inches wide, and one foot apart. The back is arranged to be turned, so that the passenger may sit with his face in either direction. . . . In winter the cars are warmed by means of an iron stove in the centre; and they are lighted at night by lamps placed at the sides. In a certain proportion of the

27. Unlike the American type of car, the bogie gained instant recognition by European railway experts. Lardner called it 'a simple and effectual arrangement'. (*Railway Economy*, p. 338.) Gerstner noted: 'There is considerably less wear and tear on both rails and carriages, and the repair costs of both carriages and locomotives are far lower than in Europe'. (*Berichte*, p. 19.) Towards the end of the nineteenth century, as European long-distance trains equipped with Waldegg's side corridor achieved American dimensions, the bogie was introduced there as well.

28. August Mencken, *The Railroad Passenger Car* (Baltimore, 1957), pp. 9ff.

passenger cars, a portion, about seven feet long, three feet six inches wide, is partitioned off, in which is a small room for the convenience of ladies nursing, and a watercloset.[29]

How different this type of car was from the compartmentalized one becomes apparent merely by a glance at scale specifications. The first-class compartment of the London–Birmingham line in the 1830s was six feet six inches wide, five feet six inches long, six feet high.[30] The different spatial dimensions were an expression as well as a cause of different attitudes toward travel. Travel in the compartment was characterized by immobility, whereas in the American car there was a great deal of mobility during the trip. A situation of embarrassed sedentary confrontation such as the one Simmel describes was unthinkable in the American car, simply because the seats had not been arranged to face each other (their backrests could be reversed), but also because of the possibilities for general communication and mobility in the American car. Poussin stressed this autonomy of movement during the journey and went on to say: ' . . . in this manner, a traveler is free to go and sit down next to whoever he likes, and also to change places again. An American would not much care for our way of traveling in a fixed seat, in a cramped carriage, under lock and key; he would sense a lack of air, of suffocation'.[31] Americans traveling in European trains did indeed mention 'confinement in a small, locked-up compartment',[32] and found it an unpleasant experience to be unable to move freely through the cars and the entire train during the journey,[33] and to have either inaccessible sanitary facilities or none at all — a

29. Galton, p. 15.
30. C. Hamilton Ellis, *Railway Carriages in the British Isles from 1830 to 1914* (London, 1965), p. 22.
31. *De la puissance Américaine* (Paris, 1845), vol. 1, p. 157. Similarly L. Simonin thirty years later: 'A day spent on the railroad in one of these cars . . . passes quickly and effortlessly because the traveler enjoys a great number of comforts and is not imprisoned in it. He is able to move at will . . . to come and go anywhere throughout the train. . . .' (*Le Monde Américain* [Paris, 1875], p. 366. The adjustability of backrests, Simonin notes, makes it possible to have various seating arrangements, depending on the situation: 'If three or four people are traveling together, they can face each other in a kind of relative privacy' (p. 364). This statement tacitly implies that solitary travelers or those in pairs usually adjusted their seats so that they did *not* face anybody; thus there was no inevitable 'confrontation', as there was in the European compartment.
32. E. B. Dorsey, 'English and American Railroads Compared', *Transactions of the American Society of Civil Engineers*, vol. 15, (1887), p. 1.
33. Robert S. Minot, *Railway Travel in Europe and America* (Boston, 1882), pp. 11–12.

problem that persisted on European trains for a long time. The European evaluation of the American car was, as we have already seen, somewhat ambivalent. There were many statements of approval, particularly during the compartment hysteria of the 1860s. 'There is no danger of robbery, murder, or other outrage, as in the small, locked, and inaccessible compartments of European roads', wrote an English author on America, in 1864.[34]

As the history of the compartment demonstrates, the obvious advantages of the American car did not, however, seem sufficient reason to abandon the quiet and immobility of the European train compartment. Thus Captain Tyler in his report to the House of Commons: ' . . . as regards the American arrangement, it is obvious that it is so opposed to the social habits of the English, and would interfere so much with the privacy and comfort which they now enjoy, that these considerations, apart from others, nearly as important, would forbid its adoption in this country'.[35] M. Couche, a member of the French commission appointed after Poinsot's murder, was even more explicit: he said that the American car was suited to American conditions but not for those that prevailed in Europe, since Europeans were not accustomed to move around during the journey, and there was thus no advantage in mobility: 'The traveler is not, in actual fact, free to move around beyond the compartment that he occupies'.[36]

The explanation for the American railroad car's particular interior form is not as uncomplicated as the compartment's derivation from the coach chamber. There is, in fact, a whole series of explanations, all of which apply. We have mentioned the invention of the undercarriage (bogie, truck) that permitted the construction of virtually endless cars. The American car can also be described as the simplest and cheapest type of passenger car: just as the lack of capital in the United States during the early- and mid-nineteenth century had led to the cheapest mode of railroad construction, it also resulted in the least expensive kind of passenger car. That purely economic state of affairs was,

34. Thomas L. Nichols, *Forty Years of American Life* (1st ed., 1864; rep. ed., New York, 1969), vol. 2, p. 8.
35. Great Britain, *Sessional Papers* (House of Commons), vol. 50 (1865), p. 6.
36. *Voie, matériel roulant, et exploitation technique des chemins de fer* (Paris, 1873), vol. 2, p. 17.

however, closely related to the indigenous American democracy of the nineteenth century as described by Tocqueville and Chevalier. The classless open car was economically, politically, psychologically and culturally the appropriate travel container for a democratic pioneer society, while the compartment car, on the other hand, expressed the social conditions prevailing in Europe.

These general explanations are not entirely satisfactory. It obviously would have been possible to simply build a cheaper and more primitive kind of compartment car. We get closer to the core of the question of why Americans preferred to travel in a large room and Europeans in a tiny cell if we consider the remarkable difference between average travel distances in Europe and the United States. The first American lines on the East Coast were still relatively short, although they did bridge larger distances than the first European connections between cities. With the westward expansion the American lines grew ever longer. By the 1830s, when European train journeys were merely a matter of hours and were undertaken only in the daytime, the first sleeping cars appeared in the United States.[37]

Couche refers to the development of new forms of travel due to longer distances. While a train journey in Europe took place in the surrounding environment of stations and their installations — such as buffets, toilets, etc., — America boasted very few of these. Thus, Couche argues, the American traveler had to find those facilities in the train itself. 'A train has to be self-sufficient. The travelers have to be able to find all that is necessary on board, as would be the case on a steamship that puts into port only rarely and briefly'.[38]

The steamship, mentioned by Couche as a convenient analogy, does indeed upon closer scrutiny yield many clues to the rise of a certain type of car on American railroads.

River Steamboat and Canal Packet as Models for the American Railroad Car

Noting that the American train car differed from European

37. Mencken, pp. 5ff.
38. Couche, p. 25.

compartment cars in its spaciousness and ease of communication, some contemporary authors claimed that this type of car reminded them more of the interior of a seagoing vessel than of a stagecoach. Von Waldegg was reminded of the 'cabin of a ship'.[39] Galton, in the report to the House of Commons in 1857: 'In designing their rolling stock, the Americans appear to have taken their ideas more from a ship than from an ordinary carriage'.[40] The French railroad engineers Lavoinne and Pontzen found that the opportunity to move around during the journey was 'analogous to what is possible on board a ship, instead of the immobility imposed on European travelers'.[41]

In the literature (sparse, and more popular than scientific)[42] dealing with the development of design on the railroads, we do not find that anyone has pursued this obvious resemblance between American railroad car and ship design. The only mention known to me of their analogous form, in the framework of a serious study, occurs in John Gloag's *Victorian Comfort*. Gloag speaks of the extreme importance of the river steamboats in American travel before the railroad era and concludes: 'The design of these river steamers had a permanent effect on American standards of comfort and travel'. He then conjectures: 'The long and spacious saloons may well have been the prototypes for the American railroad cars'.[43] In corroboration, he presents side by side illustrations of a riverboat saloon and a Pullman car interior. The similarity of these spaces seems even less accidental when considering what a dominating role the river steamers played in American transportation, and thus in American transportation consciousness, during the early part of the nineteenth century. In other words, the riverboat became for the American railroad train what the stagecoach had been for the European: a means and form of travel that was representative of the period before

39. *Handbuch* . . ., vol. 2, p. 5.
40. Galton, p. 16.
41. E. Lavoinne and E. Pontzen, *Les chemins de fer en Amérique* (Paris, 1882), vol. 2, p. 1.
42. Ellis' monograph on the English railway carriage, and Mencken's on the American, range from the anecdotal to the technically detailed, with Mencken stressing the latter, Ellis the former aspect. In addition, there are scattered essays of a semi-scientific, almost folkloristic nature, such as E. G. Young, 'The Development of the American Railway Passenger Car' (*The Railway and Locomotive Historical Society Bulletin*, no. 32 [1933]), as well as more or less accessible pictorial volumes with varying amounts of text, such as Lucius Beebe, *Mr. Pullman's Elegant Palace Car* (New York, 1961), which mentions the river steamboat as the model of the Pullman car (pp. 279 seq.).
43. *Victorian Comfort: A Social History of Design from 1830–1900*, (New York, 1973, p. 139, 142).

the introduction of railroads, and thus one upon which the railroad modeled itself.

There is one singularly striking piece of proof for that formal influence which otherwise manifested itself indirectly, becoming evident only by means of historical reconstruction: it is Morgan's never-realized design for a railroad car, published in the Boston journal *The American Traveler* in 1829, when the first American railroad had not yet been built. As the designer himself noted, what was proposed and illustrated was not so much a carriage as rather 'what may be emphatically termed a *Land Barge*, and to the Traveler will furnish an idea of all the convenience and comfort which belong to the best steam boats'. (Italics in original.) The spatial divisions corresponded exactly to those of a steamer: 'It is constructed with a cabin, berths, etc. below; a promenade deck, awning, seats, etc. above' — with 'below' and 'above' referring to the two decks of the car, similar to those of a steamer. Final proof for the immediacy with which steamboat concepts were transferred to the railroad in this proposal is the fact that the locomotive was not expected to pull several of these novel cars (in other words, a train), but just one.

This proposal, together with a considerable number of similar ones that were published in the nineteenth century,[44] was never realized, but that does not diminish its validity as proof of the persistence of the image of the steamship in American transportation consciousness. It is precisely Morgan's eccentrically literal transposition of the steamer design that casts light on the steamship's formal influence on the American railroad car, the influence being less immediately recognizable in the standardized car. Different spatial dimensions prevented the envisaged total adoption of steam forms. 'Obviously the difference in clearances and functional organization of railroad cars inhibited their designers from taking a leaf bodily from the book of the river steamers', says Beebe, 'but that they looked at them with longing eye and appropriated what they could is abundantly evident in the record'.[45]

44. Benjamin Dearborn's proposal of 1819 for a ship-like rail carriage; General James Semple's illustrated proposal for a 'Prairie Steam-Car', a vehicle that looked like a river steamboat and locomoted across the plains on rollers, not on rails. (*The Scientific American*, 12 March 1846.)
45. *Mr. Pullman's Elegant Palace Car*, p. 280.

What the railroad car was unable to adopt from the riverboat, due to different spatial relations, it copied from another model, the canal packet, which played a far greater role in passenger traffic in the United States than it ever did in Europe, although it did not gain the spectacular eminence of the steamer. In the American Northeast, on the much-traveled stretches of the Erie Canal and on the canal network connecting Philadelphia and Pittsburgh, the packet was an integral part of the traveling experience. On the Philadelphia–Pittsburgh Canal, which was actually a combination of canal and railroad, the canal packet and the train entered into a curious symbiosis. During the journey the packets, with their passengers on board, were mounted on bearing carriages and hauled to the next stretch of canal — a combination that one can well imagine to have been part of the inspiration for Winans' car, which made its appearance shortly thereafter.[46]

The canal packet of the 1820s and 1830s provided a good model for the railroad car due to its compatible form and dimensions. Its saloon consisted of a long rectangle with windows on the sides and entrances at both ends. Contemporary representations of both its exterior and interior demonstrate a similarity to the later railroad car that a comparison of dimensions corroborates with almost mathematical precision. In 1838, an English engineer stated that the main saloon cabin of a canal packet was forty feet long and eleven wide;[47] by the 1850s the standard railroad car was thirty to forty-five feet long and nine to ten feet wide.[48]

As we have seen, the difficulty in reconstructing the genesis of the American railroad car is based on the fact that there was no single model to be found among prior means of transportation, such as the European coach, but two models that had to be

---

46. In Ezra Reed's patent application of 6 April 1833, the sectional canal boat was described as follows: 'This canal boat is to be built in parts, or sections, each having its four sides, and bottom. Of these sections there may be six, or more; the two forming the stem and the stern may differ in shape from the others, which may be nearly, or quite, alike. The separate parts are to be united by two pieces of plank on each side, extending from stem to stern, fastened by spikes, or bolts, to the bow and stern sections; the intermediate ones to be kept in their place by chains'. (*Journal of the Franklin Institute*, vol. 12 [1833], p. 235.) In this separation and reassembly of interchangeable parts we recognize, once again, the Colt–Whitney principle characteristic of American technology and also expressed in the bogie.

47. D. Stevenson, *Sketches . . .*, p. 197.

48. Galton, p. 15; Mencken, pp. 12 seq.

synthesized to produce the final result. Whatever the particulars of that synthetic process, it is quite obvious that the result was of a different form, and even a different mode of travel than that of the European railway compartment.

Sea Voyage on Rails

The basic situation of travel in the European compartment, the immobility of the passenger, harked back to the situation in the stagecoach, which was the means of travel that put its stamp upon West European travel culture in the late eighteenth and early nineteenth centuries. This ascendancy of the stagecoach became possible because of the reasonably well developed highway network then existing in Western Europe.

The characteristics of the American transport situation at the beginning of the nineteenth century were under-developed traffic by land, but highly developed traffic on the inland waterways. In American travel, the river steamer was a far more important factor than the stagecoach. 'The innumerable steam boats . . . are the stage coaches and fly wagons of this land of lakes and rivers', wrote Frances Trollope in 1832, and this impression of American travel recurs in contemporary reports by European visitors.[49]

Being the second mechanized means of transportation, the railroad became closely linked with the steamer in American transportation development and consciousness. These links were reinforced, on the one hand by the American notion of steam power as the force that joined the parts of the country into a living nation and, on the other, by the reality of an under-developed highway system; highway building continued to be neglected after the arrival of the railroads, until the beginning of the twentieth century and the arrival of the automobile.[50] 'The Americans', wrote a French author discussing the situation in the mid-nineteenth century, 'seem to have been so entirely

49. *Domestic Manners of the Americans* (1st ed., 1832; rep. ed., New York, 1949), p. 15. On the ubiquitousness of ships even in the heart of the country: 'I hardly remember a single town where vessels of some description or other may not constantly be seen in full activity' (op. cit., p. 303).
50. 'The great development of traffic [in America] skipped the era of highways and began, in contrast to all European countries, immediately with the construction of the most

predestined to the exclusive use of steamboats and railroads that they have no taste for the use of carriages nor for the construction of the great roads necessary for such carriages'.[51]

The social relations of the river steamer, as described by L. C. Hunter, were the very opposite of those of the class-stratified European train:

> A 'world in miniature' was the phrase with which literary travellers were wont to describe the western steamboat, and such in truth it was. Here all the essential processes of living went on, keyed to a higher pitch than in the ordinary course of land-bound existence. Here people laboured, ate, slept, amused themselves, suffered illness and hardship, and, not infrequently, died. Here luxury and poverty, overindulgence and deprivation, freedom and bondage were found in close proximity. Here all ranks and classes were represented: proletarian and chattel slave, frontiersman and emigrant, merchant and manufacturer, farmer and planter. Here was a society with a distinctive life and folkways of its own. Here was a freedom of intercourse among persons of different rank and from different walks of life which impressed foreign observers as symbolic

---

rapid and profitable means of transport, the railroad. Especially after the union of all the states it became necessary to master the enormous space they covered. Only the railroad could answer this need. Thus the promising beginnings of a highway network, particularly in New England and in the vicinity of great cities, were inhibited or even thwarted. Thus a gap was created in the development of overland traffic that remained open until the beginning of the twentieth century. Only then, after the introduction of the automobile, that gap was slowly closed,' (Hans Kicia, 'Die Landstrassen in den Vereinigten Staaten von Nordamerika', *Zeitschrift für Verkehrswissenschaft*, vol. 6 [1928], p. 109). Discussing the development of highways in the latter half of the nineteenth century, an American publication of the year 1896 goes so far as to state that, due to the exclusive attention paid to the railroads, the highways were 'in a poorer state than they were fifty years ago'. (N. S. Shaler, *American Highways* [New York, 1896], p. 242.) The early-nineteenth century's neglect of the highways is only one side of the matter. After the automobile became the mode of mass transportation, highways were built again, but their mode of construction broke away from its own ancient tradition and acquired a new orientation based on the railroad. The German *Autobahnen* (highways) of the 1920s and 1930s were associated with the *Eisenbahn* (railroad), not only in name, but were even administered by the national railway corporation. The highway constructed exclusively for automotive traffic no longer integrated urban and rural traffic, stationary and moving traffic, but, like the railroad, served only *moving* traffic. Benton MacKay, proponent of the 'limited access highway', justified his demand for an exclusively automotive highway that no longer ran through the cities by stating that the automobile was, in fact, a locomotive. By a similar transfer we have until recently looked upon the motor road as a fitting frontage for our home lot, instead of regarding it realistically as a causeway, as much to be shunned as a railroad. Once these conventional prejudices are abolished, we see that the motor road is a new kind of railroad. . . .' (Benton, MacKay, *The New Exploration* [Urbana, Ill., 1962], p. 231.)

51. 'L'Illustration', *Journal Universel*, 22 July 1848, p. 316.

of the egalitarian quality of American life.[52]

Quite apart from the democratic aspect, Europe did not have anything comparable to these 'Floating Palaces' and 'Moving Hotels':[53] the European counterparts of these boats were modest by comparison. 'The model of this steamer is beautiful', said one American reporting on a steamer trip down the Rhine in 1844, 'but the room is extremely limited'.[54]

European visitors, on the other hand, found the American river steamer alien in form (for Charles Dickens, 'these Western vessels are . . . foreign to all ideas we are accustomed to entertain of boats') and singular in their roominess and the attendant conviviality. Thus David Stevenson, in 1839, on the doings in the main saloon: 'The scene resembles much more the coffee-room of some great hotel than the cabin of a floating vessel'.[55] Or Charles Sealsfield (Friedrich Gerstäcker) in 1827, when the river steamer had a virtual monopoly on American travel:

No one is more at home when traveling than the American, particularly when traveling in his own country. He regards the steamboat as a hostelry in which he is staying, as his temporary property, and acts quite accordingly. The citizen of the United States travels so extensively and his journeys are of such great duration that they do not present him with the notions of discomfort or fear that the European might have. His traveling facilities (I am speaking of travel by water) are far more comfortable and better equipped than those of any other nation, not excluding the English.[56]

In our discussion of the development of design we have seen how the spaciousness of the riverboat was regarded as a desideratum for the railroad car. The earliest record of this can be found in Benjamin Dearborn's proposal of 1819, which suggested that the passenger cars of the future railroad be furnished 'with accommodations for passengers to take their meals and their rest during the passage, as in packets; that they be suf-

52. L. C. Hunter, p. 391.
53. 'Floating Palace' and 'Moving Hotel' are popular nicknames for the steamboats on the Ohio and Mississippi rivers. (See Hunter, p. 390.)
54. Derby, *Two Months* . . ., p. 32.
55. *Sketches* . . ., p. 136.
56. Charles Sealsfield, *Die Vereinigten Staaten von Nord Amerika* (*The United States of North America*), Stuttgart and Tübingen, 1827, 2 vols., vol. 2, p. 136).

ficiently high for persons to walk without stooping, and so capacious as to accommodate twenty, thirty, or more passengers, with their baggage'.[57]

Thus it was not only the motive power they shared (steam) that caused river steamer and railroad to be seen as two manifestations of one and the same thing, but also their capacity to provide the same form of travel with ample space and mobility during the journey. 'We have moving palaces on the water and the land', gushed an article in the 1840 *Merchant's Magazine and Commercial Review*, reflecting the popular notion of 'saloons with gilded columns, carpeted with the costly fabrics of foreign looms, adorned with mirrors and paintings and rich tapestry . . . '.[58]

The only strange thing about this text is its date: by 1840, the spacious car was firmly established on American railroads, but in a very sober, plain, almost primitive form not easily compared with 'steamboat gothic'.[59] That the figure of speech about 'moving palaces on the water and the land' could nevertheless become so popular, despite the obvious differences, demonstrates how deeply anchored the analogy of steamer and train had become in popular consciousness.

Although the similarity between the interiors of river steamers and railroad trains was merely a figment of the imagination in 1840, it became a reality twenty years later. From 1859 on, Pullman built cars that openly allude to the model of the 'floating palace' steamer in their very name of 'palace cars': as contemporary illustrations show, their interiors were hard to distinguish from the luxury saloon of a riverboat.

These Pullman cars reflected the nation's wealth, which became increasingly apparent after the end of the Civil War in 1865. With them, a 'first class' was introduced into the until then classless American railroad system.[60] Otherwise they were merely a further development of the arrangement and the func-

---

57. 'Report of the Committee on Commerce and Manufactures', quoted in William M. Brown, *The History of the First Locomotives in America* (New York, 1874), p. 73.

58. Lanman, in *Merchant's Magazine and Commercial Review*, vol. 3 (1840), p. 274.

59. 'Steamboat gothic' is the popular term for what became a stylistic concept in the nineteenth century. For a detailed description, see Hunter, pp. 396ff.

60. Pullman cars had a dual function, transportation and comfort. They permitted the passengers to stay in the car while it was being shunted from one line to another and, as the railroad network expanded, such shunting became increasingly frequent. They were operated by the Pullman company, which entered into cooperative contracts with the individual lines. The travelers using these cars paid an additional fare.

tions that have been characteristic of the American railroad car from the beginning. As the railroads reached the West Coast, American rail journeys became even longer than before. The need for mobility and communication during the journey increased in direct proportion to the traveled distance: although the need was always typical of American travel, new distances and new wealth added fresh quality to it. The train consisting of Pullman cars looked like a steamer on rails: 'Baths, both tub and shower, barbershops, manicures, lady's maids, valet service, news tickers, libraries, current periodicals and hotel and railroad directories, smokers' accessories and, of course, the fullest possible facilities for sluicing and gentling the patrons with wines and strong waters were taken for granted on all luxury trains of the era'.[61] For a while, the Union Pacific Railroad published a newspaper on its transcontinental run,[62] according to which two organs had been installed on the train so that passengers were able to attend religious services and musical performances while on board.[63]

With the image of that Pullman train traversing the Western plains like a steamship on rails we end our consideration of the American railroad: without doubt, that was its finest hour. This image of a ship on land, crossing the prairie so frequently described by travelers as an ocean of land,[64] gave the American railroad's nautical associations vivid confirmation.

The American railroad's original and fundamental task was to create transportation where no natural waterways existed. This function became more obvious than ever on journeys through the vast dry reaches of the Great Plains: if, until then, the railroad had been merely reminiscent of the waterway it was a surrogate for, the train that then ran on it now became a ship on dry land in a concrete sense. In 1846, Thomas Hart Benton suggested that the two coasts of the American continent should

---

61. Beebe, p. 285.
62. The paper was called the *Trans-Continental*. It appeared for the first time in May 1870, on the occasion of a special trip arranged by the Union Pacific for a group of Boston businessmen. I do not know if further issues appeared.
63. *Trans-Continental*, 26 and 30 May 1870.
64. Thus, Charles Dickens calls the prairie 'a tranquil sea or lake without water' (quoted in D. A. Dondore, *The Prairie and the Making of Middle America* [Cedar Rapids, Iowa, 1926], p. 290). An 1871 German text remarks: 'No land in sight. As far as one can see, this ocean. . .. .' (Alexander F. von Hübner, *Ein Spaziergang um die Welt* [Leipzig, 1882], p. 53.)

be joined not by a railroad but by a system of waterways.[65] Although this notion, born out of the tradition of water travel, never stood a chance against the technically superior railroad, the latter was to pay its respects to that same tradition by crossing the continent like a steamship engaged in what Daniel Webster once called 'land navigation'.[66]

Postscript

The question as to why the traveling situation in the American railroad car provided so much more mobility than did its European counterpart cannot be answered entirely satisfactorily by reference to that general mobility which, since Tocqueville at least, has been regarded as an American national characteristic. One may assume that the 'passion for locomotion' that Michel Chevalier and countless other European visitors observed in the nineteenth century applied not only to general commercial and technological dynamics in America but was also characteristic of individual American bodies. Chevalier has a passage that seems to demonstrate why Americans did not travel in a state of compartmentalized immobility: he says that the American

> is always in the mood to move on, always ready to start in the first steamer that comes along from the place where he had just now landed. He is devoured with a passion for movement, he cannot stay in one place; he must go and come, he must stretch his limbs and keep his muscles in play. When his feet are not in motion, his fingers must be in action; he must be whittling a piece of wood, cutting the back of his chair, or notching the edge of the table, or his jaws must be at work grinding tobacco. . . . He always has something to do, he is always in a terrible hurry. He is fit for all sorts of work except those which require a careful slowness. Those fill him with horror; it is his idea of hell.[67]

65. See n. 11 above.
66. *The Writings and Speeches* (Boston, 1903), vol. 4, p. 113. A curious similarity between railroad train and steamboat was apparent in their relative speeds at the time. According to Gerstner, the steamers reached 12 mph, the trains 12–15 mph (*Berichte . . .*, p. 44). Even later on, American rail velocities differed considerably from the European ones. In 1864, the average speed of American express trains was 32 mph (*Appleton's Railway Guide*, quoted in John H. White, *American Locomotives, 1830–1880* [Baltimore, 1968], p. 74). English trains had reached that figure by the 1840s.
67. *Society, Manners, and Politics in the United States* (Ithaca, New York, 1961), p. 270.

A coalfield, 1812 (Chap. 1). The process of mechanization is
clearly seen. The horse is still a source of power but is now a small image in
the background, while the foreground is dominated by a steam-powered coal
train.
Columbia University, Parsons Collection.

The train cuts through the landscape (Chap. 2). *Science Museum, London,*
On opposite page: (*above*) The cutting as part of the nineteenth-century
landscape. *Science Museum, London.*
(*below*) The London–Greenwich line blazes a trail through the city like a
modern expressway. *Columbia University, Parsons Collection.*

The railroad journey as panorama (Chap. 4).
For the opening of the Paris–Orleans line in 1843 the landscape along the journey was reproduced as a sequence of pictures on three large sheets, the first of which is reproduced here.
Columbia University, Parsons Collection.

On opposite page: (*above*) The idyllic preindustrial foreground is dominated by the railroad running along the viaduct in the background (Chap. 2).
British Museum, London.
(*below*) Daumier's sleeping travellers show the monotony of the railroad journey (Chap. 4).
Archive Roger Viollet, Paris.

(*above*) The railway originated as a means of transporting coal (Chap. 1). The train that opened the Stockton–Darlington line was both coal and passenger train.
Science Museum, London.

(*below, left*) This illustration from Thomas Gray's *Observations . . .* of 1825 documents a concept for combining a coal wagon with a passenger car (Chap. 1).
(*below*) Travelling third-class in France in the 1840s (Chap. 5).
Musée Carnavalet, Cabinet des Estampes.

Chemin de fer de Paris à Orléans.

Travelling sociability (Chap. 5).
(above) Third-class passengers as seen by Gustav Doré.
Musée Carnavalet, Cabinet des Estampes.
(below) First-class traveller, France, 1900. *Archive Roger Viollet, Paris.*

The railroad car (Chap. 6).
(*above*) A European view of the American railroad car, 1848.
(*below*) Pullman car interiors, 1870s and 1880s. *The Railway Gazette*, 1887.

The riverboat cabin as model for the American passenger car, 1850s (Chap. 6).
(*above*) Daytime cabin of a small riverboat.
(*below*) The main cabin of a riverboat at night.
(*above, right*) A railroad passenger car, daytime.
(*below, right*) A sleeping car of the New York Central Railroad.
All illustrations: New York Public Library Picture Collection.

A railroad disaster on the Paris–Versailles line, 8 May 1841 (Chap. 8).

The railroad in the city (Chap. 12).
On opposite page: (*above*) Haussmannism in Paris in the 1860s.
(*below*) Haussmann's new boulevards, reorganizing the city for traffic.
All illustrations: *Musée Carnavalet, Cabinet des Estampes.*

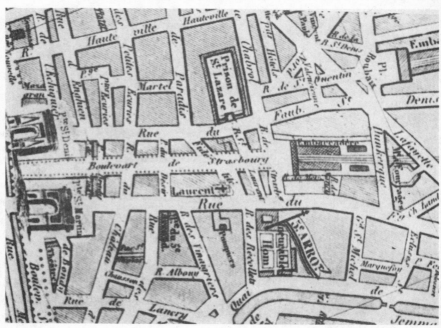

The railroad in the city (Chaps. 11 and 12).
(*above*) The train hall, Euston, London, 1835.
Science Museum, London.

On opposite page: (*above*) The façade of the terminus, Gare de l'Est, Paris, 1830.
Musée Carnavalet, Cabinet des Estampes.
(*below*) The Boulevard de Strasbourg continues the line of the railroad, 1855.
Musée de la Ville, Paris.

'Across the Continent': the opening and civilizing of the wilderness by the
railroad (Chap. 6), Currier & Ives, 1869.
New York Library Picture Collection.

[7]
The Pathology of the Railroad Journey

> The man, for the time being, becomes a part of the machine in
> which he has placed himself, being jarred by the self-same
> movement, and receiving impressions upon nerves of skin and
> muscle which are none the less real because they are
> unconsciously inflicted.
> — *The Book of Health*, 1884

Until the end of the 1850s, medical science exhibited only spor-
adic interest in the effects that rail travel had on the health of
passengers and railway personnel.[1] The first systematic study
appeared in 1857: it was E. A. Duchesne's *Des chemins de fer et
leur influence sur la santé des mécaniciens et des chauffeurs* (*On the
railroads and their influence on the health of the engineers and the
firemen*) an industrial-medical survey of the type introduced by

1. The index of the leading English medical journal, *The Lancet*, did not mention 'railway'
time in the 1830s. In the 1840s it appeared in connection with accidents, but only in
passing. In the mid-1830s, several physicians, discussing the projected London–
Brighton line, concerned themselves with the problems of smoke, sudden changes of
temperature, noise, etc.; those problems, however, did not specifically relate to the
actual process of rail travel. Medical views on the latter — i.e., on the effects of the novel
velocity, vibration, etc. — varied and contradicted each other to an extent that makes it
impossible to consider them as serious scientific investigations of the new mode of
transport. For instance, in 1835 Bavaria's *Obermedizinalkollegium* predicted that rail
travelers would succumb to brain damage, or 'delirium furiosum'. (Cf. Gisela Koch and
M. Hoffman, 'Geschichte der Verkehrsmedizin für den Verkehr mit Landfahrzeugen
von den Anfängen bis zum Ende des 2. Weltkrieges', *Zentralblatt für Verkehrsmedizin,
Verkehrspsychologie, Luft- und Raumfahrt-Medizin*, vol. 15, fas. 4, p. 193). Here we quote
several contrary evaluations of the effects of the vibration experienced on the train. In
1836, in C. W. Hufeland's medical journal, the swaying motion of coach travel is

Gaskell in England in the 1830s to study the health of factory workers. The engine-drivers and firemen, whose health Duchesne discussed were seen as industrial workers. The machine they operated was the locomotive, the cause of the various symptoms of disease that Duchesne verified and codified under the heading *maladie des mécaniciens* (engineers' malady). These consisted in part of pseudo-rheumatic pains that resulted from the drivers' and firemen's exposed working position on the locomotive and from the alternation of heat and cold.[2] There were also the consequences of the specific mechanical vibration peculiar to the motion of the locomotive and the train. On the one hand, the train proceeded so very smoothly — which is why early travellers felt that they were 'flying' — but, on the other, wheel and rail produced a new kind of vibration that was quite different from the jolts experienced on a coach journey on the highway. This vibration resulted from the exact interaction between steel rail and steel wheel, from the speed and, particularly, from the distance between the rails. What differentiated it from pre-industrial forms of mechanical shock was the train's velocity, which caused the jolts to be so brief and to follow in such rapid succession that they were no longer felt as individual jolts but as a condition of continuous vibration. There is an excellent description of this in a German text of 1838: 'The motion of the cars is quite regular; there is no shaking or jolting whatsoever. The noise caused by the wheels resembles that of a mill mechanism and makes it impossible to conduct a conversation with one's neighbor'.[3]

If this vibration was felt in the entire train, it was particularly strong in the locomotive, where the steam engine contributed its own vibration. Duchesne's *maladie des mécaniciens*, characterized

---

described as salutary, whereas 'this great advantage of continuous beneficial vibration . . . entirely disappears in railway travel'. (*Neües Journal der praktischen Heilkunde . . .*, vol. 75 [1836], p. 119.) Then the exact opposite, in the *Medico-Chirurgical Review, and Journal of Practical Medicine:* 'The vibratory, or rather oscillatory motion communicated to the human frame, is very different from the jolting and swinging motions of the stage-coach, and is productive of more salutary effects. It equalizes the circulation, promotes digestion, tranquilizes the nerves'. (Quoted in the *American Railroad Journal*, vol. 6 [1837], p. 689.)

2. 'At the beginning of railroad traffic, the train personnel had no shelter from the weather. The train conductors and brakemen stood on the open carriage platform or huddled on top of the carriages on uncovered seats.' (Koch and Hoffmann, op. cit., p. 198.)
3. Georg Kuhl, *Die westeuropäischen Eisenbahnen in ihrer Gegenwart und Zunkunft* (Karlsruhe, 1838), p. 21.

by 'generalized, continuous, and persistent pains, accompanied by a feeling of weakness and numbness',[4] was mostly due to this mechanical vibration from the engine: 'Without exception, all the firemen and drivers complain about the trepidation of the machines, the regular but perpetual movements that it transmits to the entire body and to the lower extremities in particular'.[5] Von Weber, in his 1860 article 'Die Abnützüng des physischen Organismus beim Fahrpersonal der Eisenbahn' ('The wear and tear of the physical organism of railroad train personnel'), gave a more exact account of the way in which the vibration affects the body: 'In the locomotive workers these shocks express them- selves as a continuous tremor in all the joints of the body that is only interrupted by sudden vertical jolts or sideways motions: this tremor is so intense and rapid that if the engine-driver or fireman were to attempt to rest his body on its bone structure in a rigid fashion by planting his feet firmly on the floor, it would be impossible for him to stand even for a short time'.[6]

Both von Weber and Duchesne described how the locomotive workers tried to counter the mechanical tremor by keeping their bodies in an elastic state. The engine-drivers did not plant their feet on the locomotive floor but stood on tiptoe, thus creating the spring suspension that the locomotive did not possess.[7] As this was very fatiguing some drivers invented arrangements designed to cushion the shocks. Duchesne found that: 'Some place a doormat under their feet, others a wooden board sup- ported at both ends by a brace. That board thus becomes a kind of springboard on which they stand and which absorbs the shocks; still others equip the board with five metal springs or rubber buffers. Some have even designed an elastic stool on which they can sit down from time to time'.[8]

Obviously, these machine tremors did not affect only the locomotive workers but also, in a somewhat lesser measure, all the people traveling in the train. Von Weber was explicit about

---

4. E. A. Duschesne, *Des chemins de fer et leur influence sur la santé des mécaniciens et des chauffeurs* (Paris, 1857), p. 183.
5. Op. cit., p. 146.
6. *Wieck Deutsche Illustrirte Gewerbezeitung*, vol. 25, (Leipzig, 1860), p. 228.
7. Duchesne, pp. 145–6; Von Weber, p. 228: 'In order to ameliorate the jolts and to react to the engine's motions with greater ease, these people spend almost all their time standing on the front part of their feet, raising their heels up from the floor'.
8. Op. cit., p. 146.

this, distinguishing between locomotive workers and train personnel: in his opinion, the shocks to which the train personnel are subjected 'are far less intense, partly because the suspension of the cars is much closer to perfection than that of the engines and particularly the tenders; furthermore, the shocks can be considerably ameliorated by the use of seat cushions etc.'[9] If locomotive and train personnel suffered from the same vibration — although to a varying degree — one must assume that the passengers, too, were subjected to it. In principle, their situation was the same as the train personnel's — that is, they were sheltered in closed cars, resting on springs and upholstery, yet not entirely removed from the shocks caused by the machinery that transported them.[10]

In 1862 *The Lancet*, the leading English medical journal, published a pamphlet called *The Influence of Railway Travelling on Public Health*; here we find corroboration that the same factors applied to travelers. The mechanical vibration and tremor was said to be caused by the 'inelasticity' that characterized the railroad and distinguished it from all earlier means of transportation:

In animal bodies the means of motion are muscle and tendon. Tigers or cats can leap from many times their own height without damage. A railway engine or carriage would be destroyed by a very small fall. Removed from the rail to a paved road, either it or the road, or both, would be rapidly destroyed. The reason is that there is great deficiency in the mechanical appliances which should represent muscle. If a malformed man has one leg shorter than the other, he can compensate for the difference of radius by more or less of muscular action. No such compensation is found in railway vehicles. Again: a horse works over hard pavements for years, saving the jolts by the action of his muscles and tendons. After a time his tendons

---

9. Op. cit., p. 228.
10. Only travelers in the first and second classes enjoyed the shelter of closed and roofed cars; the situation of the third- and fourth-class passengers, riding in open quasi-freight cars, was almost identical to that of the locomotive personnel. 'People sat on crowded benches, with the wind roaring over them so that they were unable to talk, the smoke stinging their eyes and nostrils; when it rained, they had to open up their umbrellas. . . . One can see how they endure, patiently, hour by hour, and how they then clamber down from the cars, literally racked, sooty, covered in dust.' (E. Stich, 'Über die Massnahmen zur Erhaltung eines gesunden Eisenbahnpersonals', *Verhandlungen des Verbandes deutscher Bahnärzte* [Cologne, 1889], quoted in Koch and Hoffmann, op. cit., p. 200.)

lose their power, and his footing becomes uncertain. The veterinary surgeon interferes and rehardens and tempers his springs or tendons by the process which is called firing. The railway carriage, even at the outset, is the condition of a worn-out horse. It is a framework of bones without muscles.[11]

The *Lancet* pamphlet's description of the passenger's state comes up with similar results to those of Duchesne and Von Weber. Due to the mechanical rigidity of the machine parts, i.e. the rails and wheels of the railroad, the journey became a 'series of small and rapid concussions'.[12] Inevitably, the passenger reacted to these in the same way that the locomotive workers did — by trying to absorb with their own bodies what the suspension mechanisms were unable to absorb. According to the pamphlet, the passenger's body compensated for the railroad's rigidity by the elasticity of its own muscles, which were inadvertently set into motion: 'The immediate effect of being placed in a vehicle subjected to rapid, short vibrations and oscillation . . . is that a considerable number of muscles are called into action, and maintained in a condition of alternating contractic effort throughout the whole journey. . . . The frequency, rapidity, and peculiar abruptness of the motion of railway-carriages keep thus a constant strain on the muscles; and to this must be ascribed a part of that sense of bodily fatigue, almost amounting to soreness, which is felt after a long journey'.[13]

The muscles grew tired, and so did the individual sense organs. The rapidity with which the train's speed caused optical impressions to change taxed the eyes to a much greater degree than did pre-industrial travel,[14] and the sense of hearing had to cope with a deafening noise throughout the trip.[15] Thus the

11. *The Influence of Railway Travelling on Public Health* (London, 1862), pp. 23–4. This is a pamphlet from the medical journal, *The Lancet*: referred to hereafter as the *Lancet* pamphlet.
12. Op. cit., p. 41.
13. Op. cit., pp. 40–1.
14. Op. cit., p. 44.
15. 'No less detrimental to the human organism than the shocks are the powerful noises that literally inundate the locomotive personnel; most of these are of an intensity and pitch that are truly damaging to ears and nerves. The volume of noise experienced while riding in the locomotive (and, at times, even in the carriage) is uncommonly great. . . . Thus any attentive person has noticed that when he rides on a train and passes large groups of people who are engaged in some festive occasion and *shouting*, the latter fact

traveler's entire organism was subjected to a degree of wear and tear that did not exist in pre-industrial travel, as well as the purely psychological stresses which were repeatedly emphasized by contemporary authors.[16]

Some twenty years after the *Lancet* pamphlet, in 1884, a medical text explained this unprecedented degree of strain as an outgrowth of the new ratio between traveling time and traversed space, claiming that this multiplied the formerly known symptoms of fatigue:

There is pulling at the eyeballs on looking out of the window; a jarring noise, the compound of continuous noise of wheels, and this conducted into the framework of the compartment; with the obligato of whistle and of the brake dashing in occasionally, and always carrying some element of annoyance, surprise, or shock; there is the swaying of the train from side to side, or the jolting over uneven rails and ill-adjusted points; and the general effect of these upon the temper, the muscles, and the moral nature. Let all that is especially, or accidentally, out of the order be left out of consideration, and suppose that all is as good as it can be, and yet there are the residua that have been mentioned. There are 'impressions' that are made, and that unavoidably, by the very conditions of the journey; and they involve fatigue. The eyes are strained, the ears are dinned, the muscles are jostled hither and thither, and the nerves are worried by the attempt to maintain order, and so comes weariness.[17]

---

can only be perceived visually, not *heard* at all.' (Von Weber, op. cit., p. 229.) See also *Lancet* pamphlet, p. 45.

16. The *Lancet* pamphlet discusses 'an often experienced condition of uneasiness, scarcely amounting to actual fear, which pervades the generality of travellers by rail. The possibility of collision is constantly present to such persons, and everyone knows how, if by change a train stops at some unusual place, or if the pace be slackened, or the whistle sounds its shrill alarm, a head is projected from nearly every window, and anxious eyes are on 'the look-out for signs of danger. . . . The pace, also, prevents the traveller from that observation of natural objects and sights of interest on the road, which made coach travelling a source of mental relaxation and a pastime. The passenger is forced into subjective sources of mental activity; and where the tendency to excitement exists, this also, *quantum valeat*, must be esteemed an undesirable feature belonging to this manner of locomotion'. (Op. cit., p. 43.) Another psychic strain is caused by the fear of missing the train. Thus an article of 1855 in the *Journal of Public Health and Sanitary Review*: 'The causes of the evil are not to be found in the noise, vibration, and speed of the railway carriage . . . but in the excitement, anxiety, and nervous shock consequent on the frequent efforts to catch the *last* express; to be in time for the fearfully punctual train'. (Vol. 1, p. 425.) The frequent mention of this aspect demonstrates the generality of such anxiety in the 1850s and 1860s. In 1868, there was even a monograph dedicated to this subject: Haviland's *Hurried to Death*.

17. Russell Reynolds 'Travelling: Its Influence on Health', in *The Book of Health*, ed. Malcolm Morris (London, Paris and New York, 1884) p. 581.

The symptoms that the *Lancet* pamphlet diagnosed in first- and second-class travelers as a state of fatigue specific to railroad travel were, in a somewhat ameliorated form, the same as those subsumed by Duchesne as *maladie des mécaniciens*. Only the rheumatic troubles were missing, since the travelers were transported in sheltered compartments. Nevertheless the compartment travelers were subject to the same tremors, the same noise and the same speed as the train personnel. Commuters were particularly subject to these stresses. One of the authors describes his impression, gained by years of observation, of daily business commuters between London and Brighton: 'I have had a large experience in the changes which the ordinary course of time makes on men busy in the world, and I know well to allow for their gradual deterioration by age and care; but I have never seen any set of men so rapidly aged as these seem to me to have been in the course of those few years'.[18] Let us compare the preceding description of bourgeois travelers, those in the first- and second-class carriages, with the following account of the general state of health of industrial workers, given in 1836 by Peter Gaskell, who was later to be regarded by Marx and Engels as the foremost authority in the field of industrial medicine: 'On the whole, it may be said that the class of manufacturers engaged in mill labour, exhibit but few well-defined diseases; but that nearly the entire number are victims to a train of irregular morbid actions, chiefly indicated by disturbances in the functions of the digestive apparatus, with their consequent effects upon the nervous system; producing melancholy, extreme mental irritation, and great exhaustion'.[19]

It would seem risky to use these scant medical texts to construct a thesis according to which railroad travel in the nineteenth century was, for the bourgeois public, an experience analogous to the work experience of the industrial proletariat. The difference between the situation of the laborer, e.g. the locomotive driver, expending his energy on a machine by the sweat of his brow, and that of the passenger sitting in his comfortable upholstered compartment is quite obvious: it is the

18. *Lancet* pamphlet, p. 53.
19. Peter Gaskell, *Artisans and Machinery: The Moral and Physical Condition of the Manufacturing Population Considered with Reference to Mechanical Substitutes for Human Labour* (London, 1836), pp. 237–8.

difference between an active-productive and a passive-consumptive participation in the same industrial process of production. Yet the simultaneous nature of the participation that joins worker and traveler permits us to speak of the 'industrial experience' of the latter. He, too, is experiencing industrial production, although from the consumer's standpoint. The railroad's industrial product is transportation, change of locality. What makes this production fundamentally different from all other industrial production is exactly that *simultaneity* of production and consumption. The consumption of industrially manufactured objects takes place at a temporal and spatial distance from their production. Their industrial character finds only indirect expression (e.g. in their uniformity, great quantity, etc.). But in the production of transportation, where the traveler is the instant consumer, the industrial character is experienced in the act of travel itself. This utility is inseparably connected with the process of transportation, which is the productive process of transportation. 'Men and commodities travel by the help of the means of transportation, and this traveling, this change of location, constitutes the production in which these means of transportation are consumed. The utility of transportation can be consumed only in this process of production. It does not exist as a use-value apart from this process.'[20] Elsewhere, even more explicitly: 'The useful effect that they [the means of transportation] create during their productive function, i.e., during their time in the sphere of production, the change of locality, becomes simultaneously assimilated in the individual consumption, as, for instance, the traveler's'.[21] To which we might add that not only the change of locality, but also its material, technological, and industrial production, is assimilated in the traveler's consumption: the vibrations of the maximally exploited rolling stock and rails, the noise of the machinery at work, the interaction, characteristic of large industries, of gigantic machine complexes that make human beings appear as 'mere living appendages'[22] of themselves.

20. *Capital*, (Chicago, 1906–9), vol. 11, p. 62.
21. Op. cit., p. 164.
22. *Capital*, vol. 1 (164), p. 455; identical or similar formulations can, of course, be found in almost any text by Marx. Gaskell's characterization of the industrial worker is very similar: '. . . he will have lost all free agency, and will be as much a part of the machines

All this gives new significance to the previously mentioned complaint of bourgeois travelers of the first half of the nineteenth century that one no longer traveled as a person but was transported like a parcel.[23] This figure of speech contains the implication that the railroad was to travel as industry was to manufacture. The industrial revolution, in the production of goods as well as in travel, destroyed what one might call the 'esthetic freedom' of the pre-industrial subject. This pre-industrial subject had a live interaction with its object engaging all the senses, whether as an artisan working at a craft or as a traveler participating in the 'organic' motion of the vehicle through the landscape.

The 'esthetic freedom' of the pre-industrial subject was discovered at the very moment when the pre-industrial methods of production and transportation seemed threatened by mechanization: this is a typical process of romanticization, one that even the young Marx was not entirely immune to. As long as the pre-industrial methods and their forms of work and travel were the dominant ones, a Carlyle or Ruskin or Morris would never have thought of seeing them in an esthetic light. As every travel journal and every social history of artisanship demonstrates, they were quotidian and cumbersome. When industrialization suddenly caused these old forms to be seen from an esthetic and romanticizing viewpoint, we learn less about those forms themselves than about general attitudes towards industrialization. On the other hand, the estheticization of the outworn forms brings out one of their aspects that had not been noticed before because there was no conscious need for it. Thus 'organic' travel and artisan manufacture became a conscious need, i.e. a valued esthetic quality, only at that moment when a new technology arrived and demonstrated the monotony of industry.

Machinery, in its ever more powerful intervention, destroyed

around him as the wheels or cranks which communicate motion'. (Op. cit., p. 338.)

23. Cf. Chap. 4, n. 8, above. The Ruskin quote reads in full: 'The whole system of railroad travelling is addressed to people who, being in a hurry, are therefore, for the time being, miserable. No one would travel in that manner who could help it — who had the time to go leisurely over hills and between hedges instead of through tunnels and between banks: or at least, those who would, have no sense of beauty so acute as that we need consult it at the station. The railroad is in all its relations a matter of earnest business, to be got through as soon as possible. It transmutes a man from a traveller into a living parcel'.

that 'live' connection between the producer or consumer of the product and the production process. The nineteenth-century English bourgeoisie gained no authentic experience of the reality of the great industries of Manchester and Sheffield. Its members became aware of them only indirectly, by means of the displays of world exhibitions and humanitarian fiction. Yet the railroad, the industrial process in transportation, did become an actual industrial experience for the bourgeois, who saw and felt his own body being transformed into an object of production.

As incontrovertible and physically palpable as that industrial experience was, everything possible was done to reduce it. This is where upholstery originated as a central cultural-historical phenomenon of the nineteenth century. It started out on the railway train as something merely functional: its initial purpose was simply to protect the human body from the mechanical shocks caused by machinery. The engine drivers observed by Duchesne and Von Weber could only deal with these by means of their own muscles and a few primitive aids; their bodies themselves bore the brunt of the problem. The first- and second-class passengers were more fortunate, being protected by the interior furnishings of their compartments. Discussing the possibility of amelioration of the railroad's 'peculiar jerking vibrations' and their unpleasant effects, the *Lancet* pamphlet alluded to several prevalent means to that end and identified the principle underlying them:

> . . . the means whereby their influence may be counteracted can be expressed in one word — elasticity — the natural antagonist of jerk. The provision of a sufficient intervention of elastic materials reduces the movement, which in a springless railway waggon is inconceivably distressing, to a gentle swaying motion. The springs of railway carriages, the horse-hair seats (and the elastic floor of cork supplied to the new royal carriage), are recognitions of the principle, which the habitual traveller may wisely extend for himself by many expedients, if he keeps in view what he has to attain — elasticity.[24]

In the course of the century, the functional purpose of that elastic upholstery fell by the wayside: it became an end unto itself and expanded in direct ratio to the expansion of industry.

24. Op. cit., p. 137.

Siegfried Giedion has hinted at this connection by remarking that the over-stuffed furniture typical of late-nineteenth-century culture arose in the West European countries simultaneously with the rise of the new industrial bourgeoise.[25] Such upholstery ceased to be functional when it appeared in realms such as the living room, where there were no mechanical-industrial jolts or jerks to be counteracted. Thus the jolt to be softened was no longer physical but mental: the memory of the industrial origin of objects, from railway stations or exhibition halls constructed out of steel to chairs constructed out of wood. The opulent Baroque and Renaissance fronts that covered the steel girders, were nothing but, on a larger scale, the braided and tasseled upholstery cushions that rendered the true construction of the armchair or sofa invisible and thus forgettable.[26]

---

25. *Mechanization Takes Command* (New York, 1969), p. 365.
26. Siegfried Giedion, in the section of *Mechanization* entitled 'The Reign of the Upholsterer', gives the following description of Second Empire lounge furniture: 'The skeleton of the chairs and sofas has retreated deep into the cushions: a process that the French have called "la victoire de la garniture sur le bois" ("the victory of the trimmings over the wood"). Every and any means are used to make the armchairs, sofas, divans, ottomans, as heavy and as bulky as possible. Foot-long fringes sometimes veil even the stumps, all that remain of the legs. The furniture increasingly tends to suggest bloated cushions'. (Op. cit., p. 366.) Compare this with Erich Schild's description of Garnier's Paris Opera: 'The entire structure consists of constructions of iron girders and pipes that have been covered up with masonry, marble, and stucco, and transmuted into forms that all but obliterate the skeleton. . . . There is no rivalry here between construction and form. The outward shape is everything, the underlying structure merely a helpmeet, subordinated into service'. (*Zwischen Glaspalast und Palais des Illusions* [Frankfurt, Berlin, and Vienna, 1967], p. 92.) What the interior, invisible, steel girders are to Beaux Arts architecture, the steel spring is to upholstered furniture. The spiral spring, until then used only 'for purely technical purposes' (Giedion, op. cit., p. 382), now facilitated the unprecedentedly lavish upholstery that rested upon and around it, concealing it from view just as the Paris Opera concealed its girders. In France, the Second Empire marked the full flowering of the upholstery principle in both architecture and furniture. For all of Europe, the reign of upholstery extended from approximately 1855 to 1890. Between 1850 and 1855 the principle of free and unconcealed construction prevailed in the utilitarian architecture of exhibition buildings, railroad terminals, market halls, etc., in the wake of the success of London's Crystal Palace of 1851. In 1855 a reaction set in, signalled by the Parisian World Expo building of that year. 'A sharp shift in taste at this time, leading to a predominant preference for the massively plastic in architecture, made unfashionable both the delicate membering suitable to iron and the smooth transparent surfaces provided by large areas of glass.' (Henry Russell Hitchcock, *Architecture: Nineteenth and Twentieth Centuries* [Baltimore, 1958], p. 115.); and, on the Paris Expo building of 1855: 'The great iron-and-glass arched interiors were all but completely masked externally by a very conventional masonry shell'. (Hitchcock, op. cit., p. 128.) From 1890 on, construction started to emancipate itself again, most notably in Dutert's famous hall of machines at the Paris World Expo of 1889, a steel construction without any masonry shell at all. Roughly at the same time, the furniture industry manifested tendencies to reduce upholstery. Thus we find the following in an article published in August 1897, in *Furniture and Decoration and the Furniture Gazette*: 'It is

[123]

Excursus
Industrial Fatigue

The curves of fatigue for metals coincided in a remarkable way
with the curves of fatigue for muscular effort.
— *Yearbook* of the Smithsonian Institution, 1911

According to the 1862 *Lancet* pamphlet, the state of fatigue that
apparently overwhelmed travelers after train journeys of some
duration was due to the mechanical shocks they experienced.
These 'rapid, short vibrations and oscillations' did not affect
only the human body but equally the materials of the machine
transporting it; not only the travelers suffered from fatigue, the
materials did, too.

In the mid-nineteenth century the concept of fatigue acquired
this additional connotation, the technical one. It was first documented in a lecture given in 1854 to the London Institution of
Civil Engineers; the lecture, entitled 'On the Fatigue and Consequent Fracture of Metals', proposed the new concept as follows:
'There are reasons for believing, that many of the appalling, and

---

necessary now that the system of thin stuffing has become prevalent to pay more careful
attention to the frames of our couches than was commonly done a few years ago. The
frames of some of the old-fashioned thickly-stuffed Chesterfield sofas bore little or no
relation to the finished piece of upholstery. The lines of the wood formed merely a
skeleton which was padded out and completely extinguished in an envelope of horse-
hair, flock, alva, shavings. . . . The construction of the article was completely hidden
from the lay eye. . . '. (Quoted in John Gloag, *Victorian Comfort* [New York, 1973], pp.
70–1.) Gloag points out that the simplification of furniture is an expression of the same
tendency toward functional construction manifested in architecture, roughly simultaneously, by Wright, Sullivan, van de Velde (op. cit., p. 72). The final and general
rejection of the upholstery principle in both furniture and architecture can certainly be
connected with the First World War, the destructive culmination of Europe's industrial
revolution: the Bauhaus was born in 1919.

apparently unaccountable accidents on railways, and elsewhere, are to be ascribed to that progressive action which may be termed, the "fatigue of metals". This fatigue may arise from a variety of causes, such as repeated strain, blows, concussions, jerks, torsion, or tension'.[1]

It had been known for a long time that continuous concussion causes iron to crystallize and finally break: the phenomenon received systematic attention only after iron became the mainstay of the Industrial Revolution. There are several reasons why the railroad represented the spearhead of this development as of so many others. In terms of machine technology, the railroad was the most advanced industry of its time; it was an object of public attention to a far greater degree than the manufacturing industries; and finally, railroad disasters ranked among the most spectacular events of the nineteenth century. On 8 May 1842, one of these disasters took place on the Paris–Versailles line: fifty-five travelers died and more than one hundred others were severely injured. It caused a European railroad trauma. The disaster had been caused by a broken locomotive axle, i.e., by material fatigue; in 1842, that technical term was not yet available for diagnosis. Remarkably enough, the concept of fatigue did appear, näively as it were, in a technical publication dealing with the disaster. One of the experts assigned to the study of the causes of the accident, the engineer Laignel, saw the physiology of the travelers and the material parts of the railroad as equally subject to the same concussions, when he said that 'the shocks and vibrations fatigue the travelers and destroy, in effect, all the material, and particularly the wheels and the axles'.[2] Two decades later, in the 1860s, the German August Wöhler laid the foundation for modern material-testing. He described and quantified the phenomenon of material fatigue as demonstrated by broken train-car axles, and proposed that more stress-resistant alloys be used in the future production of railroad materials.[3]

1. Lecture by Frederick Braithwaite, *Proceedings of the [British] Institute of Civil Engineers*, vol. XIII (1854), p. 463.
2. B. Laignel, *Quelques mots et remarques sur les chemins de fer, à l'occasion de l'événemant du 8 mai* (Paris, 1842), p. 2.
3. Wöhler's essays in the *Zeitschrift für Bauwesen*: 'Versuche über Biegung und Verdrehung von Eisenbahnwagenachsen während der Fahrt' (vol. 8 [1858], pp. 461 seq.); 'Versuche über die einwirkenden Kräfte und die Widerstandsfähigkeit bei Eisenbahnwagenach-

While systematic material research began with Wöhler, there were historical antecedents. One of Galileo's experiments can be seen as a test of material: to calculate the resilience of a beam anchored to a wall, he attached a weight to the other end. In general, pre-industrial material testing was identical with construction statics. A seperate development occurred in the military realm, which once again proved to be a pacemaker for the industrial revolution. In order to regulate the Prussian army's purchases of firearms, which were far from systematic in the eighteenth century,[4] military material testing institutions were founded, such as the Prussian Office for the Testing of Materials and the Military Experimentation Office.[5]

The industrial application of the steam engine raised the testing procedures to a new level. From the eighteenth-century Newcomen engine to the nineteenth-century high-pressure engine, it was not only the technology that changed but also the construction material required by the machines. If the early low-pressure engines still consisted in part, of wood, the more modern machines had to be constructed entirely of iron. Even that was to prove insufficient. In the United States, where Evans' high-pressure engine was mass-produced for the river steamboats, the 1830s witnessed a series of boiler explosions whose toll of casualties far exceeded that of the major European railroad disaster that was to occur in 1842.[6] These explosions provided a further impulse for the study of materials. In the 1830s, Alexander Dallas Bache conducted studies at the Franklin Institute in Philadelphia to determine the necessary strength of

sen' (vol. 10 [1860], pp. 583 seq.); 'Versuche über die Festigkeit von Eisenbahnwagenachsen' (vol. 13 [1863], pp. 233 seq.); 'Versuche über die relative Festigkeit von Eisen, Stahl und Kupfer' (vol. 16 [1866], pp. 67 seq.).

4. In a contract between firearms manufacturers and the Prussian army, 1722: 'The rifles will be received by an officer who has the barrels tested by shooting and, if they are found to work well, has those barrels stamped with an eagle; he likewise examines and tests each rifle lock'. Quoted in Walter Ruske, *100 Zahre Materialprüntüng in Berlin. Ein Beitrag zur Technikgeschichte* (West Berlin, 1971), p. 217.

5. About one hundred pages (almost a quarter) of the *Festschrift* of the German Federal Institute of Material Testing is devoted to the history of military testing institutions.

6. According to an estimate made in 1848, there were 233 boiler explosions on American river steamboats between 1816 and 1848, and these caused 2,563 deaths (John G. Burke, 'Bursting Boilers and the Federal Power', in *Technology and Culture*, ed. M. Kranzberg and W. R. Davenport [New York, 1972], p. 109). The year 1838 witnessed 14 explosions and 496 deaths (op. cit., p. 98); the explosion on the *Moselle*, for example, took the lives of all 151 passengers and crew members; another, the lives of 140. (Op. cit., p. 106.)

the steel out of which boilers were constructed.[7] The main attention of this research was directed toward material flaws and material resistance to pressure and temperature: thus the concept of fatigue had not yet emerged. The mechanical jolts and vibrations that further attacked the material had not yet been recognized as significant.

What revealed to material research the new concept of material fatigue was precisely the new kind of vibration to which the machine parts were increasingly subjected. It resulted from the working of the machine, from the interaction of its individual parts. The static element — the subject of investigation from Galileo to Bache — was replaced by the dynamic.[8] That it was the 'working' of the machine, the work performed by it, which caused its component materials to suffer 'fatigue' was no mere figure of speech: there was an obvious connection between the rise of modern material testing and what Marx calls the 'intensification of labor'. Capitalist industry exploited, in fact, both material and human labor power. Marx described this as the 'increased expenditure of labour in a given time, heightened tension of labour-power, and closer filling up of the pores of the working day'.[9]

We find a corresponding statement with regard to machinery in a more recent standard work on metal fatigue: 'The continuing trend towards higher strength/weight and power/weight ratios, more refined static design techniques, and the use of higher working stresses, increased speeds of operation, with the resultant accumulation of large numbers of cycles in a small period of time'.[10]

What Taylorism did for the optimal exploitation of human labor power, material testing did for the exploitation of material labor power. The time and motion studies that Frederick Winslow Taylor instituted in American factories between 1880 and

7. Ruske, p. 29.
8. Braithwaite gives a clear description of the distinction between statically and dynamically stressed material: 'Metal, in a state of rest, although sustaining a heavy pressure, or strain, as in a girder, and exhibiting the deflection due to the superposed weight, will continue to bear that pressure, without fracture, so long as its rest is not disturbed, or the same strain is not too often repeated, but, if its rest is too frequently disturbed, the metal becomes deteriorated, and worn out, at the part subject to the reiterated strain, and fracture will, ultimately, ensue'. (Op. cit.)
9. *Capital*, vol. 1 (Chicago), 1906–9, p. 448.
10. J. Y. Mann, *Fatigue of Metals* (London and New York, 1967), p. 3.

1900 had the same functions as the studies done by modern material researchers. In both cases the task was to find out how a given potential could be rearranged, and thus improved, to increase yield.

Chronology suggests that material research encouraged the development of Taylorism. After the most rational mode of construction had been ascertained for machines, this formulation pointed the way to investigation of how human labor could be utilized in the most rational way.[11] The manner in which the concept of fatigue migrated back and forth between physiology and technology demonstrates how the two realms exerted a mutual influence upon each other. At first the physiological phenomenon of fatigue was a diffuse and scientifically negligible concept; then technology borrowed it in order to name a novel condition that had been discovered in the context of the Industrial Revolution. After the fatigue concept had received its precise technological definition and quantification, it proceeded to migrate back to physiology. Its physiological meaning was no longer diffuse: it gained exactitude as a concept in labor medicine. Its increasing importance can be clearly perceived in the development of medical literature dealing with physiological fatigue. The *Index Catalogue of the Library of the Surgeon-General's Office*; an authoritative international medical bibliography, listed in its 1883 edition two dissertations and five articles under the heading 'Fatigue'. In the 1900 edition, the 'Fatigue' bibliography extended over almost two large pages of fine print; by 1925 there were three and a half pages; in 1940, hundreds of titles were crammed into more than six pages.

1. Cf. Marx's comment on Descartes' understanding of animals as machines: 'It may here be incidentally observed, that Descartes, in defining animals as mere machines, saw with eyes of the manufacturing period, while to eyes of the middle ages, animals were assistants to man'. (*Capital*, vol. I, op. cit., p. 426.)

[8]
The Accident

*— die Krisen des Unfalls (der unbeherrschten Dinge) werden ebenso
länger bleiben wie sie tiefer liegen als die Krisen der Wirtschaft
(der unbeherrschten Waren).*

[. . . the crises of the accident (of the uncontrolled things) will
remain with us longer to the degree that they remain deeper
than the crises of economy (of the uncontrolled commodities).]
— Ernst Bloch

Let us glance at Thomas Creevy's description of a train journey
in 1829: 'It is really flying, and it is impossible to divest yourself
of the notion of instant death to all upon the least accident
happening'.[1]

Early perception of the railroad was characterized by a curious
ambivalence. The journey was felt to be uncannily smooth,
easy, secure, like flying. 'When I closed my eyes this sensation
of flying was quite delightful, and strange beyond description;
yet strange as it was, I had a perfect sense of security, and not
the slightest fear', related Fanny Kemble, the famous London
actress, giving her impressions of a train journey from Liverpool
to Manchester in 1830.[2] At the same time, the train journey
entailed a sensation of violence and potential destruction. This
sensation became concretized in the metaphor of the railroad
train as a projectile shot through space and time. Thus all the
ease, comfort and security that were superficial characteristics of

1. Cf. Chap. 1, n. 27.
2. Quoted in Cyril Bruyn Andrews, *The Railway Age* (London, 1937), p. 31.

the train journey were always accompanied by an ever-present subliminal fear: as one German author of 1845 put it, there was a 'certain dampening of the spirits that never quite goes away despite all the pleasant aspects of train journeys'. And that anxiety can be explained by the always 'close possibility of an accident, and the inability to exercise any influence on the running of the cars'.[3]

The ever-present fear of a potential disaster remained, however, only until the railroad had become a part of normal everyday life. By the time Western Europe had culturally and psychically assimilated the railroad, that is, by the mid-nineteenth century, these anxieties had vanished, as had that turn of phrase so typical of the early period, 'the annihilation of space and time'. The expression became nonsensical because the new geography created by the railroad (and first experienced as a shock) had become second nature. The same applies to the travel process itself. The new activities and forms of behavior (reading while traveling, 'panoramic' perception etc.) have institutionalized the new reality of the new technological standard of travel. They have formed a new psychic layer that obscures the old fears and lets them lapse into oblivion. These old fears are forgotten concurrently and commensurately with the preceding technology, whose replacement by the new one was the prime cause of those fears.[4]

If the normal functioning of the railroad was thus experienced as a natural and safe process, any sudden interruption of that functioning (which had become second nature) immediately reawakened the memory of the forgotten danger and potential violence: the repressed material returned with a vengeance. Bloch has characterized this aspect of the technological accident. He speaks of the demonic nature of the first railroads, and of its gradual metamorphosis into the quotidian, and says: 'Only the accident still reminds us of it sometimes, with the crash of

3. *Zeitung für Eisenbahnwesen, Dampfschiffahrt und Maschinenkunde*, vol. 1 (1845), pp. 114–15. (The article reprinted from *Frankenstein's Allgemeines Industrie- und Gewerbeblatt*.)
4. This process of the assimilation of initially disturbing new phenomena has been excellently described by Peter Wexler in the context of the development of French railroad vocabulary (*La formation du vocabulaire des chemins de fer en France, 1778–1842* [Geneva and Lille, 1955]). Wexler states that the initial phase is a 'descriptive' one, characterized by cumbersome and pedantic circumlocutions for processes and parts of machinery that are still unknown; in the last phase, we get a new concretized conceptual vocabulary, which is an expression of the new 'almost unconscious familiarity' with the formerly frightening technology.

collision, the roar of explosion, the cries of maimed people — a production that knows no civilized schedule'.[5]

One might also say that the more civilized the schedule and the more efficient the technology, the more catastrophic its destruction when it collapses. There is an exact ratio between the level of the technology with which nature is controlled, and the degree of severity of its accidents. The pre-industrial era did not know any technological accidents in that sense. In Diderot's *Encyclopédie*, 'Accident' is dealt with as a grammatical and philosophical concept, more or less synonymous with coincidence. The pre-industrial catastrophes were natural events, natural accidents. They attacked the objects they destroyed from the outside, as storms, floods, thunderbolts, and hailstones. After the Industrial Revolution, destruction by technological accident came from the inside. The technical apparatuses destroyed themselves by means of their own power. The energies tamed by the steam engine and delivered by it as regulated mechanical performance destroyed that engine itself in the case of an accident. The increasingly rapid vehicles of transportation tended to destroy themselves and each other totally, whenever they collided. The higher the degree of technical intensification (pressure, tension, velocity, etc.) of a piece of machinery, the more thorough-going was its destruction in the case of dysfunction. The breaking of a coach axle in the eighteenth century merely interrupted a slow and exceedingly bumpy trip on the highway; the breaking of a locomotive axle between Paris and Versailles in 1842 led to the first railroad catastrophe that caused a panic in Europe. In 1844, two years after this disaster, the *Encyclopédie des chemins de fer et des machines à vapeur* devoted a nine-page article to the subject of 'Accidents'. The accident was seen as a negative indicator of technological progress:

All man-made things are subject to accidents. By a kind of compensation . . ., the more these things are perfected, the greater the gravity of the accidents that happen to them. That is why, without rigorous surveillance at all points, the most powerful and most perfected industrial means, that is, steam engines and railroad trains, can cause the most grave and fatal mishaps. The mass of the

5. Ernest Bloch, *Spuren* (Frankfurt and Berlin, 1962), p. 208.

objects they set in motion, the velocity they engender, their very power, once halted or turned from its proper objective, is transformed into a terrible agent of destruction. Steam power, while opening up new and hitherto unknown roads to man, also seems to continually put him in a position best compared to that of a man who is walking along the edge of a precipice and cannot afford a single false step. It is a situation analogous to the one engineers term an unstable equilibrium, which can be upset by the least little effort.[6]

Accident and Crisis

The modern technological accident, the sudden collapse of a highly developed machine, is a result of the management of industry according to capitalist principles, as is industrially applied technology as a whole. This technology is subject to the dictates of the profit motive. Bloch's comparison between the 'crises of the accident' and the 'crises of economy' is based on this interrelationship between technology and economy. The phenomenon of material fatigue has demonstrated for us how the exploitive interest affects even the molecular structure of the materials. In *Das Kapital* Marx provided a definition of economic crisis that reads like a translation of the technological accident back into the economic sphere. If the nineteenth century perceived the cause of technological accidents to be the sudden disturbance of the uncertain equilibrium of a machine (i.e., the relationship between curbed energy and the means of curbing it), Marx defined the economic crisis as the disruption of the uncertain balance between buying and selling in the circulation of goods. As long as buying and selling work as a balanced and unified process, the cycle will go on functioning, but as soon as the two become separated and autonomous, we arrive at a crisis: 'To say that these two independent and antithetical acts [purchases and sales] have intrinsic unity, are essentially one, is the same as to say that this intrinsic oneness expresses itself in an external antithesis. If the interval in time between the two complementary phases of the complete metamorphosis of a commodity becomes too great, if the split between the sale and

6. Felix Tourneux, *Encyclopédie des chemins de fer et des machines à vapeur* (Paris, 1844), pp. 2–3.

the purchase becomes too pronounced, the intimate connexion between them, their oneness, asserts itself by producing — a crisis'.[7]

---

7. *Capital*, vol. 11, p. 126. In this context, reference should be made to central concepts of Freudian psychoanalysis: pyschic apparatus, economic principle, free and contained energy, etc. The balance between the Ego and the Id is assumed to be as unstable as the balance between the parts of a nineteenth-century machine. The psychic apparatus, according to Pontalis and Laplanche, 'performs a particular kind of *labor*, described by Freud in various ways: it transforms free energy into contained energy, postpones frustration, psychically *reworks* stimuli, etc.' (*Das Vokabular der Psychoanalyse* [Frankfurt, 1972], p. 358.) It might be profitable to consider, in terms of the history of these concepts, the connections between accident, crisis, and neurosis.

[9]
Railroad Accident, 'Railway Spine' and Traumatic Neurosis

The destructive force of the railroad disasters manifested itself not only in the physical demolition of the technological machinery and the passengers: it had other effects as well. In many accident victims who had suffered no injuries, or only minor ones, symptoms of psychic and physical deterioration appeared after some time and these frequently resulted in total disability or, in some cases, death. The medical profession found it difficult to diagnose these symptoms, which became an important subject of medical and legal controversy after the railroad companies had become legally liable for their passengers' safety and health. (In England this happened in 1864, in Germany in 1871.)[1] Only material, i.e., pathologically demonstrable, damage caused to accident victims qualified them for compensation. Thus the compensation of physically injured victims caused no

1. In England the corresponding law, the Campbell Act, was passed as early as 1846. However, only an amendment passed in 1864 made this act applicable to victims of railroad accidents, as literature by medical experts only began to appear after that date. It is worthwhile investigating how the industrialization process was reflected in accelerating accident rates and the new institutions such as liability laws and accident insurance policies which grew out of these. Thus the increase in railroad accidents was a part of the general increase in industrial accidents. The more sophisticated the mechanization of production became, the more vulnerable it also became, especially in the initial period of adjustment, as people were not yet accustomed to the new machines. The connection between industrialization and accident frequency can be seen in the Registrar's Office annual report of 1842, which noted the remarkably higher (i.e., double) rate of fatal accidents in England as compared to other countries, and demanded a statistical analysis of its causes: 'The violent deaths in England appear to be nearly twice as frequent as in other countries of Europe from which returns have been procured. . . . The coroners' informations, although not made at present on a uniform

problems, but those victims who suffered damage without a pathologically demonstrable cause created — in the period between 1865 and 1885 — a legal and medical problem whose solution in the courts depended on the medical profession. The medical experts called upon in compensation cases had to determine whether the claimant's ailment was an imaginary one, simulated in order to receive compensation from the railroad company, or whether it was a manifestation of a new medical syndrome.

The medical explanations given for the new symptoms changed significantly during those two decades. The initial explanation was a pathological one. The experts decided on either simulation or a supposed microscopic deterioration of the spinal cord ('railway spine') due to mechanical shock caused by the accident. This latter explanation was based on the traditional medical view that all ailments have purely pathological causes, which was bolstered by the corresponding juridical dogma that only physical injuries qualified as just cause for compensation. From the early 1880s on, the purely pathological view was superseded

---

plan, furnish many valuable facts, and when compared with the occupations and other circumstances recorded in the registers, or ascertained at the census, become doubly interesting. . . . It is very desirable that in all cases in which inquests are held the coroners should instruct the juries to state in their verdicts with greater minuteness than at present the cause of death, recording more in detail the nature of the injury, and the circumstances in which the death happened'. (Quoted in Cornelius Walford, *The Insurance Cyclopedia* [London, 1871], vol. 1, p. 4.) According to Walford, a French survey of the year 1865 shows 'that accidental deaths nearly everywhere increase more rapidly than does the population.' (Op. cit., p. 5.) In the Registrar's Office annual report of 1856 we read: 'The progress of science has created new forces often fatal, and has produced new substances, of which our forefathers had no knowledge. Machinery is organized on a large scale, so that the lives of numbers of men are liable to be destroyed, *not by malicious intent, but by the negligence of other men who have their lives in charge*'. (Op. cit.; italics added.) The notion of negligence is a modern one; it did not exist before the seventeenth century. With the increasing differentiation of bourgeois life it became ever more important. (Cf. William S. Holdsworth, *A History of the English Law* [Boston and London, 1922–52], vol. 8, pp. 449ff.) In the nineteenth century, industrialization gave a powerful impetus to this development: Eldridge even stated that 'there is practically no law of negligence prior to the nineteenth century'. (Laurence Eldridge, *Modern Tort Problems* [Philadelphia, 1941], p. 32.) It is within the context of the increasing importance of the negligence problem that the Campbell Act, 'An Act for compensating the Families of Persons killed by Accidents', passed in 1846, has to be understood. It was the legislative response to the increase in accidents; as the commentary in *Halsbury's Statutes of England* points out, it elevated negligence, for the first time, to a clearly defined breach of the law: 'No such liability existed at common law'. (*Halsbury's Statutes* . . ., vol. 12, p. 335.) In addition to liability laws, industrial development created the institution of accident insurance. This began with the railroad (W. A. Dinsdale, *History of Accident Insurance in Great Britain* [London, 1954], p. 52). According to Walford, eleven out of the thirteen accident insurance firms founded between 1845 and 1850 included the word 'Railway' in their names. (Op. cit., vol. 1, p. 7.)

by a new, psychopathological one, according to which the shock caused by the accident did not affect the tissue of the spinal marrow, but affected the victim psychically. Now it was the victim's experience of shock that was the main causative factor of the illness. By the end of the 1880s, the concept of 'railway spine' had been replaced by that of 'traumatic neurosis'.

In terms of medical history, Esther Fischer-Homberger has described this development in a masterful way that includes detailed sociological considerations.[2] In this work, we are interested in the story of 'railway spine' and traumatic neurosis not so much as part of the history of medicine but rather as a reflection in medical science of the new reality of industrialized life, concretely exemplified by the railroad and its accidents. If the novel symptoms of the traumatized accident victims originated in the new quality of railroad accidents, studying the history of the medical explanation of those symptoms must contribute to the understanding of the effects of the industrialization of travel on the human mind and body. Thus it is our intention to demonstrate how the original 'railway spine' theory represented a first attempt to explain industrial traumata, and how the subsequent attempts finally lead us to Freud's theory of stimulation and overstimulation, and the protective mechanisms against it — an explanatory model still relevant today.

Since our main interest is not in the history of medicine but in the connection between industrialization and certain symptoms of illness, we shall restrict ourselves to the development in England, using Erichsen and Page as the two definitive authors. Fischer-Homberger also deals with these authors, but only as a preamble to the history of the traumatic neurosis. She has based her description mainly on German psychiatric literature of the 1880s and 1890s, stating, no doubt accurately, that German research into traumatic neurosis — an originally German medical concept — was the leading research on the subject in the world at the time, comparable to Charcot's investigations of hysteria in France. For the researcher, developments in England

2. Esther Fischer-Homberger: 'Railway Spine und traumatische Neurose: Seele und Rückenmark', *Gesnerus* no. 27 (1970), pp. 96–111; "Die Büchse der Pandora: Der mythische Hintergrund der Eisenbahnkrankheiten des 19. Jahrhunderts," *Sudhoffs Archiv* (1972), pp. 297–317; *Die traumatische Neurose: Vom somatischen zum sozialen Leiden* (Bern, 1975).

have the advantage of beginning with the first manifestations of the problem — as in the overall history of the railroad — and of providing a manageable amount of literature. It certainly is no accident that medical attention to victims of railroad accidents began in the 1860s in England — then still the leading industrial nation in the world — while discussion began in Germany twenty years later, after that country had experienced its own great industrial leap forward.

The phenomenon of accident shock, i.e., a traumatization of the victim without discernible physical injury, naturally existed before the English medical profession started devoting its systematic attention to it in the mid-1860s, after the passage of the liability laws.[3] There are reports of railroad accidents that describe travelers as exhibiting signs of strong psychic disruption, phobias, obsessive actions, etc., without having suffered any apparent injury. Thus a newspaper report on an unhurt participant in the great disaster on the Paris–Versailles line in 1842: 'We saw a woman who had been in the first compartment of the car that followed right behind the locomotives; she had not received any injury, but had experienced a commotion so extreme when confronted by this horrible disaster that she did not remember anything of it at all'.[4]

The concept of the 'commotion', while already sounding psychological, is intended in a purely physical sense: a French medical dissertation of 1834 defined it as 'the shock experienced by certain parts of the body on the occasion of falls or when being stricken'.[5] The invariable cause of such a 'commotion', the text went on, was 'a shock that affects the same part or a contiguous part of the body to the one affected'.[6]

Two things were constant in reports given by traumatized accident victims. Immediately after the accident the victim felt completely normal; after one or two days he became overwhelmed by the memory of the event. We have a report by Charles Dickens: on 9 June 1865, he experienced a minor railroad accident and escaped entirely unscathed. Four days later

3. In an extended sense, these include shock reactions to bad news, to experienced catastrophes, etc.
4. *Moniteur parisien*, 10 May 1842, quoted in Pinard, *Relation exacte de l'affreuse catastrophe du 8 mai* (Paris, 1842).
5. J. A. Delcasse, *De la commotion* (Paris, 1834), p. 5.
6. Op. cit.; similarly, in the *Dictionnaire des sciences médicales*, 'commotion' is defined as a

he discussed it in a letter, describing how he assisted other travelers immediately after the accident occurred. After then giving a description of the scene of destruction, he continued:

I don't want to be examined at the inquest and I don't want to write about it. I could do no good either way, and I could only seem to speak about it to myself. . . . I am keeping very quiet here. I have a — I don't know what to call it — constitutional (I suppose) presence of mind, and was not in the least fluttered at the time. I instantly remembered that I had the MS of a number with me and clambered back into the carriage for it. *But in writing these scanty words of recollection I feel the shake and I am obliged to stop.* Ever faithfully, Charles Dickens.[7] (Italics added.)

The abrupt ending of the letter, caused by the suddenly overwhelming memory of the accident, is all the more remarkable for the fact that Dickens is not exactly known for such sudden shifts in his manner of writing. We find a further testimony for this kind of after-effect of accidents, popularly termed 'shock' in the nineteenth century, in the report of an American traveler who experienced an equally negligible accident between Manchester and Liverpool in 1835 and likewise survived it without any injury. After that experience he stood on a bridge across the rails and tried once again, as in former times, to enjoy the sight of an approaching train, but found it impossible: 'As it approached the bridge on which I stood, I could not bear to look at it, and seemed inclined to run off, lest it should be carried away from under me; I shrank back involuntarily, and refused to follow it with my eye to the goal. . . . But still no accident occurred, except in my creative imagination . . . '.[8]

All these examples concern accident victims who escaped unscathed but for the fright. They showed no enduring symptoms of disease and required no medical treatment. Because of their apparent innocuousness these cases fell below the threshold of medical attention. However harmless and finally without consequence the victims' fright may have been, its sudden and powerful return to their memories proves that it belonged to that class of

---

'general or local shock to the nervous system, following either a fall or a violent percussion' ([Paris, 1813], vol. 16, pt. 1, p. 152.)
7. In Jack Simmons, ed., *Journey in England* (New York, 1969), pp. 210–11.
8. Calvin Colton, *Four Years in Great Britain, 1831–35* (New York, 1835), vol. 1, p. 68.

accident traumata that would occupy the courts and their medical experts from the mid-1860s on.

In medical literature the new subject appeared for the first time in 1866. The *Lancet* published a three-part article by Thomas Buzzard entitled 'On Cases of Injury from Railway Accidents'. In the same year William Camps, an author who had previously published papers on epilepsy and hysteria, published his 'Railway Accidents or Collisions: Their Effects, Immediate and Remote, Upon the Brain and Spinal Cord and Other Portions of the Nervous System'. Finally, that year also saw the publication of an epoch-making book by John Eric Erichsen, *On Railway and Other Injuries of the Nervous System.*

After the near-absence of material dealing with such accidents in *The Lancet* of preceding years, this sudden onset of a literature was remarkable — as was the fact that not one of the three authors makes any reference either to any of the others or to previous publications. Nevertheless, all three works presented approximately the same views on the specific nature of the railroad accident, namely, that this kind of accident did not differ from other accidents in principle but in the degree of violence, with the additional observation that that degree was a new and previously unknown one. Subsequently that observation proved to be the great contradiction with which the medical authors tried to come to terms. Here is William Camps' description of the peculiar nature of the railroad accident:

> There is something in the crash, the shock, and the violence of a railway collision, which would seem to produce effects upon the *nervous system* quite beyond those of any ordinary injury. In some cases, we are told, the sufferer may not even have sustained any fracture, and the cuts and external injuries may be apparently slight to the visual perception of the medical man; whilst, notwithstanding this comparatively and apparently external trifling injury or injuries, yet there may be coincident with all this, such a *shock* to the system as for a time to shatter the whole constitution, and this, moreover, to such a degree, to such an extent, that the unfortunate sufferer may not altogether recover throughout the remainder of his life, which I apprehend, may, in some instances at least, be reasonably expected to be curtailed in its duration.[9]

9. William Camps, *Railway Accidents or Collisions: Their Effects, Immediate and Remote, upon the Brain and Spinal Cord* . . . (London, 1866), p. 12.

In essence, this is the same view as that expressed by Erichsen, although, as noted, neither of the authors has made reference to the other.

Let us now see how Erichsen described the consequences of the accident in victims who have suffered no physical injury. His text reads like a medical paraphrase of Dickens' report on his experience:

> One of the most remarkable phenomena attendant upon this class of cases is, that at the time of the occurence of the injury the sufferer is usually quite unconscious that any serious accident has happened to him. He feels that he has been violently jolted and shaken, he is perhaps somewhat giddy and confused, but he finds no bones broken, merely some superficial bruises or cuts on the head or legs, perhaps even no evidence whatever of external injury. He congratulates himself upon his escape from the imminent peril to which he has been exposed. He becomes unusually calm and self-possessed; assists his less-fortunate fellow sufferers, occupies himself perhaps actively in this way for several hours, and then proceeds on his journey. When he reaches his home, the effects of the injury that he has sustained begin to manifest themselves. A revulsion takes place. He bursts into tears, becomes unusually talkative, and is excited. He cannot sleep, or, if he does, he wakes up suddenly with a vague sense of alarm. . . .[10]

According to Erichsen, these were the subsequent symptoms: fatigue, headaches, difficulty in concentration, digestive problems, forgetfulness, stammering, reduction of sexual potency, cold sweats, states of anxiety, etc. Erichsen also mentioned dreams that reflected the victim's anxiety: 'The sleep is disturbed, restless, and broken. He wakes up in sudden alarm; dreams much; the dreams are distressing and horrible'.[11] He did not state expressly that such dreams were, in their content, repetitions of the traumatic accident — a fact that Freud later pointed out as important — but it may be assumed that the dreams in question were of that nature, especially since Buzzard has mentioned a female patient 'complaining that she saw the engine coming in at the window'.[12] The surprising thing about

10. Erichsen (1866), pp. 95–6.
11. Op. cit., p. 99.
12. Buzzard, *Lancet* (1866), p. 454.

Erichsen's book is that, on the one hand, it distinguished between two groups of accident victims — the physically injured, and those suffering from medical symptoms without physical injury — and, on the other, it recombined these groups in the diagnosis that they both suffered from concussion of the spine, caused by the violent mechanical shock of the accident. As consistent as Erichsen was in his defense of this purely pathological view, he did not succeed in proving an actual pathological change in the tissue of the spinal marrow, but had to content himself with the analogy of the magnet, in which similar changes occur that cannot be demonstrably proven:

> How these Jars, Shakes, Shocks or Concussions of the Spinal Cord directly influence its action I cannot say with certainty. We do not know how it is that when a magnet is struck a heavy blow with a hammer, the magnetic force is jarred, shaken, or concussed out of the horse-shoe. But we know that it is so, and that the iron has lost its magnetic power. So, if the spine is badly jarred, shaken, or concussed by a blow or a shock of any kind communicated to the body, we find that the nervous force is to a certain extent shaken out of the man, and that he has in some way lost nervous power. What immediate change, *if any*, has taken place in the nervous structure to occasion that effect, we no more know than what change happens to a magnet when struck.[13] (Italics in original.)

How shaky Erichsen's belief in the pathological view was in the face of his own observations is evidenced by that surreptitious 'if any' qualifying his reference to the alleged but unproven pathological change in the tissue. This internal contradiction became even more obvious in Erichsen's repeated implicit stress on the psychic factor in railroad accidents, i.e., on the experience of fright:

> It must . . . be obvious . . . that in no ordinary accident can the shock be so great as in those that occur on Railways. The rapidity of the movement, the momentum of the person injured, the suddenness of its arrest, the helplessness of the sufferers, and the natural perturbation of mind that must disturb the bravest, are all circumstances that of a necessity greatly increase the severity of the result-

13. Erichsen (1866), p. 95.

ing injury to the nervous system, and that justly cause these cases to be considered as somewhat exceptional from ordinary accidents.[14]

Although Erichsen finally stuck to his pathological explanation, the passage just quoted demonstrates sufficiently that he was unable to ignore the psychological distress resulting from the relative exceptionality (i.e., violence) of the railroad accident.[15] The confusion of pathological and psychopathological explanations was caused by Erichsen's inability to distinguish between the accident's mechanical *power* to shock and the psychic *reception* of that shock. His definition of the 'concussion of the spine' as 'a certain state of the spinal cord occasioned by external violence'[16] was intended to be read in terms of pathology, but could just as well be interpreted in a psychopathological sense. In the latter case, the outside force would no longer affect the spinal cord in a direct, mechanical fashion, but would affect psyche and organism in the form of an experience of fright.

Erichsen suppressed such an interpretation of the traumatic reaction in 1866. In the considerably enlarged and revised edition of his book, published in 1875, he did express his recognition of it.[17] Although that recognition was intended to be subsidiary, it was given sufficient space to justify the supposition that Erichsen had, as it were, changed his orientation behind his own back. This is the decisive passage in the 1875 edition: 'It is important to observe that a serious accident may give rise to two distinct forms of nervous shock. . . . The first is mental or moral, and the second purely physical. These forms of "shock" may be developed separately, or they may coexist. It is

14. Op. cit., p. 9.
15. Let us compare the previous quote on the violence and peculiarity of the railroad accident with another one that states the exact opposite, i.e., that railroad accidents are *not* essentially different from other accidents: 'I cannot, indeed, too strongly impress on you the fact that there is in reality nothing special in railway injuries, except in the severity of the accident by which they are occasioned. They are peculiar in their severity, not different in their nature, from injuries received in the other accidents of life. There is no more real difference between that concussion of the spine which results from a railway collision and that which is the consequence of a fall from a horse or a scaffold, than there is between a compound and comminuted fracture of the leg by the grinding of a railway carriage over the limb and that resulting from the wheel of a street cab across it.' (Op. cit., pp. 46–7.)
16. Op. cit., p. 18.
17. John Eric Erichsen, *On Concussion of the Spine, Nervous Shock, and Other Obscure Injuries of the Nervous System, in Their Medical and Medico-Legal Aspects* (London, 1875).

most important . . . to diagnose between these two, and if co-existing to assign to each other its proper importance'.[18]

Erichsen thus stated unequivocally — thereby correcting his inadequate distinction between psychic and physical concussion in 1866 — that the 'mental shock' resulted not from a mechanical but from a psychic blow: 'It is probably dependent in a great measure upon the influence of fear'.[19] This psychic blow is the translation of the mechanical blow into an experience of fright. In recognizing this, Erichsen furthermore arrived at a new evaluation of the specific quality of the railroad accident. In 1866, the only difference he saw between the railroad and any other kind of accident was quantitative: for example, a railway accident was usually more violent than falling off a horse.[20] In 1875, Erichsen detected a new, entirely specific quality in the rail accident that distinguished it from all other kinds of accidents:

During a hospital practice of thirty years I can scarcely recall to mind a single case in which the emotional or hysterical state that I am about to describe[21] has been met with after, or as a consequence of, any of the ordinary accidents of civil life. But I have seen many instances of it after railway concussions. Is this due to the frantic terror which often seizes upon the sufferers from railway collisions, or is it due to some peculiarity in the accident, some vibratory thrill transmitted through the nervous system by the peculiarity of the accident? I am disposed to think that terror has much to do with its production. It must be remembered that railway accidents have this peculiarity, that they come upon the sufferers instantaneously without warning, or with but a few seconds for preparation, and that the utter helplessness of a human being in the midst of the great masses in motion renders these accidents peculiarly terrible. In most ordinary accidents, as in a carriage accident from a runaway horse, the sufferer has a few minutes to prepare, is enabled to collect his energies in order to make an effort to save himself, and does not feel the utter hopelessness of his condition in his struggle for life and safety. The crash and confusion, the uncertainty attendant on a railway collision, the shrieks of the sufferers, possibly the sight of the

18. Erichsen (1875), pp. 194–5.
19. Op. cit., p. 195.
20. See n. 15 above.
21. In 1866, Erichsen strictly rejected the designation of the pathological symptoms as hysterical; however, in 1875 he said: 'It is this condition that is so apt to lead to an emotional state, which, for want of a better term, may be called hysteria'. (p. 195.)

victims of the catastrophe, produce a mental impression of a far deeper and more vivid character than is occasioned by the more ordinary accidents of civil life.[22]

The modifications that Erichsen made in his views between 1866 and 1875 did not cause him to abandon his pathological shock theory. Nevertheless, they indicated clearly how the new technological-industrial reality, so palpably demonstrated in the railroad accident, gradually and in the face of much resistance infiltrated and ultimately transformed traditional medical thought. Erichsen's hesitations and contradictions illustrate the process that Foucault calls 'reorientation' of medical vision. Such a reorientation occurred as the medical world was forced to acknowledge the existence of new qualities created by the Industrial Revolution.

With Erichsen's recognition of fright as a causative factor in the traumatization of railroad accident victims, the modernization of medical thought on this subject became an accomplished fact, even though Erichsen himself did not wish to admit this.[23] Medical literature after Erichsen, while expanding his work and criticizing it, continued primarily along the lines laid down in his work. The pathological explanation was discarded and the psychological one was granted both exclusive and universal validity.[24] The first comprehensive critique of Erichsen's theory was given in 1883 by Herbert W. Page, in his 'Injuries of the Spine and Spinal Cord without Apparent Mechanical Lesion and Nervous Shock, in Their Surgical and Medico-Legal Aspects'. Page wrote that Erichsen's failure was '[not] to have separated and differentiated those symptoms which we must have recognized are much more cerebral or psychical, from those which can only find an explanation in some actual lesion

22. Erichsen (1875), p. 196.
23. Thus Fischer-Homberger still represents Erichsen as a proponent of the purely pathological conception, while pointing out her unfamiliarity with the second version of his book.
24. In the early 1880s, the psychopathological explanation gained ground. After M. Bernhardt's initial attempts in this direction in 1876, Moeli published an article in 1881 (*Berliner Klinische Wochenschrift*, No. 18) which stated that psychic causation was the most likely one. In 1883, Hodges published an article, 'So-Called Concussion of the Spinal Cord' (*Boston Medical and Surgical Journal*), in which he criticized Erichsen and stressed the psychic component. Subsequent literature can be found in Fischer-Homberger's listing. While psychic causation gained thoroughgoing acceptance, there remained; in the background, the continued notion that even the psychic cause ultimately had a 'molecular' effect.

of the spinal cord or of the nerves which are given off from it'.[25] In direct opposition to Erichsen, Page was interested exclusively in the psychically caused symptoms; for him — and for the entire line of research begun by him — these were the only valid ones. Only the psychic fright arising out of an accident was recognized as the cause of the psychosomatic consequences, and that fright was seen as something specific to the railroad accident. According to Page, the essential difference between a person run over in the street by a carriage and a railroad accident victim was 'that in the one case [railroad accident] there is an element of great fear and alarm, which has perhaps been altogether absent from what may be called the less formidable and less terrible mode of accident'.[26]

Page described the traumatizing effect of the rail accident in words that even Erichsen could have used: 'The suddenness of the accident, which comes without warning . . . the utter help-lessness of the traveller, the loud noise, the hopeless confusion, the cries of those who are injured . . . are surely adequate to produce a profound impression upon the nervous system'.[27] The decisive difference was that these psychic concussions were now regarded as the *only* cause of traumatization: 'The incidents of every railway collision are quite sufficient — even if no bodily injury be inflicted — to produce a very serious effect upon the mind, and to be the means of bringing about a state of collapse *from fright and from fright only*'.[28] (Italics added.)

In Page's work, the psychological theory of accident trauma-tization became the dominant one, although there was still no generally accepted term for the syndrome. Having departed from Erichsen's 'railway spine', experts now spoke of 'railway brain', while also using Erichsen's concept of 'general nervous shock' in a new psychological interpretation. At the end of the 1880s Hermann Oppenheim came up with the term 'traumatic neurosis', which gained acceptance with some rapidity. In his article of 1889, 'Die traumatischen Neurosen' ('The traumatic neuroses'), Oppenheim described himself as a follower of Page, and defined the essential character of the traumatic neuroses as

25. Page (1883), p. 83.
26. Op. cit., p. 147.
27. Op. cit., p. 147.
28. Op. cit., p. 147.

consisting of the fact 'that they are not based on broad anatomical nor microscopically demonstrable changes but on cerebral functional disturbances, most probably located in the neocortex, affecting the psyche and the centers of motility, sensibility, and sensory functions'.[29] Two years later, in 1891, Page published a new edition of his book of 1883 and noted that his theory had found general acceptance in the intervening years. However, he himself did not adopt the concept of traumatic neurosis but called the syndrome he described a 'fright neurosis'. Subsequently, the literature on the subject grew by leaps and bounds, introducing competing and partially overlapping terms such as 'traumatic neurosis', 'fright neurosis', 'hysterical neurosis', 'libidinal neurosis', and (with the First World War providing new realities) 'war neurosis'.[30]

At this point, let us recall the starting point of this chapter of medical history. We began with the question that arose from the legal liability of the railroad companies and had to be resolved in courts of law: were physically undamaged, traumatized victims of railroad accidents mere malingerers, or was their suffering genuine? Even after medical science had struggled through to the notion that mere psychic fright could indeed cause a deterioration in an individual's health, it took a long time before there was any change in the legal concept of injury. Even after the turn of the century, legal handbooks denied recognition to psychic shock. Thus Street's *Foundations of Legal Liability*, 1906: 'Simple nervous shock and consequent injury to the mind, considered alone do not as a matter of law supply a ground of action. Bodily injury necessarily involves mental suffering. Being bound together the law refuses to separate one of these elements from the other and allows compensation for both'.[31] In *Mayne's Treatise on Damages*, 1899, reference was made to a precedent of the 1880s that stated, similarly, 'that damages resulting from mere sudden terror or mental shock, could not be considered the natural consequence of the negligence complained of'.[32]

---

29. Quoted in Fischer-Homberger, *Traumatische Neurose*, p. 33.
30. Cf. Fischer-Homberger, *Traumatische Neurose*.
31. Thomas Atkins Street, *The Foundations of Legal Liability* (Northport, LI, 1906), vol. 1, p. 458.
32. John D. Mayne, *Mayne's Treatise on Damages* (London, 1899), p. 51.

Thus it seems that Erichsen's pathological explanation of accident traumata was more helpful to physically undamaged accident victims seeking compensation than the later psychological theories that recognized psychic trauma as a legitimate syndrome. (We can, however, only assume this on the basis of the legal handbooks referred to, as it has not been possible to study the transcripts of compensation lawsuits.)

In Anglo-American Common Law, the recognition of psychic trauma as an actual malady that is eligible for compensation occured as late as the middle of the present century — more than fifty years after its recognition by medical science. A legal handbook published in 1963 states this general principle: 'Nervous shock is a form of personal injury for which damages may or may not be recoverable according to the circumstances of the particular case'. The handbook cites a decision made in 1943: 'The crude view that the law should take cognizance only of physical injury resulting from actual impact has been discarded, and it is now well recognized that an action will lie for injury by shock sustained through the medium of the eye or the ear without direct contact. The distinction between mental shock and bodily injury was never a scientific one, for mental shock is presumably in all cases the result of, or at least accompanied by some physical disturbance in the sufferer's system'.[33]

The specific character of the railroad and its accidents, from which the discovery of psychic trauma emanated, is no longer present in the above example of the further evolution of law and medicine. The importance that the concept of trauma gained in Freud indicates how the final reminiscences of the material-mechanical explanation of the causation of trauma gradually wear away. As Freud concentrated his attention increasingly on the psychoneuroses of sexual origin (as distinct from the actual neuroses), the patient's disposition became the decisive element, and the traumatic event itself lost objectivity. Fischer-

---

33. *Winfield on Tort* (7th ed., London, 1963), p. 249. The latest accessible handbook from the year 1970 again reduced liability to the somatic pathological symptoms that may accompany the psychological shock: '. . . mere grief, anguish, unhappiness, humiliation, outrage and so on, however distressing they may be, are never compensable at all unless they follow on some physical injury. Only if the plaintiff suffers some actual illness, usually referred to by lawyers somewhat unscientifically, as "nervous shock", does any question of compensation arise'. (P. S. Atiyah, *Accidents, Compensation and the Law* [London, 1970], p. 63.)

Homberger calls this Freud's 'psychologization of the trauma and its subsequent dissolution as an etiological factor'.[34] Similarly, Laplanche and Pontalis find that 'psychoanalytical investigation leads to a questioning of the concept of traumatic neurosis: by, on one hand, stressing its relativity in regard to the subject's tolerance, and on the other, integrating the traumatic experience in the subject's specific history and organization, it negates the determinative function of the traumatic event'.[35] Psychoanalysis tends to 'equate trauma that triggers neurosis with what Freud has elsewhere called "refusal" (*Versagung*)'.[36]

Yet Freud saw more than the psychological aspect of trauma. While he did abstract it into a psychological function within the framework of the sexual causation of neuroses, he later developed a renewed interest in the kind of neurosis that is brought about in an actual fashion, by means of violent events from outside. The stimulus-response theory he developed in *Beyond the Pleasure Principle*, which Walter Benjamin used in his reconstruction of a specifically modern structure of perception,[37] involved a recapitulation of the original concept of traumatic neurosis.

Freud's preoccupation with what he himself has called the 'old, naive theory of shock' significantly occurred soon after the end of the First World War. The drastic change in the quality of warfare (i.e., a new technology of battle *matériel*) caused medicine to renew its interest in mass psychic phenomena. This time, the mass phenomenon was shell shock, or war neurosis. Shell shock can certainly be seen as a successor to the railroad shock of the nineteenth century. In both cases the victims are psychically traumatized by a sudden and violent release of energy, without being demonstrably damaged in the physical sense.[38]

34. Fischer-Homberger, *Traumatische Neurose*, p. 79.
35. J. Laplanche and J. B. Pontalis, *Das Vokabular der Psychoanalyse* (Frankfurt, 1975), vol. 2, p. 523.
36. Op. cit., p. 517.
37. Walter Benjamin, 'On Some Motifs in Baudelaire', in *Illuminations*, pp. 160–3.
38. Fischer-Homberger, *Traumatische Neurose*, pp. 86–7: 'The shell explosion now became, as it were, the trauma *par excellence*. In that explosion . . . sense impressions and physical shock acted on the bystanders with the highest degree of intensity. According to the old doctrine of traumatic neurosis, the shell explosion had to be generative of neurosis to a greater degree than any other trauma. It proved, indeed, to be thus: as we know, World War I, particularly in its first years, was a time of enormous epidemics of neuroses, many of which were traced back to shellshock'.

As before, medical experts were called in to decide on the question of simulation, only this time the objective was not to see who deserved to be awarded damages, but to see who was a malingerer and should be sent back to the front lines, and who was a genuinely sick person requiring treatment.

If one recognizes the new quality of military technology in the First World War as the cause of the 'gigantic epidemics of neuroses' (Fischer-Homberger), and this mass phenomenon of shell shock as the reason for Freud's new interest in the old concept of shock,[39] it is possible to establish a relatively direct connection between that novel technical quality and Freud's reorientation. One might say, perhaps a little too loosely, that the period of peace in which Freud developed the sexual etiology of neurosis favored the psychologization and attendant abstraction of trauma concept, and that it took the very real mass experience of trauma of the World War to recall the original concept and render it interesting again. Without the experiential background of that war, Freud's theory of the destruction of the stimulus shield by great amounts of energy would be as hard to imagine as the nineteenth-century theories of 'railway spine' and traumatic neurosis would be without the railroad and its accidents.

That Freud's new orientation was based essentially on a novel quality in warfare technology is not surprising, considering the important effects that military technology has had on civilian life, the economy and the human psyche over the last five hundred years. The emergence of the shock concept from military life, and its subsequent application to civilian cases, paralleled the way in which the military developments of early modern Europe repeatedly anticipated forms and symptoms that later reappeared in the civilian life of the period of the industrial revolution.

---

39. On Freud's preoccupation with war neuroses, see Fischer-Homberger, *Traumatische Neurose*, pp. 151–9.

Excursus
The History of Shock

That Freud in his later years developed his concept of shock and his theory of the stimulus-shield on the basis of the mass phenomenon of shell shock during the First World War, would seem a direct continuation of the history of shock, as such, which is, in large measure, part of military history.

According to the *Oxford English Dictionary*, the word 'shock' has carried since the seventeenth century the connotations of 'blow', 'strike', 'concussion', in a material-physical as well as a borrowed psychological sense. The original meaning, first noted in the sixteenth century, was a military one. 'First adapted as a military term', says the *OED*, it denoted 'the encounter of an armed force with the enemy in charge or onset; also, the encounter of two mounted warriors or justlers charging one another.'

The French word 'choc' received the same meaning about the same time. Hans Delbrück quotes Field Marshal Blaise Monluc describing the encounter of the opposing troops in the battle of Ceresole, 1544: 'Tous ceux des premiers rangs, soit du *choc* ou des coups, furent portés par terre'. ('All those in the front lines had fallen to the ground, either from *shock* or blows'.)[1]

Before the word received this military meaning in English and French, it denoted, in the Germanic languages, 'a pile of sheaves', later the exact number sixty; but even then *Schock* is 'used more generally, as a concept of indefinite amount . . .

---

1. Hans Delbrück, *Geschichte der Kriegskunst im Rahmen der politischen Geschichte* (Berlin, 1908), vol. 4, p. 62.

mostly in regard to crowds of people and hordes of soldiers'. (Grimm, *Deutsches Wörterbuch*.)

According to Trübner,[2] the word 'shock' entered the Romance languages via the Middle Dutch *schokken*, meaning to collide. A possible explanation for the process by which this general concept of colliding became a specifically military form can be found in the work of Lynn White, who describes the evolution of a new mode of battle, 'mounted shock combat', as the result of the technical innovation of the stirrup in the first half of the eighth century:

> The stirrup, by giving lateral support in addition to the front and back support offered by pommel and cantle, effectively welded horse and rider into a single fighting unit capable of a violence without precedent. The fighter's hand no longer delivered the blow: it merely guided it. The stirrup thus replaced human energy with animal power, and immensely increased the warrior's ability to damage his enemy. Immediately, without preparatory steps, it made possible mounted shock combat, a revolutionary new way of doing battle.[3]

Here we have the beginning of that development toward the consolidation of energies that later became the military phenomenon of shock. The nature of that shock consisted in creating a situation where it was no longer the individual muscular force of the single combatant that counted, but the fusion of his individual power with one extraneous to it.

If the fusion of the energies of horseman and steed into a powerful new force behind the lance was the first decisive step towards the development of military shock, the second step occurred with the rise of modern armies, at the beginning of the Early Modern era. Sombart, who called these armies one of the most important motive forces behind the early development of capitalism, gave an excellent description of the differences between companies of knights on horseback and modern mass armies, demonstrating therein how the military shock was no longer executed by the rider–horse unit, but by the new mass unit of the army. Sombart wrote that the modern army is characterized by 'its working by means of its size, being a large

2. *Trübners Deutsches Wörterbuch* (Berlin, 1955), vol. 6, p. 192.
3. Lynn White, Jr., *Medieval Technology and Social Change* (Oxford, 1962), p. 2.

band of warriors combined into one tactical unit. When you had a thousand knights in the field, they still did not constitute one unified mass: they were a thousand individual warriors, fighting together. But a thousand modern cavalrymen collaborate to deliver *one blow*, when they charge'.[4] (Italics added.)

The basic principle of this new tactical organization was that the warriors no longer did battle individually but as parts of the new combat machine; the squadron (*Geviert Haufen*), developed in the fourteenth century, is frequently compared to a machine.[5] As Delbrück says, it 'forms the self-contained tactical body whose parts are used to finding and understanding their strength in exactly that containment and cohesion'.[6] Sombart, who saw in this new military form an analogy to other modern capitalistic forms of the division of labor, recognized that it put an end to the personal development of the individual warrior, because the individuals now joined into one military body were merely the executive organ of an authority exterior to themselves: 'Thus the functions of (spiritual) leadership and (physical) action have become separated and are performed by different persons, while they had previously been conjoined in one and the same person'.[7]

In the single-combat bouts of warriors of the era of chivalry, the combatants related to each other so intensely that the event can be seen as a form of dance:[8] while it ended with the death of one of the warriors, it created a highly animated relationship between the participants, and a series of functional body motions. By contrast, the modern body of soldiers functions according to an abstract discipline that has nothing to do with the fighting *per se*, but merely serves the cohesion of that body. Its

4. Werner Sombart, *Krieg und Kapitalismus* (Munich and Leipzig, 1913), p. 28.
5. While Delbrück perceived the modern squadron formation as in many ways a kind of resurrection of the phalanx of antiquity, he believed that the impact of collision experienced in the warfare of modern times was not known in antiquity (vol. 4, p. 63), because the phalanx, although it was a closed formation, did not function as a unified body of troops, but rather as a sequence of individual warriors who were replaced by others as they fell or were wounded. (Delbrück, vol. 1, p. 32.)
6. Delbrück, vol. 4, p. 12.
7. *Krieg und Kapitalismus*, p. 28.
8. 'Observation and anticipation of the intentions of the adversary are the objective. . . . For their own interest, adversaries in battle are in closer communication and are compelled to cooperate with each other far more intensively and deliberately than dancers. . . .' (Rudolf zur Lippe, *Naturbeherrschung am Menschen*, vol. 2, *Geometrisierung des Menschen und Repräsentation des Privaten im französischen Absolutismus* [Frankfurt, 1974], p. 152.)

function, according to Sombart, 'is to create, by mechanical means, the connection between leading and executive organs'.[9]

Thus we see how, in the creation of the modern military, there was a mechanization of the 'human material' analogous to the mechanization in the more or less simultaneously emerging process of mass manufacture. Sombart: 'I believe that we have not yet given sufficient credit to the influence that the development of the modern army has had on the entire culture and on its economic life in particular. During the decisive seventeenth century we experience the fragmentation and demolition of that natural man who still dominated the years of the Renaissance'.[10]

As significant as the analogy between military and economic organization is, we are mainly interested in the fundamental difference that exists between the two. In the economic realm, the new mechanized collectivity of manufacture, and later of industrial production, appeared, as it were, peacefully. It was productive and it reproduced itself linearly. In the military realm, on the other hand, the purpose of the mechanical organization was the annihilation of the enemy, the performance of the military clash — the initial meaning of 'shock'. The new military organization concretized the entirely specific sense of the word: the clash of two bodies of troops, each of which represented a new unified concentration of energy by means of the consolidation of a number of warriors into one deindividualized and mechanized unit. What was new in this military clash was its unheard-of violence (due to the concentration of energy) as well as the degree of attrition of its elements; the latter occurred in direct proportion to the degree of energy concentration. Again, we encounter what we have called, in the context of technical accidents, the 'falling height' of a mechanical apparatus: the greater the degree of concentration/mechanization of the two colliding bodies of troops, the more violent the shock of their clash, the greater the attrition of the elements that consti-

9. *Krieg und Kapitalismus*, p. 28; see also Zur Lippe, vol. 2, *Kövpererfahrung als Entfaltung von Sinnen und Beziehungen in der Ära des italienischen Kaufmannskapitals*, p. 102.
10. *Krieg und Kapitalismus*, pp. 28–9. In M. D. Feld's extremely interesting paper, 'Middle-Class Society and the Rise of Military Professionalism' (*Armed Forces and Society*, no. 4 [1975]), pointed out to me by Lutz Unterseher, the development of the modern Dutch army in the seventeenth century is described as a process of industrialization. According to Feld, this army was 'the only industrialized system of the age' (p. 429), its creation 'this earliest of industrial revolutions — the industrialization of military behavior' (p. 434).

tute the whole. The definition of 'shock' in the *OED* relates to this military clash situation: 'A sudden and violent blow, impact, or collision, *tending to overthrow or produce internal oscillation in a body subjected to it*'. (Italics added.)

The modern organization of armies, i.e., the gathering of deindividualized warriors into a single body, caused the concept of shock to become identified with an event involving the discharge of violence.

The initial development of the new military form began within the framework of traditional weapons technology. In the seventeenth century, the standard weaponry of armies did not consist of firearms but of pikes and halberds. Only in the course of the eighteenth century did hand firearms become standard issue in the European armies. They not only strengthened the tendency to mechanize the military units but raised that mechanization to a new level. This role of the hand firearms can be compared to the one played by the steam engine in the Industrial Revolution: it was the continuation of existing developments on a new technical level. The use of simple offensive weapons such as pikes required certain craftsmanlike skills on the part of their users, whereas the new firearms were easily mastered mechanical tools. They were the technical counterpart to the already firmly-established mechanics of troop organization. 'This reform of warfare', Feld comments on the transition from pikes and halberds to firearms in the eighteenth century, 'was analogous to the change, in industrial production, from a craft to an assembly line mode'.[11]

The new quality of combat with hand firearms consisted of the final loss of a 'personal' relationship between combatants such as was still inherent in battle waged with pikes. The characteristic trait of the new method of fighting was the 'salvo', the collective, unaimed discharge of firearms by the entire unit. Delbrück has discussed this new tactic of the eighteenth century: 'Due to the great inaccuracy of the single shot, the decision was made to forego taking aim or training soldiers in marksmanship: effectiveness was sought by means of collective fire repeated as rapidly as possible, the salvo, delivered on command. While Frederic [II, of Prussia] still ordered his troops not to fire

11. Op. cit., p. 427.

too hastily — "because the fellow has to look and see what he's shooting at" — later orders even *prohibited* such deliberate taking of aim. The main stress now was as on split-second timing of the salvo so that it would sound like one shot'.[12]

The salvo tactic already presaged the later psychological significance of the shock concept. The desired effect of the salvo, the *simultaneous* slaying of as many soldiers as possible within the closed ranks of the enemy unit, was seen quite consciously as a psychological one that led to the demoralization of the enemy. In paragraph 178 of Scharnhorst's *Taktik* the salvo was preferred over single fire 'because ten men falling to the ground at the same time will cause a battalion to retreat sooner than fifty that drop at different times and in different places'.[13]

We saw how the original military concept of shock changed its meaning after the introduction of hand firearms. The force of the clash lost its concrete physical manifestation. The collision was no longer performed directly by the participating military units but occurred at a distance, by means of the salvo.

Quite obviously connected with this military-technical and tactical change was the additional significance the concept of shock received in the eighteenth century. It no longer applied only to the military clash but also to the consequences it caused, by means of the use of firearms, in the organisms of the affected soldiers. In Henri-François Le Dran's *Treatise, or Reflections, on the Use of Firearms* (1743), an English translation of the French military surgeon's account, we find this: 'The Bullett . . . thrown by the Gun Powder acquires such rapid force that the whole Animal Machine participates in the Shock and Agitation'.[14] Groeningen, in *Über den Shock* (1885), described this alteration or enlargement of the concept, although he did so without mentioning the initial military meaning of the word: 'Towards the middle of the eighteenth century the common demotic English word for blow, strike, etc., the word shock . . . had acquired next to its

---

12. Delbrück, vol. 4, pp. 307–8.
13. Summarized by Delbrück, op. cit., p. 308. Due to the use of the salvo as a tactic, there was hardly ever any hand-to-hand combat in the eighteenth century (Delbrück, op. cit., p. 309).
14. Quoted in H. A. Davis, *Shock, and Allied Forms of Failure of the Circulation* (New York, 1949), p. 1. In the original French edition of 1737 the word *choc* does not yet occur; the corresponding passage is as follows: '. . . le bale . . . poussé par la poudre à canon, l'est avec tant de vitesse et de force, que toute la machine animale se ressent plus ou moins de la *secousse* et de l'*ébranlement*'. (Pp. 1–2; italics added.)

active meaning a passive one, and even in medical nomenclature shock no longer describes only the blow but also its consequence, the concussion, and the pathological general state of the victim caused by it'.[15]

The fact that a certain state that occurs after being wounded by a firearm was discovered in the eighteenth century and described by the word 'shock' would seem to indicate that this state has to do with the evolution of army organization and military technology. One can assume that the mechanization of combat, which gave the individual combatant a consciousness different from that involved in medieval modes, not only made that individual behave differently while engaged in combat but also caused different reactions in him when he received a wound. A wound caused during a medieval duel was essentially different from one caused by a salvo of firearms. The intense relationship between the duelists may be seen as one of alert expectation. The individual combatants were able to see from exactly which direction the possible wound may be caused: they were, as it were, well prepared for it. From the eighteenth century on, such a state of readiness no longer existed. The wound caused by mass fire occurred suddenly, invisibly; it came 'out of nowhere'. (The earlier specific state of readiness should be distinguished from the generalized readiness of a soldier who is aware that he is in a war and that he can get wounded or even killed: the latter is not an alert expectation but a dull routine state of mind.)

The wound shock discovered by military medicine in the eighteenth century was obviously not only a consequence of the lesion itself but was equally a result of the specific situation involved in receiving wounds caused by firearms, i.e., from the lack of effective readiness. Observations made by military surgeons in the nineteenth century seem to confirm this conclusion. 'The wounded man', wrote Pirogoff, 'does not experience the wounding as such but rather feels the concussion or a shock similar to an electric one.'[16] The receptive situation could even be so unexpected and diffuse that the wound was not noticed at first. Groeningen gives an example: 'McLeod tells us about an officer who had lost both his legs below the knee and only

---

15. G. H. Groeningen, *Über den Shock* (Wiesbaden, 1885), pp. 3–4. Like most non-English authors of the period, Groeningen used the English spelling of the word.
16. Ibid., p. 101.

noticed it as he was trying to get up'.[17] Rose clarified the connection between lack of expectation and 'unnoticed' firearm wounds: 'Most warriors do not feel their wounds at all, not only because of the rapidity of the damage but rather because of the total exertion of all their psychological powers towards other goals. Every sensation requires a degree of attention, however small'.[18]

It would be outside of the framework of this discussion to try to ascertain whether the mechanization of the modern military, and the introduction of firearms in particular, has actually altered human organic reaction upon the receipt of a serious wound so that the new reaction is a more serious wound shock than was previously the case.[19] Within our context, the main interest lies in the psychic state of receptivity before getting wounded, and this state obviously has changed radically due to the organizational and technical innovations of the military in the past five hundred years.

The lack of readiness is what connects the military-medical concept of shock with the later psychological concept of shock developed in the wake of railroad accidents and makes the earlier concept the forerunner of that later one. The history of shock, its origin in military innovations (e.g., stirrup, mass army, firearms), conveys its own modernity: this consists of the fact that 'shock' no longer describes any simple blow or strike but a violent act compounded from the concentration of many individual elements. *Now 'shock' describes the kind of sudden and powerful event of violence that disrupts the continuity of an artificially/*

---

17. Ibid., p. 101.
18. Quoted from ibid., p. 101. Ernst Jünger provides an example from first-hand experience: ". . . a blow on my left thigh felled me to the ground. I thought that I had been struck by a flying clod of earth, but the copiously flowing blood soon convinced me that I had been wounded'. *Stahlgewittern* [Berlin, 1929], p. 25.
19. It would be of some interest to investigate the relation between shock and pain. As modern bullet wounds are generated unexpectedly, one might assume that the sensation of pain occurs after a longer interval than in former times. Copland, among others, had noted that shock and absence of pain are closely connected: 'In most of these severe injuries, and especially those produced by fire-arms, the amount of pain is very small compared with the intensity of the shock; and even where the shock is the greatest, the pain may be the least, or may even be entirely absent'. (James Copland, *Dictionary of Practical Medicine* [London, 1858], vol. 3, p. 785.) Following wound shock, there is an absence of pain, due to the unexpectedness of the physical trauma. This may be parallel to what happens in cases of psychological trauma. In these, according to Freud, the traumatic neurosis will occur due to the absence of *fear* on the occasion of the traumatic experience.

mechanically created motion or situation, and also the subsequent state of derangement. The precondition for this is a highly developed general state of dominance over nature, both technically (military example: firearms) and psychically (military example: troop discipline). The degree of control over nature and the violence of the collapse of that control, in shock, are proportionate: the more finely meshed the web of mechanization, discipline, division of labor, etc., the more catastrophic the collapse when it is disrupted from within or without.

The history of modern armies demonstrates this proportional relationship between the control of nature and shock so clearly because the destructive application of productive energy is an integral part of military history, as opposed to the situation in manufacture and industrial production. Not only did the new capitalistic productivity manifest itself first in the European armies but it also manifested itself most clearly there, in the negativity of destruction. The level that the development of the productive forces had reached became visible as 'falling height' in the military clash. In a sense, the technical and organizational development of the military is a paradigm for the simultaneous or immediately subsequent analogous development of the civilian productive forces, and the military shock is a paradigm for what threatens man in the event of the collapse of those productive forces.

[10]
Stimulus Shield: or, the Industrialized Consciousness

> These discoveries [i.e., the new technical devices such as the railroad] . . . bend our senses and our organs in a way that causes us to believe that our physical and moral constitution is no longer in rapport with them. Science, as it were, proposes that we should enter a new world that has not been made for us. We would like to venture into it; but it does not take us long to recognize that it requires a constitution we lack and organs we do not have.[1]
>
> — G. Claudin, 1858

It is now easy to perceive why the originally military and military-medical concept of shock experienced a revival in the nineteenth century in the context of the railroad and its accidents. The railroad related to the coach and horses as the modern mass army relates to the medieval army of knights (and as manufacture and industry do to craftsmanship). In the railroad journey, the traditional experience of time and space was demolished the way the individual experience of battle of the Middle Ages is abolished in the modern army (and the individual craft activity is abolished in manufacturing and industrial production). The early descriptions of the train journey as an experience of being 'shot' through space (with the train as projectile) no longer seem merely accidentally associated with the military realm. Structurally, the train passenger is analogous

1. G. Claudin, *Paris* (Paris, 1867; pp. 71–2).

[159]

to the soldier in the mass army in being conditioned by the unit in which he functions as an integral part. The conditioning of the individual in a military context can now be seen as the earliest model of all subsequent and similar conditioning in the civilian economic world. In the modern army individuals are for the first time mechanized, or even subsumed, into an organizational scheme that is completely abstract and exterior to them. In the further history of the modern age, this condition becomes increasingly common in all spheres of life.

We have seen how the nineteenth-century travelers gradually got accustomed to what at first seemed frightening: the demolition of traditional time-space relationships and the dissolution of reality. The travelers developed new modes of behaviour and perceptions, forms in which the new experiential content extended itself. 'Panoramic vision' was one of these innovations, as were the new general consciousness of time and space based on train schedules and the novel activity of reading while traveling.

These new modes of behavior and perception enabled the traveler to lose the fear that he formerly felt towards the new conveyance. The process by which human beings get accustomed to new technical means that initially evoke mistrust and fear can be characterized as a process of repression of fear, or, more neutrally, as a diminution of fear. In the early descriptions of the railroad, open fear or subliminal apprehension is evident as a fear of derailment, of velocity, of collisions. People used to the more leisurely technology of the previous era were still unable to comprehend that it had become possible to travel safely in something that seemed like an enormous grenade. These fears had an actual technological base, as railroad technology in its first phase still suffered from 'gaps', or infantile maladies, which were real enough sources of danger. In that phase, technology still had one foot in the realm of obsolete forms and the other in that of the new form of production. This interim situation was conducive to fear, but it did not last long. The conveyance was perfected, it worked ever more smoothly, and its disquieting idiosyncrasies were, if not abolished totally, at least ameliorated, or 'upholstered'.[2] The sinister aspect of the

---

2. Mumford has posited an inverse ratio between actual technical differentiation of ma-

machinery that first was so evident and frightening gradually disappeared, and with this disappearance, fear waned and was replaced by a feeling of security based on familiarity. The traveler who sat reading his newspaper or novel instead of worrying about the ever-present possibility of derailment or collision no doubt felt secure. His attention was diverted from the technological situation in which he found himself and directed to an entirely independent object. One might say that he felt secure because he had forgotten how disquieting the technological conveyance still was, how tremendous and potentially destructive were the amounts of energy it contained. This forgetfulness was possible because the technology itself helped it along by eliminating or obfuscating all its initially anxiety-producing manifestations (vibration, mechanical jolts, etc.).

Every airplane traveler experiences this process today, and re-remembers it, while anxiously and attentively observing the mighty vibrations of the machine in its takeoff phase, then relaxing entirely during the flight, and then again, when it is time to land, attentively listening to the technological noises to detect any irregularity that might herald catastrophe.

In their empirical psychological study *Zur Psychologie des Sicherheitsgurtes (On the psychology of the safety belt)*, H. J. Berger, G. Bliersbach and R. G. Dellen pursued the question as to why the introduction of the safety belt in automobiles still meets with considerable resistance on the part of the driving public. In contrast to all the other manual motions required to start and drive the car, the one of fastening the seat belt has not so far been assimilated by the drivers of automobiles: '. . . for the majority of drivers of private vehicles, the safety belt appears as an *unsafety* belt. Instead of reducing anxiety, it actualizes a great deal of it simply by the fact that it has to be fastened time and

---

chinery on the one hand, and its external surface presented to the consumer for use, on the other: '. . . . a simplification of the externals of the mechanical world is almost a prerequisite for dealing with its internal complications. To reduce the constant succession of stimuli, the environment itself must be made as neutral as possible'. (*Civilization and Technics*, p. 357.) Mumford has also hinted at an analogy between the development of technological and social forms: 'The machine has thus, in its esthetic manifestations, something of the same effect that a conventional code of manners has in social intercourse: it removes the strain of contact and adjustment'. (Op. cit.)

again.' (Italics in original.)

This is so because the latent danger is permanently present in the safety belt, and so very visibly that it cannot be repressed: 'The safety belt *confronts* the driver with the actual dangers of traffic on the road, and he has to come to terms with them whether he wants to or not. Feeling the safety belt against his body, the driver is constantly reminded of the possibility of an accident, since that is what the belt is for'. (Italics in original.) 'Most persons tested, when asked for spontaneous associations with the belt, came up with the images of injury or death.'

While the safety belt thus perpetuates the fear of accident, which makes it impossible to get used to, the air bag is a popular safety device. The reason is its invisibility, which enables the driver to forget/repress the danger of accident. Thus it is a modern version of train upholstery: while upholstery in nineteenth-century first-class compartments ameliorated the technological vibrations and thus aided the travelers in forgetting their fear of the technology, the air bag serves an analogous function without even being visible. It provides actual safety from the results of a collision and by its invisibility ensures that the fear of an accident is not perpetuated.[3]

It is obvious how closely such a feeling of safety is joined to the technology upon which it is based. The technology has created an artificial environment which people become used to as second nature. If the technological base collapses, the feeling of habituation and security collapses with it. What we called the 'falling height' of technological constructs (destructivity of accident proportionate to technical level of construct) can also be applied to the human consequences of the technological accident. The web of perceptual and behavioral forms that came into being due to the technological construct is torn to the degree that the construct itself collapses. The higher its technological level, the more denaturalized the consciousness that has become used to it, and the more destructive the collapse of both.

In the technological accident and the shock released by it, the fear that has been repressed by the improvement in technology reappears to take its revenge. It becomes obvious that the

3. H. J. Berger, G. Bliersbach, R. G. Dellen: *Zur Psychologie des Sicherheitgurtes* (Frankfurt, 1973, pp. 128–33).

original fear of the new technology has by no means dissolved into nothingness during the period of habituation, but that it has only been forgotten, repressed, one could even say, reified[4] as a feeling of safety. It then appears in a new form — as it were, from behind the victim's back — as fright. If the original anxiety anticipated the imagined or actual danger that emanated from the new technology, and protected people to a certain degree from actually occurring accidents by creating an attitude of readiness, the later fright works in the opposite direction. The disposition that has enjoyed a sense of security which is then proven to have been spurious is attacked suddenly and unexpectedly by that fright.

Freud has dealt with this distinction between anxiety and fright and has drawn far-reaching conclusions from it. It is particularly interesting that Freud discussed these in connection with his theory of the stimulus shield, in *Beyond the Pleasure Principle*, the work in which he developed the theory which originated in his immediate response to the context of the First World War and its neuroses.

'Anxiety', wrote Freud, 'describes a particular state of expecting the danger or preparing for it, even though it may be an unknown one. . . . "Fright", however, is the name we give to the state a person gets into when he has run into danger without being prepared for it; it emphasizes the factor of surprise. I do not believe anxiety can produce a traumatic neurosis. There is something about anxiety that protects its subject against fright and so against fright-neuroses.'[5] The precondition for fright, Freud specified, 'is the lack of any preparedness for anxiety'.[6] Thus he was working in the tradition of the psychological

---

4. In connection with the concept of reification developed by Lukács in *History and Class Consciousness* on the basis of Marx's concept of commodity fetishism, we would like to quote an *aperçu* by Adorno, conveyed in a letter to Benjamin in 1940, concerning the relationship between reification and forgetting: 'All *reification* is a forgetting: objects become mere things at the moment they are fixed without being actually present in all their parts — the moment when some part of them has been forgotten'. (Adorno to Benjamin, 29 February 1940, Benjamin, *Gesammelte Schriften* [Frankfurt, 1974] vol. 1, pt. 3, p. 1131.)

5. Sigmund Freud, *The Standard Edition of the Complete Psychological Works*, London, Hogarth Press, vol. 18, p. 12. (1) 'Anxiety (angst) has an unmistakable relation to expectation: it is anxiety *about* something.' (p. 165.) (2) 'Anxiety is a reaction to a situation of danger.' (p. 128) (3) 'The ego subjects itself to anxiety as a sort of inoculation, submitting to a slight attack of the illness in order to escape its full strength.' (p. 162)

6. Ibid., vol. 18, p. 32.

explanation of the traumatic neurosis: for him, too, the moment of fright was decisive, that sudden, violent, and unexpected accident experience that the psyche finds itself unable to deal with.

Yet Freud went far beyond the traditional explanation, in his theory of the stimulus shield. This theory, an explanation of the conditions necessary for the development of traumatic shock, was described by Freud himself, very cautiously, as 'speculation, often far-fetched speculation'. Walter Benjamin, in his writings on Baudelaire, has demonstrated that we can find in it a very useful suggestion for the understanding of what modern civilization does to human consciousness.[7]

Having described the traces that the railroad has left on the actual and psychic landscape of the nineteenth century, we can elevate these observations to a more general level by applying Freud's theory. It provides a possible answer to the question how the industrialization of travel is reflected in the traveler's psychic structure — or, more broadly speaking, as in one of Marx's well-known formulations, how 'production not only creates an object for the subject but also a subject for the object'.[8]

To illustrate the relationship between consciousness and the outside world, Freud reduced the elements of the relationship to the highest possible degree of abstraction:

> Let us picture a living organism in its most simplified possible form as an undifferentiated vesicle of a substance that is susceptible to stimulation. Then the surface turned towards the external world will from its very situation be differentiated and will serve as an organ for receiving stimuli. . . . It would be easy to suppose, then, that as a result of the ceaseless impact of external stimuli on the surface of the vesicle, its substance to a certain depth may have become permanently modified, so that excitatory processes run a different course in it from what they run in the deeper layers. A crust would thus be formed which would at last have been so thoroughly 'baked through' by stimulation that it would present the most favourable possible conditions for the reception of stimuli *and become incapable of any further modification.*[9] (Italics added.)

7. *Illuminations*, pp. 160–3.
8. *Grundrisse*, op. cit., p. 92.
9. Op. cit., p. 27.

What Freud developed here with his model of the small vesicle, we can imbue with historical concreteness in tracing the history of the development of railroad perception. One of the essentially new stimuli of the train journey was its speed, which expressed itself as the dispersed perception of foreground objects, as the feeling of the annihilation of space and time. This new stimulus at first merely irritated the traveler, who was still accustomed to the old velocity of the coach. Yet gradually everything connected with the new velocity became psychically assimilated: as Freud would have said, the stimuli burnt their way into the skin layer of consciousness and 'its substance to a certain [depth] may . . . become permanently modified'. The train passenger of the later nineteenth century who sat reading his book thus had a thicker layer of that skin than the earlier traveler, who could not even think about reading because the journey still was, for him, a space-time adventure that engaged his entire sensorium. (When the later traveler stopped reading and looked out the compartment window, he did so with a gaze that was quite different from his predecessor's. The development of what we have called the panoramic vision perhaps demonstrates most clearly how the 'baking' of the stimuli into the skin layer of consciousness changes it. A comparison between the traditional and the panoramic vision demonstrates which technological developments the latter has assimilated.)

Freud's conclusion that the skin layer modified by the impact of stimuli 'has become incapable of any further modification' seems an important one. It indicates that the stimuli, once they have been pyschically assimilated, determine consciousness and perception to the extent that stimuli of a quality entirely different from the assimilated ones no longer register, or at least not adequately. Once the traveler had reorganized his perception so that it became panoramic, he no longer had an eye for the impressions of, say, a coach trip, no more than pre-industrial travelers like Ruskin were capable of panoramic vision, as their skin layer had been similarly conditioned, once and for all, and was 'incapable of any further modification'. (An analogy from military history: the skin layer/consciousness of the soldier in the modern mass army has been so deeply conditioned by the stimuli specific to modern battle organization that this soldier would find himself totally helpless in the battle situation of the chivalrous duel — not for reasons of weapons technology, but for psychic ones.)

The creation of this skin layer by the effects of outer stimuli was, indeed, the development of what Freud calls the stimulus shield. It exemplified a function of consciousness that was, according to Freud, just as vital as the reception of stimuli: the ability to ward off stimuli. Freud wrote of the small vesicle:

> This little fragment of living substance is suspended in the middle of an external world charged with the most powerful energies; and it would be killed by the stimulation emanating from these if it were not provided with a protective *shield against stimuli.* It acquires the shield in this way: its outermost surface *ceases to have the structure proper to living matter, becomes to some degree inorganic* and thenceforward functions as a special envelope or membrane resistant to stimuli. In consequence, the energies of the external world are able to pass into the next underlying layers, which have remained living, with only a fragment of their original intensity; and these layers can devote themselves, behind the protective shield, to the reception of the amounts of stimulus which have been allowed through it. By its death, the outer layer has saved all the deeper ones from a similar fate — unless, that is to say, stimuli reach it which are so strong that they break through the protective shield.[10] (First italics in original; second italics added.)

Freud's explanation of the traumatic neurosis assumed such a possibility, an onslaught of stimuli powerful enough to pierce the shield: 'We describe as "traumatic" excitations from outside which are powerful enough to break through the protective shield. It seems to me that the concept of trauma necessarily implies a connection of this kind with a breach in an otherwise efficacious barrier against stimuli'.[11]

Thus relating trauma to a prevention mechanism that becomes shattered in the traumatic event, Freud advanced the theory of traumatic neurosis by an important step. The concept of the stimulus shield proved to be a suitable model for what one might call the formation of *an inorganic protective layer due to civilization.* The strength or density of the stimulus shield indicates the strength or density of the stimuli that it receives and,

10. Op. cit., pp. 28–9.
11. Op. cit., p. 31.

again, the strength or density of these stimuli is an indicator of the prevailing historical stage of civilization.

Although Freud's vesicle model was intended as a pure abstraction for the demonstration of psychic processes, its vocabulary does have immediate, specifically modern connotations. An outside world 'charged with the most powerful energies' cannot be all that timeless. That Freud's model is based on an experience of modernity, even if that experience is not subjectively known to the author, can be demonstrated by a glance at Georg Simmel's essay, written twenty years earlier, 'The Metropolis and Mental Life'. Describing the fate of the psyche in metropolitan life, Simmel arrived at conclusions that are remarkably similar to Freud's. One only has to substitute concepts — Freud's 'stimulus shield' for Simmel's 'intelligence', Freud's 'deeper psychic layers' for Simmel's 'heart' — to realize that the description concerns the same event. The urban dweller distinguishes himself from the small-town or rural person in that his intelligence — according to Simmel — is more developed due to the many impressions/stimuli that it has to deal with. The intelligence, however, 'has its locus in the transparent, conscious, higher layers of the psyche; it is the most adaptable of our inner forces'. Furthermore: 'Thus the metropolitan type of man — which, of course, exists in a thousand individual variants — *develops an organ protecting him against the threatening currents and discrepancies of his external environment which would uproot him*. He reacts with his head instead of his heart. In this an increased awareness assumes the psychic prerogative. Metropolitan life, thus, underlies a heightened awareness and a predominance of intelligence in metropolitan man. The reaction to metropolitan phenomena is shifted *to that organ which is least sensitive and quite remote from the depth of the personality*'.[12] (Italics added.)

Freud's model is so well suited to the description of the psychic process of civilization because it demonstrates the relationship between subject and outside world to be a synthesis of both. The stimulus shield is subject as well as outside world in that it *is* outer world (i.e., stimuli of that world) assimilated into the subject, absorbed and interiorized by it.[13]

12. *The Sociology of Georg Simmel*, ed. Kurt Wolff (Glencoe, Ill., 1950), pp. 410–11.
13. The proposal to call this process of assimilation of the journey 'interiorization' was made

On the other hand, the stimulus shield model is so abstract that it can be applied to all possible kinds of stimuli: to technically caused ones (i.e., velocity) as well as cultural ones (laws, customs, etc.). Thus the 'civilizing process' described by Norbert Elias can be understood as the formation of a stimulus shield, just as we have understood the process of travel by rail to be one. The 'stimuli' that the individual becoming civilized in Elias' sense absorbs during the civilizing process are the social rules that are interiorized by the courtly upper strata in the seventeenth and eighteenth centuries. A violation or breaking of these rules was commonly described as 'shocking': it was the shattering of a stimulus shield of convention — an analogous event to 'shock' in military clash or railroad accident, with the sole difference that the tissue torn in the former consisted of interiorized forms of social intercourse and not of interiorized technically caused stimuli.

Thus we have to distinguish between two different formations of stimulus shields or psychic civilizing processes, occurring at different levels: on one hand, interiorization of social rules, on the other, interiorization of technologically caused stimuli. As qualitatively different as the sources are, their stimulus effect on the psychic structure is comparable. Social rules and technologically produced stimuli structure the individual in a similar manner, regularizing, regulating, shaping him according to their inherent laws.

Conceptually, we can comprehend the distinctness and the similarity of both these sources of the civilizing process by describing them as external and internal domination of nature. Technology is an expression of external domination: by means of technological constructs (machines) nature's powers and materials become disciplined to produce cultural, i.e., economic achievements. The social rules are constructs designed to serve internal domination: they structure the individual in such a way that he fits into the social context and performs constructively

---

by Fritz Heubach, in a letter to the author: 'By means of it [the concept of interiorization] we can understand the development of fearlessness, the taking for granted of structures formerly connected with fear and expectation, and finally the congruence of psychic matter with what the psyche has at some point experienced; the "dulling" of a stimulus (qua stimulus) — i.e., the cancellation of a sensibility — can thus be seen as its recession into the interior, its interiorization. Thus we also find the repressive mechanism of "identification with the aggressor"'.

within it.

The technological constructs affect the natural forces in the same way social rules affect the individuals; furthermore, the constructs of external domination themselves demonstrate progress in terms of increasing self-discipline, as do the individuals who internalize the social rules. Let us compare how Elias describes the process of human self-discipline to Franz Reuleaux's description of the corresponding process in the development of machines. Elias: 'The behavior of an increasing number of people has to be co-ordinated, the web of actions organized ever more precisely and rigorously, in order for the individual action to perform its social function within that web. The individual is forced to regulate his behaviour in an ever more differentiated, ever more regular and stable fashion'.[14]

According to Reuleaux the progress of machine technology consists in the increasing elimination of *play*. Play signifies the relation of the elements of a machine to each other. The more primitive the technology, the less attuned the parts of the machine to each other, the greater the degree of play. The more perfected the technology, the less play the individual parts have in regard to each other. 'I am convinced', wrote Reuleaux in 1875, 'that the cogwheel working entirely without play will be the rule within a few years.'[15] Creating an almost poetic image, Reuleaux described how the increasing density of the machine grasped the forces of nature ever more firmly: 'As waterwheels have become perfected, the water jets left to the free play of forces have disappeared; the Strauber wheel [which Reuleaux previously says is technically so deficient that the propelling stream of water still washes over it like a natural waterfall] has developed into the smoothly and quietly running turbine, which produces hardly any of that spray and diffusion of small water particles. . . . The cosmic freedom of the natural phenomenon becomes transformed by the machine into an order and law that outside forces of an ordinary kind are unable to disrupt'.[16]

We return to the civilizing process understood as the forma-

14. Norbert Elias, *Über den Prozess der Zivilisation*, 2nd ed. (Bern and Munich, 1969), vol. 2, p. 317.
15. Franz Reuleaux, *Theoretische Kinematik*. p. 234.
16. Reuleaux, op. cit., p. 37.

tion of a stimulus shield. After making the distinction between culturally and technologically caused stimuli and relating it to the distinction between internal and external domination of nature, we still have to demonstrate why, in our opinion, the technological stimuli deserve at least as much attention as agents in the civilizing of psychic life as the cultural 'stimuli' of social forms, which Elias has described in such a magnificent manner. The answer is simple. The technologically produced stimuli, as signals emanating from the external domination of nature, are *more immediate* expressions of the productive forces than are the social rules; like all ideological forms, the latter develop as functions of productive forces, but only through a complex process. It might not be equally useful in regard to all periods of human history to describe the civilizing process of consciousness in terms so closely related to the development of technology; however, it does seem appropriate to an epoch as permeated and even overwhelmed by technology as that of the Industrial Revolution. Marx's remark that production not only provides an object for the subject but also provides a subject for the object would appear applicable, and it ought to be possible to describe what an 'industrialized consciousness' is.

[11]
The Railroad Station:
Entrance to the City

We find ourselves in the gigantic vestibule of a large city, with
millions streaming into and out of it. The space encloses
thousands of people in any single minute, and then disperses
them in all directions in the next.
— Richard Lucae, 1869

In the pre-industrial era, overland traffic was confined to the
space of the landscape through which it proceeded, and this
remained the case even at its destination, the city. The stagecoach related to the city in exactly the same way that it related to
the open country. The stagecoach depot was located in the
center of the city, usually adjacent to an inn that was named
after it (Zur Post, The Coach and Horses), and thus was practically indistinguishable from the surrounding buildings in architectural terms. The stagecoach was completely integrated into
urban life.

The railroad, however, terminated that intimate relationship
between the means of transport and its destination. Railroad
depots and stations were as different from the old coach depots,
as the train from the coach and the rails from the highway. The
newly-built railroad station was not an integral part of the city: it
was located outside the traditional city limits, and for a long
time it remained an alien appendage. The immediately adjoining parts of the city were soon stigmatized as being industrial

[171]

and proletarian: they became the disreputable 'railroad district' (the 'wrong side of the tracks'). A remark in Perdonnet's handbook — in its third edition (1865), not the first of 1855 — shows that this was an unexpected development. The rubric is 'La Répulsion des habitants des villes par les gares' ('The repulsion felt by the city dwellers towards the railroad stations'): 'It was long assumed, erroneously, that the railroad stations would become points of attraction for the city dwellers. Far from it: today we see them trying to stay as far away as possible from those noisy centers. Only rarely do the hotels located too close to the stations prove successful'.[1]

If the surroundings of the rail station appeared tainted by industry, then the station itself must have had an extremely noticeable industrial character. As an architectural type, it belongs clearly and exclusively to the category of typically nineteenth-century steel and glass edifices that have been termed 'traffic buildings'.[2]

The 'traffic' function found its architectural expression in a far more immediate way in the railroad station than it did in the other types of steel and glass architecture. In market halls, exhibition pavilions, arcades and department stores the traffic of goods took place in a stationary fashion, in the form of storage and display; in the railroad station, the human traffic literally poured through, actively, in the form of travelers streaming in and out of the trains. Unlike the other 'traffic buildings' of this period, the railroad station appeared as a palpably industrial building, in which the railroad's industrialization of transport was perceptible to all the senses.

Nevertheless, the industrial aspect was only one of the railroad station's characteristics. The metropolitan passenger terminal with which we are exclusively concerned here was not merely a utilitarian industrial construct of steel and glass. The total installation was curiously dual: first we have the actual

---

1. Auguste Perdonnet, *Traité élémentaire des chemins de fer* (Paris, 1865), vol. 4, pp. 401–2.
2. Hermann Muthesius in his lecture 'The Unity of Architecture', 1908: 'In the commercial buildings, the railroad stations, the market halls, the convocation halls, modern conditions have been able to create modern types of buildings. . . . These edifices of novel form served commerce and traffic, which experienced rapid development in the nineteenth century. In the requirements of that traffic we see the shaping idea that the art of architecture now uses preferentially'. (Quoted in Monica Hennig-Schefold and Helga Schmidt-Thomsen, *Transparent und Masse: Passagen und Hallen aus Eisen und Glas, 1800–1880* [Cologne, 1972], p. 19.)

train hall, built out of steel and glass; then the reception building, erected out of stone. The former faced the open country, the latter, the city. This division into two entirely different realms, once aptly apostrophized as 'mi-usine, mi-palais' ('half-factory, half-palace'),[3] was, as Alfred Gotthold Meyer noted, a novelty in the history of architecture: 'Architecturally, these are two entirely separate worlds. Heretofore, architecture has failed to create another species of building in which one single edifice combines two main parts that are formally totally different as is the case in our great railroad stations that conjoin the stone-built reception buildings with the steel and glass halls of the actual *railroad* terminal'.[4]

This two-facedness of the metropolitan railroad station was the result of two decades of railroad expansion. The train halls were not built out of steel and glass until the early 1850s; when this finally happened, it was, no doubt, partly due to the European success of London's Crystal Palace of 1851, which furthered the cause of commercial glass architecture generally.[5] The decisive factor, however, arose out of the development of the railroad itself, which demanded new technical solutions even for the terminals. In the 1830s, when railway traffic was still restricted to bilateral connections between cities, the dimensions of the stations were modest; most consisted of a single train platform with separate buildings for arrivals and departures and an overall roofing that was often a plain wooden structure.[6]

As the railroad network grew denser during the 1840s, traffic put greater demands on the terminals. A greater number of tracks now converged on them, requiring a greater number of platforms. These had to be connected with each other in order to enable the passengers to transfer from one train to the next. Finally, the entire, now considerably enlarged, structure had to

3. P. J. Wexler, *La formation du vocabulaire . . .*, p. 83.
4. A. G. Meyer, *Eisenbauten*, p. 146.
5. ' . . . ferrovitreous construction . . . certainly moved to a climax around 1850 and before 1845 had amounted to little.' (Henry Russell Hitchcock, *Early Victorian Architecture in Britain*, 2 vols. [New Haven, 1954], vol. 1, p. 511.)
6. See Meeks' hitherto unsurpassed standard work on the architectural history of the railroad station (Carrol L.V. Meeks, *The Railroad Station: An Architectural History* [New Haven, 1956], pp. 37ff.) The roof of Euston Station (1839) was only 40 feet wide, and the railroad station of Liverpool (1850) was the widest in the world at 153 feet (op. cit., pp. 38–9.)

be roofed. The solution was a new type of building with a midway connecting the platforms and with a train hall constructed out of steel and glass.

From the mid-nineteenth century on, this kind of station became a characteristic feature of the great European cities. Situated on the periphery of the inner city, these stations, as Meyer described them, 'receive traffic from the city in their vestibules, conduct it to the midway in the main building, and thus distribute it by means of individual access platforms to the trains. Simultaneously, an equally intense volume of traffic proceeds in the opposite direction, from the rails to the city, at first cohesive, then divided and dispersed'.[7]

Thus the station functioned as a gateway which had to connect two very different kinds of traffic and traffic space with one another: the traffic space of the city, and that of the railroad. One part of it, the neoclassical stone building, belonged to the city; the other part, the steel and glass construct, was a pure function of the railroad's 'industrial' side.

By means of this two-facedness, the railroad station's function as a gateway found its architectural expression. As the departing traveler proceeded from the city, through the reception building, to the train hall, traversing these qualitatively different spaces, he experienced a process of expansion of space, one might even say, of industrialization of space. Leaving the urban space of the city (in the 1850s, still relatively reassuring), he entered the station's space, which in turn prepared him for the actual industrial space of the railroad. Conversely, the arriving traveler experienced a process of spatial reduction. The boundless and shapeless space of the railroad journey was first delimited by the hall in which the train arrived, and then reduced further in the traditional stone architecture of the reception building which provided a continous transition to the urban spaces of the city.

This function of the station as a spatial gateway is what Richard Lucae had in mind when he described the differing effects that the train hall had on departing and arriving passengers. Lucae wrote that the space of the train hall, 'with one of its sides wide open to the world, may, by contrast with the closed

---

7. Meyer, p. 146.

buildings of the city, create an unpleasant or perhaps even frightening impression. But to one who arrives from outside, the gigantic hall with its solid stone enclosure and its wide-spreading protective roof, may, despite the enormous dimensions, seem positively cozy after the limitless space through which the train wheels have been carrying him for miles and miles'.[8]

The neoclassical character of the facades of the station buildings was quite certainly another expression of the typical nineteenth-century desire to disguise the industrial aspect of things by means of ornamentation.[9] And yet, unlike the exhibition halls of the Second Empire, whose stucco facades had no other purpose than the concealment of the steel and glass constructions they covered, the stone fronts of these railroad station buildings exercised a real function, that of a kind of stimulus shield: they were there to connect two fundamentally different realms, city space and railroad space. The stone reception building that obscured the train hall from view remained necessary as long as the city itself remained essentially pre-industrial in character. Throughout the 1850s, an abrupt entry of the industrial apparatus of the railway into the city, not ameliorated, not 'filtered' in some way, would be far too shocking.[10] But very soon thereafter, and helped along by the railway in a

8. Richard Lucae, 'Über die Macht des Raumes in der Baukunst', *Zeitschrift für Bauwesen*, vol. 19 (1869), p. 298.
9. It is interesting to consider, in this context, the idea of the railroad station as the modern successor to the town or city gate. The gate certainly exerted some influence on the form of the reception buildings; this is most clear in Philip Hardwick's Euston Station (1835–9), with its monumental Greek portico, which was deemed provocative even by contemporary architecture critics, as the ornamental aspect had become entirely emancipated from the practical function, leaving a facade without a building behind it. (Meeks, pp. 40ff.)
10. Here, too, American development proceeded quite differently. In the nineteenth century, Americans did not see the railroad as entirely different from other thoroughfares, as Europeans did. Frequently the railroads were simply referred to as 'roads', and this familiarity gives rise to a situation unheard of in Europe: the train appeared in the middle of the city, but with the locomotive disengaged and replaced by horse teams. 'In several of the principal American cities, the railways are continued to the very centre of the town, following the windings of the streets and turning without difficulty the sharpest corners', observed Lardner, describing the American railroads of the 1840s (*Railway Economy* [London, 1850], p. 338). That situation continued until the turn of the century: 'The railroads proceed for long distances at the same level as the highways, and railroad crossings within the city disrupt traffic, but the public endures this disruption with incredible patience. Furthermore, while it travels through inhabited streets, the locomotive continuously rings a loud and nervewracking bell.' (Alfred von der Leyen, *Die Nordamerikanischen Eisenbahnen in ihren wirtschaftlichen und politischen Beziehungen* [Leipzig, 1885], p. 221.)

crucial sense, the city lost its medieval character and assumed an industrial character determined by modern traffic. This transformation rendered both reception building and train hall redundant.[11]

The change, simplification, and acceleration of the process of transition from the city realm to the railroad realm is apparent in an interesting modification that took place in the interior spatial arrangement of the railroad station around 1860. Before that time, there was no direct access between reception area and station platforms: the latter could be reached only by moving through the waiting rooms. In these, the passengers (like air travelers in our day) had to congregate and wait until the doors to the midway were opened shortly before the train's departure. This regulation prevented the travelers from reaching their trains in an uncontrollably individual fashion: especially in continental Europe, which at that time had not yet achieved a high degree of industrialization, there were doubts as to the general public's ability to deal with industrial machinery in the absence of precise regulations.[12] But that changed in the 1860s and the reception building and the train hall became directly connected. Thus, the waiting rooms lost their function as gateways and became peripheral to the main stream of traffic. The reception hall assumed the function of both waiting rooms and midway and became a 'concourse', a 'vast mixing chamber . . . serving as a self-adjusting traffic center'.[13] 'Once the function of the concourse was comprehended', writes Meeks in his summary of this development, 'it became possible to abandon the

11. The spacious railroad station hall disappeared at the beginning of the twentieth century, and did so first in the US. It was replaced by the less expensive roofing of the individual platforms by means of 'bush sheds': 'Such a shed was cheaper to build and more economical to maintain, and gave nearly as much protection as the colossal ones'. (Meeks, p. 122.) As the train hall disappeared, the reception halls clearly adopted the form of the train halls of the nineteenth century, i.e., the form of their 'adversary': this, too, was a kind of architectural variation of the 'interiorization' principle discussed in chapter 10, n. 13.

12. Perdonnet, describing this regulation of access to the platforms, contrasted it with the freedom of such access in England and recognized this freedom as the result of advanced industrialization: ' . . . this is truly a grand and beautiful spectacle which gives a good idea of the power and liberalism of the companies that have given their country these magnificent instruments. The travelers, who can freely enter the station at all hours, familiarize themselves with the machines by studying them. By admiring them, they lose their fear of them, and thus the railroads become popular'. (*Traité . . .*, 1st ed., [Paris, 1856], vol. 2, p. 30.)

13. Meeks, p. 79.

midway altogether and to provide separate quiet waiting areas while all moving traffic was handled in the concourse.'[14]

The new spatial arrangement quite obviously reflected a speeding-up of the process of spatial transition. The traveler's sojourn in the waiting room, that hiatus in the passage of traffic from city to railway, was perhaps the clearest indication of the station's function as a gateway. One might say that the pause was necessary to enable the traveler to cope with the change in the quality of space. However, it became possible to master the change of space in a continuous movement, merely by walking through the reception hall (now the 'concourse') and out onto the platforms — a further indication of the rapprochement between city space and railroad space. Direct access from the city to the railroad had become possible because the city itself, to paraphrase Lucae, had become as 'frightening' (i.e., industrialized) in its aspect as the train hall.

14. Op. cit.

[12]
Tracks in the City

The Attila of the straight line.
— Victor Fournel, speaking of
Georges Haussmann, 1865

The transformation of the still largely medieval aspect of the European city in the nineteenth century; the explosion of its spatial enclosures; its horizontal expansion of urban space, with the creation of specialized districts (residential, business, and industrial; bourgeois and proletarian, etc.) — all were results of the industrial revolution in general, and of the railroad's transportation revolution in particular. Where this development was not caused directly by the railroad, the latter nevertheless functioned as an accelerating factor for existing tendencies. Kellett, who has researched the railways' influence on urban development in nineteenth-century England, gives a summary that is fundamentally applicable to developments in all the other West and Central European countries as well: '. . . it was the influence of the railways, more than any other single agency, which gave the Victorian city its compact shape, which influenced the topography and character of its central and inner districts, the disposition of its dilapidated and waste areas, and of its suburbs, the direction and character of its growth; and which probably acted as the most potent new factor upon the urban land market in the nineteenth century'.[1]

1. John R. Kellett, *The Impact of Railways on Victorian Cities* (London and Toronto, 1969), p. xv.

The railroad made its most immediate and visible impression on those parts of the city with which it interacted physically, i.e., the districts immediately adjoining the tracks and the stations. Here, the railroad changed the physiognomy of the old cities with bold strokes. 'The plans of British towns, no matter how individual and diverse before 1830', says Kellett, 'are uniformly superinscribed within a generation by the gigantic geometrical brush-strokes of the engineers' curving approach lines and cut-offs, and franked with the same bulky and intrusive termini, sidings, and marshalling yards.'[2]

These changes did not affect the actual heart of the city. Apart from some exceptions,[3] the railroad lines were drawn merely to the peripheries of the old centers, and that is where the terminals were built. This was due not so much to reverence for the historical architecture of the centers — although that may well have had something to do with it, considering the nineteenth century's generally ambiguous relationship to machinery and industry — but to the high cost of real estate in the middle of town. The railroads required considerable space for their tracks, stations, storage halls and other technical installations and therefore located themselves in a part of the city that met the requirements of optimal location in terms of traffic and of optimal (i.e., minimal) real estate prices. Perdonnet, commenting on the location of passenger terminals: 'The passenger stations are not located close to the centers of the cities unless the expenditure involved in such close location, which is mostly a considerable one, is justified by the advantages gained.'[4]

A glance at the city plans of European metropolises in the 1850s shows clearly exactly where in the city the terminals were located, in each instance. The terminals of Paris were sited between the inner and outer rings of the boulevards. In London, the social difference between the East End and the West End is demonstrated by the fact that the western terminals were located on the outskirts of the city, while the eastern lines penetrated deep into the industrial-proletarian region.[5] A map of

2. Op. cit., p. 2.
3. The stations of English industrial cities such as Birmingham, Liverpool and Manchester were located in the center of the city. (Kellett, pp. 9ff.)
4. A. Perdonnet, *Traité élémentaire* . . . (Paris, 1865), vol. 4, p. 401.
5. In London, the railroads were built exclusively through proletarian residential districts, because the real estate prices (and those of the buildings that had to be demolished)

Berlin from 1846 shows the terminals on the periphery of the old city; later maps demonstrate how, starting about 1860, this old inner city grew around and beyond the terminals, and became a new, expanded inner city. This explains the comparatively central situation of the terminals in typical European city development.[6]

The railroad did not influence only those parts of the city that were in its immediate vicinity; more generally, it increased the volume of traffic, an increase that led finally to the demolition of the city's traditional interior structure. The effects of increased traffic volume became apparent as soon as a city was attached to a railway network: the streets in the environs of the station changed character overnight. 'Walking along the Leipziger Strasse that leads to the railroad, one has difficulty recognizing it', observed a newspaper article after the opening of the railroad between Berlin and Leipzig, 'there is a constant stream, in both directions, of pedestrians, coaches, cabs and other vehicles; the solid, massive buildings reverberate from the continuous shocks, and inhabitants who formerly thought to find here a quiet, beautiful street, with its advantages of proximity to the countryside, green trees and fields, are now moving back into the city to find their lost serenity. In the future, the great Leipziger Strasse will most probably be a thoroughfare of factories. . . .'[7]

Thus, even the volume of traffic that the railroads directed into the cities became most clearly apparent in the vicinity of the stations. These were the bridgeheads of the new traffic that would now spread over the entire city. The first main arteries were those between railroad station and city center, as well as

---

were the lowest there, and the properties belonged mostly to a few wealthy individuals — thus, negotiations were simple (Kellett, pp. 324ff.) Kellett estimates that at least 120,000 inhabitants had to be resettled (p. 328). In a historical irony, the arches of the viaducts that enabled the trains to cross over former proletarian housing districts were turned into shelters for those who had been evicted from their homes (Kellet, pp. 344–6).

6. This *ex post facto* incorporation of the stations into the city has not been noted by the otherwise knowledgeable historian of urban development, Lewis Mumford, who writes that the railroad 'was invited to plunge into the very heart of the town and to create in the most precious central portions of the city a waste of freight yards and marshalling yards'. (*The City in History* [New York, 1961], p. 461.)

7. *Morgenblatt für gebildete Leser*, 1838, no. 294, p. 1176 (quoted in Manfred Riedel, 'Vom Biedermeier zum Maschinenzeitalter', *Archiv für Kulturgeschichte*, vol. 43 [1961], no. 1, p. 121.)

those between the various main terminals of a metropolis. Around 1855, London's daily traffic on these thoroughfares amounted to seventy-five thousand vehicles.[8]

The street system of the old cities was unable to cope with the new volume of traffic, and thus modernization and modification become necessary. 'The greatly increased internal circulation of people and goods, by day and night, in the expanding cities, had to be accommodated by expensive street realignments and improvements.'[9]

Baron Haussmann's renovation of Paris is an exemplary case. In a mere fifteen years the physiognomy of that city underwent a complete transformation, a 'regularisation' (Haussmann) that is unique in European history. In London, where traffic was certainly as pervasive a problem as in Paris, the accommodation of the city to the needs of modern traffic occurred during a longer period of time and in more 'civilized' forms. The authoritarian, highly structured, even brutal methods with which Haussmann 'renewed' old Paris is often seen only as a modification of the city to make it conform to the counter-revolutionary strategic needs of the Second Empire. It is obvious that the avenues and boulevards were designed to be efficacious army routes, but that function was merely a Bonapartist addendum to the otherwise commercially orientated new system. The form and methodology of Haussmann's street plan was authoritarian and military; its purpose, like the overall intention of the Bonapartist regime, was the advancement of the bourgeoisie's business interests.[10]

Thus the underlying authoritarian intentions do not entirely explain the drastic obviousness of Haussmannism. In the preparation and realization of his work, Haussmann used the rail-

8. Kellett, p. 313; also, on the stations as traffic nodes in the city: 'No single business-district function attracted and focused more traffic than the railway stations. They were the originating points of a great part of the cab traffic, and their names figured on the destination boards of many of the new horse omnibuses which replaced the short-stage coaches in London in the 1830s'. (p. 312.)
9. Kellett, p. 287.
10. It would be worthwhile to investigate exactly which of Haussmann's thoroughfares were indeed motivated by exclusively strategic considerations, how the strategic and commercial interests were balanced out, and what conflicts, agreements and compromises resulted therefrom. Basically, then, the process of Haussmann's constructions was a variant of what happened to the railroads during the era of the July monarchy: they were planned in as centralized a fashion as was Paris when it was remodelled under Napoleon III (this is in contrast with the English practice of *laissez-faire*).

road as his technological model, not subjectively but objectively. To describe the straight lines of Haussmann's avenues, Victor Fournel could not think of a better parallel than the railway line: 'To avoid any curve invisible to the eye and unnoticeable to the foot, cuts are made across the terrain, as in the case of tunnels for the railroad'.[11] Haussmann approached Paris as a railroad engineer approaches any terrain through which a line has to be laid. He began his labors by surveying the city; until 1853, no complete street map of Paris existed, but only partial maps, indicative of the mutual isolation of the individual *quartiers*.[12]

The survey produced a complete street map, upon which the envisaged new thoroughfares were inscribed. Before the actual street construction began, there was 'a general levelling of Paris, to eliminate the minor humps and hillocks which could play havoc with a road intersection or a long perspective'.[13] Finally, the completed thoroughfares were opened ceremonially, not so much as memorials (as Walter Benjamin assumes),[14] but in the manner of new railway lines.

The first thoroughfare thus completed, the Boulevard de Strasbourg, became, as André Morizet notes in his history of Paris, 'much more essential . . . as the rapid development of the railroad network shakes the Parisians out of their old domestic habits and revolutionizes their circulation'.[15] The Boulevard de Strasbourg not only began at a terminal, the Gare de l'Est, its arrival and departure gate to the inner city,[16] but it then ran as a direct continuation of the rails, mathematically parallel and just as linear. Like the railway line in open terrain, the boulevard struck across the cityscape, cutting heedlessly through whatever was in its way. Thus the Gare de l'Est, which received the railroad on one side and permitted it to continue on the other,

11. Victor Fournel, *Paris nouveau et Paris futur* (Paris, 1865), p. 40.
12. J. M. and Brian Chapman, *The Life and Times of Baron Haussmann* (London, 1957), p. 77; Françoise Choay, *The Modern City: Planning in the Nineteenth Century* (New York, 1969), p. 17.
13. Chapman, pp. 77–8.
14. Walter Benjamin, 'Paris, die Hauptstadt des 19. Jahrhunderts', in *Illuminationen* (Frankfurt, 1961), p. 197.
15. Andre Morizet, *Du vieux Paris au Paris moderne* (Paris, 1932), p. 195. The only access to the Gare de l'Est before the construction of the Boulevard de Strasbourg was 'the narrow Rue de Chabrol [which could] ill accommodate the 12,000 vehicles that used it daily'. (David Pinkney, *Napoleon III and the Rebuilding of Paris* [Princeton, 1958], p. 39.)
16. In every European city connected to the railroad, the street becomes the *Bahnhofstrasse/ Station Street* etc.

transformed into a thoroughfare, would seem the most exemplary of all European city terminals. As a clearly recognizable direct continuation of the railroad line in the city, the Boulevard de Strasbourg is unique, but even Haussmann's other main thoroughfares can be perceived as complements to rail traffic. They either connect the terminals with the center of the city, or with each other.[17] In Paris, as well as in all the other European metropolises, the terminals functioned as bridgeheads for the new traffic that slowly expanded from them over the entire city. The farther this expansion of traffic proceeded, the more it became emancipated from its points of origin, the railroads and the terminals. What finally characterized the new streets was no longer any specific reminiscence of the railroad but their general function, which became mere subservience to the flow of traffic. Françoise Choay says:

> Problems of traffic flow were given priority. Haussmann's first step was to conceive a network of through streets which have no significance in themselves but are essentially a means of connection. They form new lines of communication, general ones between districts (east, west, north, south), specific ones between certain old or new key points such as railway stations or market places. . . . This overall network of arterial connections constituted what Haussmann described as a kind of 'general circulatory system', which he subdivided into hierarchized tributary systems, each organized around a plaza, which is no longer a place in itself but a traffic node, or what the Prefect [Haussmann] termed *nodes of relation*.[18] (Italics in original.)

The streets that Haussmann created served only traffic, a fact that distinguished them from the medieval streets and lanes that they destroyed, whose function was not so much to serve traffic as to be a forum for neighborhood life; it also distinguished them from the boulevards and avenues of the Baroque, whose linearity and width was designed more for pomp and ceremony than for mere traffic.[19] It is not even necessary to go back as far as

17. Chapman, p. 181.
18. Choay, pp. 17–18. Siegfried Giedion on Haussmann's streets: 'The streets themselves, not squares or single buildings, dominate the scene'. (*Space, Time and Architecture* [Cambridge, Mass., 1976], p. 770.)
19. If the avenue of the Baroque era was straight, it was so for reasons of symmetry and perspective. 'The straight road provides its triumphal, *dominating*, regulating note in the antique manner; it also expresses the need for order and classification that systematized

the Baroque to recognize the 'modernity' of the traffic function of Haussmann's streets. Even Pierre Patte's Englightenment-oriented proposal of 1765 demonstrates the difference between a type of city planning that is primarily traffic-oriented and one to which management of traffic does not yet exist as a task. Patte's plan envisaged modernizations such as water supply, the removal of cemeteries to the outskirts of the city and even traffic improvements between individual districts — so that one might assume, as Pinkney does, that 'he might be easily taken for a nineteenth-century urban reformer or city planner'. This impression, however, is deceptive: 'When he came to recommendations of specific improvements in the city's streets he remained a man of his age'. According to Pinkney, Patte's plan remained 'a work of embellishment; the needs of communication were forgotten'.[20]

With the remodeling of Paris to allow for flowing traffic, with the construction of streets 'which have no significance in themselves but are essentially means of connection', the inhabitants familiar with the old Paris experienced a situation similar to that of the first railroad travelers. As the latter, accustomed to the space–time perceptions of coach travel, experienced the railroad journey as a destruction of space and time, the former saw the new traffic-oriented city of Paris as destroyed — in a double sense: demolished physically as well as in its spatial and historical continuity. The railroad put an end to the lyricism of old modes of travel; the new thoroughfares signaled the end of the poeticism of Paris. (Contemporaries did not recognize the fact that, in both cases, the old appeared 'poetical' only at the very moment when the new technology announced its termination.)[21]

Descartes and this desire for perspective.' (Gaston Bardet, quoted in Michel Ragon, *Histoire mondiale de l'architecture et de l'urbanisme modernes*, vol. 1, *Idéologies et pionniers, 1800–1910*, p. 95.) Haussmann's avenues were rectilinear for the sole reason that, in terms of traffic technology, the straight line is the shortest connection between two given points. The Baroque avenue had as its destination and vanishing point an edifice representing regal might: its essential function was to point to and lead to that building in terms of perspective. Haussmann's avenue either totally rejected such vanishing points or created artificial eye-catchers such as the Opera House. Haussmann, Pinkney says, 'thought of the streets first as traffic arteries, then sought architectural embellishments that might be attached to them'. (Op. cit., p. 218). In addition to this, Haussmann's traffic arteries were so long that any building at the vanishing point would literally vanish 'in the blue distance' (Giedion).

20. Op. cit., p. 32.

21. 'That which one knows one will soon no longer have in front of one's eyes becomes an

Haussmann's work, observed Victor Fournel in 1865, caused Paris to lose 'the picturesqueness, the variety, the unexpectedness, that charm of discovery which made a walk in old Paris an exploratory voyage through always new and always unknown worlds, that multiple and living physiognomy that gave each great district of the city its special traits like those on a human face'.[22] The spatio-temporal disorientation of the first railway passengers was caused by the collision of two space–time relationships, the traditional with the new; similarly, a comparable disorientation of the Parisians of the 1850s and 1860s can be understood as a result of their seeing, with their own eyes, one Paris intersecting and colliding with another in the process of demolition and reconstruction.

'Buildings arise in place of old roads; new roads make their way across the debris of demolished houses. From all sides, the avenues advance as if to attack, overturning, bulldozing, flattening everything in their way', wrote Fournel, that implacable critic of Haussmann.[23] This obliteration of the old Paris and its subsequent replacement with a new city must have seemed both as unreal and as speedy to its contemporaries as a change of stage scenery. The new avenues, spreading out where only a short while before there had been vacant demolition lots, and before that, part of a medieval city, tried to compensate for their lack of historicity by means of pompous opening ceremonies and organizational and technological perfection. They were given over completely to traffic and, as if to conceal it, were stagily adorned with thirty-year-old trees planted by means of a machine specially invented for this purpose.[24]

If contemporaries attached to the old Paris, such as Fournel and Adolphe Thiers,[25] no longer felt at home in this new Paris of

---

image', wrote Walter Benjamin, discussing Meryon's etchings of the old Parisian quarters, 'that is what seems to have happened to the streets of Paris of that time.' (*Charles Baudelaire: Ein Lyriker im Zeitalter des Hochkapitalismus* [Frankfurt, 1969], p. 94.)

22. Fournel, p. 220.
23. Fournel, p. 22.
24. Giedion, pp. 758–9.
25. Thiers complained: 'For the promenaders, what necessity was there to walk from the Madeleine to the Étoile by the shortest route? On the contrary, the promenaders like to prolong their walk, which is why they walk the same alley three or four times in succession'. (Quoted in Giedion, op. cit., p. 771.) 'The straight line has killed the picturesque and the unexpected. The Rue de Rivoli is a symbol — a new, long, broad cold street on which people travel as cold and formal as it. The Paris of yesterday still had its Cour des Miracles, whose multicolored inhabitants we knew; they have just

flowing traffic, others were able, nevertheless, to arrive at a consciousness adequate to the new cityscape. The broad, tree-lined streets were seen as providers of light and air, creating sanitary conditions in both a physiological and a political sense — the latter favorable to the rule of Napoleon III. Gautier who, unlike other apologists for Napoleon[26] was not quite able to suppress a feeling of melancholy in the face of the destruction of the old Paris, saw the avenues as indices of 'civilization, which needs air, sun and space for its frenzied activity and constant motion, advances along great avenues into the dark labyrinth of narrow streets, squares and dead-ends of the old city; it strikes down buildings the way the American pioneer fells trees. In its own way, it also opens up new territory'.[27]

In Zola's *La Curée*, we find a description of the new Paris and its appropriate consciousness, in which there no longer is a trace of reminiscence of the bygone city. Renée and Maxime, relatives of the unscrupulous speculator Saccard, ride along one of the new boulevards:

> While gliding along in their carriage, they observed, amicably, the endless, broad, grey bands of sidewalks with their benches, multi-colored advertising kiosks, scrawny trees. This bright channel, stretching, growing ever narrower and ending in a square of blueing emptiness, all the way to the horizon; the uninterrupted double row of the great department stores . . .; the flowing masses of people, the noise of their footsteps and intermingling voices, slowly filled the

---

expropriated it for the cause of public utility. . . . The street [in the old sense] existed only in Paris, and now the street is dying; it is the reign of the boulevards and their outcome, the great arteries.' (Charles Yriarte, in *Paris guide: Par les principaux écrivains et artistes de la France* [Paris, 1867], part 2, p. 929.) Even the overall street plan of Haussmann was misunderstood by those who did not recognize its traffic orientation: 'One cannot grasp the intention and scope of the plan . . .', says one commentator in 1867, 'one sees only long straight lines striking out at random, illustrating all possible variations of the triangle and quadrangle'. (Quoted in Chapman, pp. 183–4.)

26. Thus, for instance, Claudin remarked that Haussmann's work had 'hardly changed anything in the beautiful quarters. War has been waged only on side streets of obscure thoroughfares and on those insanitary labyrinths in which the fractious, in times of trouble and mutiny, tended to entrench themselves. Their amputation has been complete: entire quarters have disappeared under the hammer. The Boulevard Sébastopol on both banks, the prolongation of the Rue de Rivoli, the isolation of the tower of Saint-Jacques and the Hotel de Ville, the new Louvre all exist on terrain previously occupied by smoky factories and unsalubrious shops'. (G. Claudin, *Paris* [Paris, 1867], p. 57.)

27. In Alexandre Dumas, Arsène Houssaye, Paul de Musset et. al., *Paris et les parisiens au XIXe siècle* (Paris, 1856), p. 40.

two women with unconditional, unadulterated joy, with an impression of the excellence of this street life. . . . They drove on and on, and it seemed to them that the carriage was rolling over carpets stretching along this straight and endless highroad that had been expressly constructed to save them from the sight of the small dark streets. Each boulevard became a hallway in their own house. The gaiety of sunlight smiled at them out of the new house fronts, made the window-panes light up, rebounded from the awnings of the stores and cafés, warmed the asphalt under the busy footsteps of the crowd. . . .[28]

28. Émile Zola, *La Curée* (*The Rush for the Spoils*). The novel, written in 1869–72, around the time of the final phase of Haussmanization, can be read as a contemporary description of the newly-completed boulevards.

[13]
Circulation

While Haussmann transformed the old Paris into a new city of flowing traffic, a similar change was taking place in the realm of retail business. In 1852 Aristide Boucicaut opened the first Parisian department store, the Bon Marché. The simultaneity was not coincidental: the department store, as a new form of retail merchandising, was predicated on a well-developed intra-urban traffic system. 'It only became possible to exploit such large retail outlets after the development of the omnibuses during the following decades and the appearance of the first horse-powered tramways in the period between 1850 and 1860.'[1] As Haussmann's traffic arteries were connected to the rail network by means of the railway stations, and thus to all traffic in its entirety, the new department stores, in turn, were connected to the new intra-urban arteries and their traffic. The *Grands Magasins* that arose during the second half of the nineteenth century were concentrated on the boulevards that supplied them with goods and customers.

There are three fundamental differences between a department store and the traditional retail business: the department store makes its profit by means of high turnover at a low rate of profit; prices are low, but fixed; and customers are encouraged to enter the store without any obligation to buy. Retail business became industrially revolutionized by means of these cheaper prices based on mass turnover. From the beginning of the nineteenth century there had been attempts to bring retail merchandising into line with the new industrial productivity;

1. H. Pasdermadjian, *Le Grand Magasin: Son origine — son évolution — son avenir* (Paris, 1949), p. 2.

for example, the *Magasins de Nouveauté* and the arcades, in which several independent retail businesses joined to form a kind of bazaar. However, those new arrangements consisted merely of a collection of autonomous businesses — there was no new quality to the organization of retail merchandising. In the traditional retail shop, buyer and purchaser still confronted one another in person: when a customer entered this presaged, if not necessarily a transaction, at least a dialogue between him and the shopkeeper.

The department store put an end to this sales conversation, as travel by rail put an end to verbal exchanges among travelers. The latter were replaced by travel reading; the former, by a mute price tag. This change resulted from the increased turnover of goods; the increase in quantity required new forms of distribution and behavior in travel space as well as in commercial space.

Not only did the department store change the relationship between seller and buyer, it also changed the buyer's attitude toward the goods sold. In the transition from the traditional retail shop to the department store, the customer's perception of the goods changed in a manner analogous to the traveler's perception during the transition from coach to train, and to the Parisian's perception during the process of his city's Haussmannization. The department store encouraged the development of the kind of perception that we have called 'panoramic'. To recapitulate its essential characteristics as seen in the context of the train journey: as speed caused the foreground to disappear, it detached the traveler from the space that immediately surrounded him, that is, it intruded itself as an 'almost unreal barrier' between object and subject. The landscape that was seen in this way was no longer experienced intensively, discretely (as by Ruskin, the critic of rail travel), but evanescently, impressionistically — panoramically, in fact. More exactly, in panoramic perception the objects were attractive in their state of dispersal. That attraction was generated by the motion that created this perception of the objects in the observing subject. We have observed a similar process at work in the kind of perception that esthetically enjoyed Haussmann's new thoroughfares as much as it loathed the old Parisian streets: here, the attraction lay in the width, the lightness, the continuous traffic of those new streets. We called this perception 'panoramic', by contrast with the traditional one that involved a static, intensive relationship with the objects observed.

We can call the appearance of the goods in the department store 'panoramic' — to distinguish them from their appearance in shops of the old type — because those goods participated in the same acceleration of traffic which generated the new mode of perception on the railways and boulevards. In the department store, this meant an acceleration of turnover. This acceleration changed the relationship between customer and goods to the same degree that the railroad's accelerated speed changed the traveler's relationship with the landscape. In both cases, the relationship became less static, less intensive, less discrete and more mobile.

The price-tag system introduced by the department stores did not only silence sales conversation, it also transformed the appearance of the goods. No longer did this appearance speak for itself, as in the traditional retail store, where the price of goods was determined by their visible and tangible qualities as evaluated by the customer and shopkeeper in the sales dialogue; that intrinsic quality, the use value, became obscured by the price tag. (The price tag interposed itself between goods and customer as the train's speed interjected itself between traveler and landscape.) On the side of the goods, the price tag corresponded to money as the carrier of exchange value; on the side of the buyer, it indicated the degree to which that exchange value has become a dominant part of the appearance of the goods. From that point on, the goods were perceived primarily in terms of price, while they had formerly presented themselves as concrete, individual objects whose price only emerged in the give and take of the sales dialogue.

This change stripped the goods of their former immediate, individual presence and sensuous quality and provided them with a new one. The attractiveness of an item no longer consisted in its individuality (its use value) but resulted from the totality of *all* the goods assembled in the salesroom. The gathering of a mass of heterogeneous goods under one roof, and its arrangement according to a concept, produced that 'extraordinary power of attraction to the public',[2] i.e., the motive power of

----

2. Pasdermadjian, p. 8.

the accelerated turnover, and thus led to the department stores' triumph over the traditional shops.

Zola's carefully researched novel about a department store, *Au Bonheur des Dames*, casts light on the sales dynamics and sales psychology of the last third of the nineteenth century that are based on this new relationship between customer and goods. *Motion* appeared in this book as the foundation of that relationship. This motion originated in the actual street traffic that led in and out of the building and thus the steady expansion of the department store proceeded apace towards one of the main traffic arteries. 'As long as the main entrance fronted onto the Rue Neuve-Saint-Augustin, a dark street of ancient Paris, his work remained mere dilettantism and lacked consequence', begin the musings of Zola's department store tycoon. 'He wanted to flaunt it in the face of the new Paris, by one of these newly constructed avenues, where the noisy throngs of the second half of the century paraded by in broad sunlight'.[3] One of this protagonist's fantasies involves not only situating the store *by* that artery but even incorporating it: 'Had he seen his way of doing it, he would have liked to let the thoroughfare run right through his store'.[4]

If the connection with street traffic was necessary to ensure the numbers of customers and goods required by accelerated turnover, it is also true that that turnover itself depended on motion. The influx from the street was of a new kind: it was channeled by means of a carefully manipulated display of goods. Zola's tycoon knew this: 'He made it a law that not one far-flung corner of the Bonheur des Dames should remain tranquil. There had to be noise, commotion, life everywhere, because life, he said, attracts life, bears new life, and multiplies quickly'.[5]

The customer was kept in motion; he traveled through the department store as a train passenger traveled through the landscape. In their totality, the goods impressed him as an ensemble of objects and price tags fused into a pointillistic overall view:

3. Émile Zola, *Au Bonheur des Dames* (Paris, 1883), conveys a vivid impression of the great new emphoria, the Louvre, the Samaritaine and the Bon Marché.
4. Ibid.
5. Ibid.

Mme Desforges saw everywhere only the great big signs with enormous numerals whose garish colors contrasted with the bright calico, the radiant silk, the muted wool materials. People's heads almost disappeared behind piles of ribbons; a wall of flannel protruded like a headland; everywhere around, mirrors made the salesrooms seem even more huge, reflecting displays and parts of the public, appraising heads, half-glimpsed shoulders and arms; while to the right and left, the side corridors allowed glimpses of the snowy bays of white goods, the mottled deeps of knitted things, of remote worlds illumined by a beam of light from some part of the glass roof, where the crowd became merely human motes of dust.[6]

The motion in the department store was a part of the general motion of traffic that generated the panoramic perception of railroad and boulevard landscapes. In the store, however, the panoramic eye was not dealing with landscapes or boulevards but with goods. This called for another perspective on the panoramic concept. The department store customer's new relationship to the goods proved to be less a result of his own physical motion (although this, too, was occurring) than the result of the new economic relationship that had found its expression in the form of the department store, where the goods achieved more of their character *as* goods — their appearance as items of exchange value. One might say that their 'commodity-esthetic' aspect became ever more dominant.

It seems questionable to describe two such widely-differing subjects as the appearance of goods in a department store and the appearance of the landscape seen from the train compartment by the same term, 'panoramic', since one is the result of actual, i.e. physical, speed, the other a reflection of an economic relationship. Yet the problem solves itself as soon as we look at the railway journey, not in its aspect of physical motion, but in economic terms: economically speaking, the railway journey is a commodity, a service performed, transportation purchased in the form of a ticket.[7] Thus the panoramic view from the compartment window can be understood not only as a result of

6. Ibid.
7. The railroad 'made personal travel a "commodity" whereas previously it had usually been undertaken only under some compulsion. The main effects of the railways were not on production possibilities in other sectors, but in making available a much-improved consumer service'. (G. R. Hawke, *Railways and Economic Growth in England and Wales, 1840–1970* [Oxford, 1970], p. 54.)

physical acceleration but also, and simultaneously, as a consequence of the new economic relationships which made the railroad journey a commodity to a qualitatively new extent.[8] The fragmentation and panoramic reconstruction of the railway journey's landscape *did* correspond, structurally, to the fragmentation and pointillistic reconstruction of the appearance of the goods in the department store. The city names on the station buildings are evidence of the same process that attaches price tags to the commodities.

We have to recognize both of the sources that fed the panoramic perception — physical speed and the commodity character of objects — to an equal degree. They were intimately connected in that the physical speed achieved by means of a vehicle of transportation was merely the base for the economic circulation of the commodities: that circulation increased the commodity character of the goods with a rapidity that is in direct proportion to the physical rapidity of the vehicles. Finally, to recognize such a close interaction between commodity character and change of location does seem to be quite in accord with the previously cited observation by Marx which states that 'this moment of locality' may be assumed to be the 'transformation of the product into a commodity'. We also gain further insight into that turn of phrase so well-liked by the railroad's critics — the claim that this form of travel transformed the traveler into a parcel. The realization that one no longer felt like a person but like a commodity indicates some awareness that one had been assimilated not only by physically accelerated speed but also by the generally accelerated process of the circulation of goods.

It now becomes possible to define panoramic perception in more general terms. It is perception based on a specific developmental stage of the circulation of commodities, with corresponding specific stages of technology in general, traffic technology in particular, retail merchandising, etc. Panoramic perception of objects, panoramic ways of relating to objects, made their appearance in connection with, and based upon, the accelerated circulation of commodities — as distinct from the traditional mode of perception, which, being still attuned to a

---

8. Naturally, even coach travel was a commodity that had to be paid for, but its commodity character was still undeveloped, pre-industrial. The coach journey still had as much 'use value' as the goods in the old-fashioned retail store.

prior development stage of circulation, found it difficult to deal with the now accelerated objects.

It is a corollary of the above that it makes sense to speak of 'panoramic perception' only as long as the archaism of such a traditional, old-fashioned perception still exists. As soon as a society's overall perceptions have reorganized themselves after a qualitative change of the production-circulation complex, the new normality is what was formerly the panoramic.[9]

By the end of the nineteenth century, the capitalist world's recomposition on the basis of modern traffic had been completed. From then on, traffic determined what belonged where. The pre-industrial contexts of location and space–time relations were no longer valid. Only the general context of traffic assigned and dictated positions to the individual elements. The nineteenth century was very aware of this achievement, the conquest of space; this can be seen in the relatively high value it assigned to the means of communication and transportation in its official self-perception: the triad of railroad, steamship, telegraph, was evoked time and again as representative of industrial progress. The world exhibitions (which in their very definition presupposed modern world traffic) gave prominent displays to the communication and transportation industries.[10] In a salute to the 1867 exhibition, Victor Hugo urged the French to disband as a nation and to join humanity.[11]

The nineteenth century's preoccupation with the conquest and mastery of space and time had found its most general expression in the concept of circulation, which was central to the scientistic social notions of the epoch. Its origin was obviously biophysiological, but it is equally obvious that it reflected the process of modern traffic. The reality of traffic was contained in the biologization of social processes and institutions that is so typical of nineteenth-century thinking. The century's social organisms were replicas of events in both the biological and the traffic sphere. In other words, when the nineteenth century saw

9. Obviously, the concept of the panoramic is used here in a general, i.e. a-historical sense, as a category, although it was initially discovered in connection with a specific historical subject. It would, naturally, be necessary to develop a corresponding concept for each and every historical reorganization of perception. The panoramic merely serves as a model here.
10. Utz Haltern, *Die Londoner Weltausstellung von 1851*, p. 182, (Münster, 1971).
11. Werner Hofmann, *Das Irdische Paradies* (Munich, 1960), p. 153.

the health and vitality of social institutions and processes as dependent on a functioning circulatory system (e.g. Jean Baptiste Say: 'One imagines that the social body will be the livelier and healthier the more general and rapid the circulation of values is'),[12] it based this view on a biophysiological notion of society and economy; yet the notion itself was merely a reflection of the actual traffic conditions.[13] This complex meaning of the circulation concept in the nineteenth century became quite explicit in French, where 'circulation' refers to the actual movement of traffic as well as to the circulation of the blood and the circulation of goods.

In this complex sense, the circulation concept serves as a key to unlock the open triumphs as well as the hidden anxieties of the nineteenth century. The formula is as simple as can be: whatever was part of circulation was regarded as healthy, progressive, constructive; all that was detached from circulation, on the other hand, appeared diseased, medieval, subversive, threatening. Haussmann's public works can now be seen in a new light. His bold thoroughfares reveal themselves as designed not only for traffic, but also for the city's physiology. (Du Camp's book on Paris, frequently reprinted during the Second Empire, bears the title *Paris, ses organes, ses fonctions, sa vie* [*Paris, its organs, its functions, its life*].) Haussmann's street system has been aptly characterized as based upon 'the dual concept of a circulatory and respiratory system'.[14] The streets have the function of connecting the old, i.e. diseased, city districts to

12. Quoted in E. Littré, *Dictionnaire de la langue française* (Paris, 1956), vol. 2. One might object that Say's definition originated at a time before the railroad was known, but if we remind ourselves that in the decades immediately preceding this, traffic capacity increased, although still based on the old technology (a great need for traffic already existed at the beginning of the nineteenth century), then we can see Say's definition as anticipatory of the modern traffic that was realized by means of the railroad.

13. The biologization of social and economic processes and, conversely, the influence of underlying social conditions on biophysiological notions, are of course older than the nineteenth century. Thus William Harvey's discovery of the circulation of the blood has been related to the bourgeois revolution in England: 'Harvey dethroned the heart in the same year as the English Republic was proclaimed'. (Christopher Hill, 'William Harvey and the Idea of Monarchy', *Past and Present*, no. 27, April 1964]; repr. in *The Intellectual Revolution of the Seventeenth Century*, ed. Charles Webster [London and Boston, 1974], p. 163.) It would be worthwhile to trace the changes that have occurred in the last 300 years in this area of the interpenetration between biological and social concepts, and to investigate which biological metaphors are stressed in which historical periods. To cite only one example, Marx's notion of 'metabolism' was obviously borrowed from the physiologists of his day.

14. Choay, p. 19.

the circulatory system that is already pulsing through modern France. Their adornment with trees merely underlines that physiological/biological intention, which cannot be separated from the traffic-oriented intention any more than from the counter-revolutionary military one. In a rare formulation, Haussmann successfully summarized these complex motives: he said that it was his intention 'to insure public tranquility by the creation of great boulevards that allow the circulation not only for air and light but also of military units and, by means of this ingenious combination, to render the people both healthier and less disposed to revolt'.[15]

The same notion of circulation, light, air, life on one hand, and isolation, stagnation, darkness, death on the other, are to be found in the work of Emile Zola, albeit with a liberal, not an authoritarian slant. In his department-store novel, what remains isolated from circulation are the small shops that become unable to turn over their wares. The mold that grows on those goods, the humidity and darkness of the shops themselves, whose owners die off one after another, demonstrate what it means to be cut off from the circulation of commodity turnover — seen in the novel as light radiating off the facade of the neighboring department store. The list of examples could be lengthened *ad libitum*. Harking back to a previous topic discussed in this book, the threatening nature of the train compartment, we will present only one more example. The bourgeois passenger found the compartment frightening because it was not connected to permit traffic between the parts of the train. The side corridor, which finally provided that connection, did for the compartment what Haussmann's boulevards did for the isolated old city districts of Paris: each shone a light into the threatening darkness by providing a connection to the general traffic. The threat disappeared as soon as the bourgeois traveler knew that his compartment and the possible events taking place in it were controled by the appropriate authority. The conductor, who could view the compartments from the side corridor, was the civilian equivalent of the prison guard who controled the cells from his central tower.[16]

15. Quoted in Ragon, p. 96.
16. Remarkable analogies can be demonstrated between the remodeling of Paris and the (slightly earlier) prison reform. The replacement of the medieval dungeon by a type of

The notion that communication, exchange, motion bring to humanity enlightenment and progress, and that isolation and disconnection are the obstacles to be overcome on this course, is as old as the modern age. The bourgeois cultural development of the last three centuries can be seen as closely connected with the actual development of traffic. In retrospect, it is easy to see what significance the experience of space and time had for bourgeois education when one considers the Grand Tour, which was an essential part of that education before the industrialization of travel. The world was experienced in its original spatio-temporality. The traveling subject experienced localities in their spatial individuality. His education consisted of his assimilation of the spatial individuality of the places visited, by means of an effort that was both physical and intellectual. The eighteenth-century travel novel became the *Bildungsroman* (novel of education) of the early nineteenth century. The motion of travel, that physical and intellectual effort in space and time, dominated both.

The railroad, the destroyer of experiential space and time, thus also destroyed the educational experience of the Grand Tour. Henceforth, the localities were no longer spatially individual or autonomous: they were points in the circulation of traffic that made them accessible. As we have seen, that traffic was the physical manifestation of the circulation of goods. From that time on, the places visited by the traveler became increasingly similar to the commodities that were part of the same circulation system. For the twentieth-century tourist, the world has become one huge department store of countrysides and cities.

---

building based on Bentham's Panopticon was caused by the same intentions as the remodeling of the city and led to very similar results. The intention, to provide more light and air, is humanitarian and sanitary; the result, as Michel Foucault has noted, is the more effective control of the prisoners. Light is what makes such control possible. It enters through the cell windows and shows the prisoners to their guards as easily controllable silhouette figures. (M. Foucault, *Surveiller et punir: Naissance de la prison* [Paris, 1975], p. 197.) 'In short, the principle of the dungeon is inverted; or rather, of its three functions — to lock in, to deprive of light, and to conceal — only the first one is retained, the other two eliminated. The strong light and the stare of a guard are better captors than the dark which, finally, was protective. The visibility is a trap'. (Op. cit., p. 202.)

Bibliographical Note

Railroads have not been a neglected subject in historical writing. Indeed, the *Bibliography of British Railway History* which George Ottley compiled some fifteen years ago lists close to eight thousand titles; the catalogue of the library of the Association of American Railroads contains over a million references. British and American social and economic historians, especially, have written many studies relating to the impact of railroads on the most varied aspects of society. What follows is a selection of topics which have been the subject of scholarly study in more recent years.

Railroads and General Economic Development

Here the New Economic historians have published a number of important, and in some cases controversial, monographs. A. Fishlow, *Railroads and the Transformation of Ante-Bellum Economy* (Cambridge, 1966), for the US, and G. R. Hawke, *Railways and Economic Growth in England and Wales, 1840–1870* (Oxford, 1970), for Britain, confirm the vital role played by railroads in the development of capitalism. R. W. Fogel's *Railroads and American Growth* (Baltimore, 1964), on the other hand, is an attempt to provide the statistical evidence that this argument does not hold true of the US. Fogel's hypothesis, which caused a sensation in its time, has meanwhile been overturned. A bibliography of his critics is to be found in T. L. Haskell, 'The True & Tragical History of "Time on the Cross"', *New York Review of Books*, 1975, no. 15, p. 33.

Railroads and Politics

An excellent study of how the American railroads spearheaded the establishment of so-called regulatory agencies is G. Kolko, *Railroads and Regulation*, 1877 to 1916 (Princeton, 1965). Officially these agencies were

[198]

to protect the consumer, but *de facto* they became agencies of the industries concerned.

Railroads and Urbanisation

See J. R. Kellett, *The Impact of Railways on Victorian Cities* (London/ Toronto, 1969).

Railroads and Medicine/Psychology

E. Fischer-Homberger, *Die traumatische Neurose. Vom somatischen zum sozialen Leiden* (Berne, 1975), deals extensively with the roots of the 'railway accident' neurosis. The same author has provided a more general survey of medicine and railroads during the nineteenth century in: idem, 'Railway Spine und traumatische Neurose — Seele und Rückenmark', *Gesnerus*, no. 27, 1970; idem, 'Der mythische Hintergrund der Eisenbahnkrankheiten des 19. Jahrhunderts', *Sudhoff's Archiv*, no. 56, 1972. A bibliography (which is far from comprehensive, however) is to be found in G. Koch and H. Hoffman, 'Geschichte der Verkehrsmedizin für den Verkehr mit Landfahrzeugen von den Anfängen bis zum Ende des 2. Weltkriegs', *Zentralblatt Verkehrsmedizin, Verkehrs-Psychologie, Luft- und Raumfahrt-Medizin*, no. 15, 1969.

Railroads and Architecture

Here the standard work is C. L. V. Meeks's *The Railroad Station: An Architectural History* (New Haven, 1956). Her study is rather traditional and concerned with architectural style, but remains important for lack of other books on the subject.

Railroads and Language/Literature

Two exemplary French studies examine the gradual introduction of railroads as a term or as a theme into French language and literature: P. J. Wexler, *La formation du vocabulaire des chemins de fer en France (1778–1842)* (Geneva/Lille, 1955); M. Baroli, *Le train dans la littérature française* (Paris, 1964). Both studies also inspired the present work because of the way they deal with the process of assimilation, even though both authors have confined themselves to the process of assimilation in language and literature.

Apart from this specialised literature, there are general cultural histories which attempt to describe the complexities of the 'railway age' (this or similarly, the title of many studies). As a rule, these are either compilations or popularised accounts of the social history of the railroads, enriched by contemporary descriptions of the speed of railroad travel. Two such works by British historians are: H. Perkin, *Age of the Railway* (London, 1962); M. Robbins, *The Railway Age* (London, 1962). Unlike earlier studies (by e.g. C. H. Ellis), both authors are less interested in elaborating on the anecdotal than in popularising the social history aspect of railroad development.

Finally, two important works that have appeared since the original edition of this book was completed: on railroads and urbanisation, see J. R. Stilgoe, *Metropolitan Corridor: Railroads and the American Scene* (New Haven, 1983); on railroads and architecture, see J. H. White, *The American Railroad Passenger Car* (Baltimore, 1977).

Index

Index

Index

Proust, M., 39
Pullman, G.M., 105, 110

Raphael, M., 48, 49
Reed, E., 106
Reuleaux, F., 19, 20, 24, 169
Reynolds, R., 118
Riedel, M., 56
Robbins, M., 200
Rostow, W.W., 90
Ruskin, J., 38, 54, 57, 58; 60, 64, 121, 165, 189

Saint-Simon, C.H. de, 70
Saulle, L. de, 68
Say, J.B., 195
Scharnhorst, G.J.D.v., 155
Sealsfield, C. (pseud. F. Gerstäcker), 109
Shaler, N.S., 108
Simmel, G., 57, 74–5, 101, 167
Simonin, L., 101
Smith, A., 2, 5
Smith, H.N., 91
Smith, W.H., 35
Sombart, W., 1–2, 73, 151, 152–3
Sorokin, P., 36, 37
Stephenson, G., 15, 55
Sternberger, D., 30, 31, 61, 63
Stevenson, D., 106, 109
Sticht, E., 116
Straus, E., 36, 53
Street, T.A., 146

Taine, H., 77

Taylor, F.W., 90, 127
Thiers, A., 185
Thrupp, G.A., 74
Tocqueville, A. de, 103, 112
Trollope, F., 107
Trübner, —., 151
Turner, W., 49
Tyler, Capt., 82, 86, 102

Unterseher, L., 153

Verlaine, P., 31

Waldegg, H.v., 83, 87–8, 104
Walford, C., 134–5
Ward, M., 60, 97
Watt, J., 3
Weber, M.M.v., 30, 75–6, 89, 90, 115, 117, 122
Webster, D., 112
Wexler, P.J., 17, 130, 199
Wheatstone, C., 30
White, L., 151
Whitney, —., 99
Whittow, G.J., 43
Winans, R., 98, 100, 106
Wöhler, A., 125, 126
Wood, N., 8, 22
Wordsworth, W., 42

Yriarte, C., 186

Zola, E., 186–7, 191, 196.

[203]